LOVECRAFTIAN PEOPLE AND PLACES

*Lovecraft of Devon, New York State, and Rhode Island
Courtesy Henry L. P. Beckwith, Jr.*

LOVECRAFTIAN PEOPLE AND PLACES

Ken Faig, Jr.

Hippocampus Press
New York

For David E. Schultz
Editor, Book Designer and Friend

Copyright © 2022 by Ken Faig, Jr.

Published by Hippocampus Press
P.O. Box 641, New York, NY 10156.
www.hippocampuspress.com

All rights reserved.
No part of this work may be reproduced in any form or by any means without the written permission of the publisher.

Cover artwork from "Map of Lovecraft's Providence"
© 2018 by Jason C. Eckhardt, eck-art.net
Cover design by Dan Sauer, dansauerdesign.com
Hippocampus Press logo designed by Anastasia Damianakos.

First Edition
1 3 5 7 9 8 6 4 2

ISBN 978-1-61498-337-8 (paperback)
ISBN 978-1-61498-369-9 (ebook)

Contents

Foreword, *by S. T. Joshi* 7

Abbreviations 9

Lovecraftian People 11
    Devonshire Ancestry of Howard Phillips Lovecraft 13
    Edward Francis Gamwell and His Family 72
    George Elliott Lovecraft: Lost Scion of the House of Lovecraft 108
    Lovecraft Was Our Neighbor: The People of The Arsdale 122

Lovecraftian Places 135
    The Story of 454 Angell Street: The Birthplace of Howard Phillips Lovecraft 137
    The People of 598–600 Angell Street 176
    The Site of Joseph Curwen's Home in *The Case of Charles Dexter Ward* 187
    Can You Direct Me to Ely Court? Some Notes on 66 College Street 226

The Fiction 245
    John Osborne Austin's Seven Club Tales: Did They Inspire Lovecraft? 247
    Ethnic Names in Lovecraft's "The Dreams in the Witch House" 276

Amateur Journalism 289
    The Providence Amateur Press Club: 1914–16 291
    The Lovecraft–Gidlow Centenary 343

Sources 353

FOREWORD

For a full fifty years, Ken Faig, Jr. has been a pioneering scholar in H. P. Lovecraft's life and work. One of his earliest accomplishments was the identification of Lovecraft's contributions to Providence newspapers, for which he wrote three separate astronomy columns between the years 1906 and 1918. In other papers dating to the 1970s, He discussed such subjects as Lovecraft's appearances in his school yearbooks, mentions of him in B. K. Hart's "Sideshow" column in the *Providence Journal,* and numerous other lesser-known aspects of Lovecraft's multifaceted life.

By the 1980s, Faig began focusing on two separate but partially linked areas of scholarship: Lovecraft's ancestry and his complex relationships with numerous friends and colleagues, literary and otherwise. The former interest led to such landmarks as *The Parents of Howard Phillips Lovecraft* (1990)—an exhaustive treatment of all that is known of Winfield and Sarah Susan Lovecraft—and an insightful study of the business endeavors of Lovecraft's grandfather, Whipple Van Buren Phillips, in Idaho. In terms of the latter interest, Faig produced a substantial monograph on R. H. Barlow, Lovecraft's literary executor. He combined these two interests by a penetrating analysis of the friendship of Sarah Susan Lovecraft and the poet Louise Imogen Guiney.

Some of Faig's papers of that era were presented in the Hippocampus Press volume *The Unknown Lovecraft* (2009). This new collection features another array of penetrating analyses, much of the raw information for which has been derived by Faig's diligent analysis of census records, genealogical data, topographical maps of Providence, R.I., and other such material. These are the sources that all sophisticated historians must use as the basis of their studies, and Faig has developed the gift of imbuing this oftentimes mundane material with the breath of life.

And so we have such pieces as "Devonshire Ancestry of Howard Phillips Lovecraft," in which Lovecraft's paternal ancestry is traced in meticulous detail; studies of Lovecraft's uncle by marriage, Edward Francis Gamwell, and of a more remote relation, George Elliott Lovecraft; and the history of the occupancy of Lovecraft's two earliest residences in Providence, 454 and 598 Angell Street.

Faig is highly sensitive to the interplay between Lovecraft's life and his work, as exhibited in his papers on *The Case of Charles Dexter Ward* and "The Dreams in the Witch House." And he has used the availability of a list of Lovecraft's library to speculate on the possible influence of Rhode Island writer John Osborne Austin on Lovecraft.

Faig has always been interested in Lovecraft's career in amateur journalism, which began in 1914 and continued sporadically throughout the rest of his life. It is a facet of Lovecraft's life that remains to be charted in detail, but Faig has contributed to it with his papers on the Providence Amateur Press Club and on Elsie Alice Gidlow.

This volume demonstrates not only Ken Faig, Jr.'s tireless efforts in illuminating the obscurer corners of the Lovecraftian realm but the degree to which the study of Lovecraft has reached a level of granular detail almost unfathomable to those who have dismissed Lovecraft as merely a pulp hack. The existence of thousands of his letters, dozens of memoirs by friends and family, and many other primary documents has made possible a monumental array of research and scholarship over the past half-century; and among the many figures who have contributed to this effort, Ken Faig, Jr. stands close to the summit.

—S. T. JOSHI

ABBREVIATIONS

AAV	S. T. Joshi and David E. Schultz, ed. *Ave atque Vale: Reminiscences of H. P. Lovecraft.* West Warwick, RI: Necronomicon Press, 2018.
AG	*Letters to Alfred Galpin and Others.* Ed. S. T. Joshi and David E. Schultz. New York: Hippocampus Press, 2020.
AT	*The Ancient Track: Complete Poetical Works.* Ed. S. T. Joshi. New York: Hippocampus Press, 2013.
CE	*Collected Essays.* Ed. S. T. Joshi. New York: Hippocampus Press, 2004–06; 5 vols.
CF	*Collected Fiction: A Variorum Edition.* Ed. S. T. Joshi. New York: Hippocampus Press, 2015–17; 4 vols.
CLM	*Letters to C. L. Moore and Others.* Ed. David E. Schultz and S. T. Joshi. New York: Hippocampus Press, 2017.
DS	*Dawnward Spire, Lonely Hill: The Letters of H. P. Lovecraft and Clark Ashton Smith.* Ed. David E. Schultz and S. T. Joshi. New York: Hippocampus Press, 2017.
DW	*Letters with Donald and Howard Wandrei and to Emil Petaja.* Ed. S. T. Joshi and David E. Schultz. New York: Hippocampus Press, 2019.
EHP	*Letters to E. Hoffmann Price and Richard F. Searight.* Ed. S. T. Joshi and David E. Schultz. New York: Hippocampus Press, (2021).
ES	*Essential Solitude: The Letters of H. P. Lovecraft and August Derleth,* Ed. David E. Schultz and S. T. Joshi. New York: Hippocampus Press, 2013.
ET	*Letters to Elizabeth Toldridge and Anne Tillery Renshaw.* Ed. David E. Schultz and S. T. Joshi. New York: Hippocampus Press, 2014.

FLB	*Letters to F. Lee Baldwin, Duane W. Rimel, and Nils Frome.* Ed. David E. Schultz and S. T. Joshi. New York: Hippocampus Press, 2016.
IAP	S. T. Joshi, *I Am Providence: The Life and Times of H. P. Lovecraft.* Hippocampus Press, 2010.
JFM	*Letters to James F. Morton.* Ed. David E. Schultz and S. T. Joshi. New York: Hippocampus Press, 2014.
JVS	*Letters to J. Vernon Shea, Carl F. Strauch, and Lee McBride White.* Ed. S. T. Joshi and David E. Schultz. New York: Hippocampus Press, 2016.
LL	S. T. Joshi and David E. Schultz. *Lovecraft's Library.* 4th rev. ed. New York: Hippocampus Press, 2017.
LFF	*Letters to Family and Family Friends.* Ed. S. T. Joshi and David E. Schultz. New York: Hippocampus Press, 2020.
Misc.	*Miscellaneous Letters.* Ed. David E. Schultz and S. T. Joshi. New York: Hippocampus Press, 2022.
MWM	*Letters to Maurice W. Moe and Others.* Ed. David E. Schultz and S. T. Joshi. New York: Hippocampus Press, 2018.
OFF	*O Fortunate Floridian: H. P. Lovecraft's Letters to R. H. Barlow.* Ed. S. T. Joshi and David E. Schultz. Tampa, FL: University of Tampa Press, 2007.
RB	*Letters to Robert Bloch and Others.* Ed. David E. Schultz and S. T. Joshi. New York: Hippocampus Press, 2017.
RK	*Letters to Rheinhart and Others.* Ed. S. T. Joshi and David E. Schultz. New York: Hippocampus Press, 2020.
SL	*Selected Letters,* ed. August Derleth et al. Sauk City, WI: Arkham House, 1965–76; 5 vols.
WBT	*Letters to Wilfred B. Talman and Helen V. and Genevieve Sully.* Ed. David E. Schultz and S. T. Joshi. New York: Hippocampus Press, 2019.
WH	*Letters to Woodburn Harris and Others.* Ed. S. T. Joshi and David E. Schultz. New York: Hippocampus Press, 2022.

LOVECRAFTIAN PEOPLE

Devonshire Ancestry of Howard Phillips Lovecraft

with Chris J. Docherty and A. Langley Searles

For Henry L. P. Beckwith

Introduction

H. P. Lovecraft's published letters provide several discussions of his paternal ancestry: most notably, the letter to Frank Belknap Long dated [24] November 1927 (*SL* 2.179–85) and the letter to Maurice Winter Moe dated 5 April 1931 (*MWM* 292–304). Based on genealogical charts compiled by his great-aunt Sarah Allgood[1] and originally copied by him in 1905,[2] Lovecraft claimed a line of direct paternal ascent as follows: Howard(4) Winfield(3) George(2) Joseph(1) Thomas(A) John(B) Joseph(C) George(D) William(E) Richard(F) John(G) (*SL* 2.182). Lovecraft's charts indicated that the emigrant Joseph(1) married Mary Fulford, daughter of Rev. Francis Fulford and Ellen Edgecombe, and arrived in North America in 1827 with his wife and six children: John, William, Joseph, George, Aaron and Mary (*SL* 2.183; *MWM* 294).

---

1. Sarah Allgood was born 8 July 1830, in New York, the daughter of William Allgood (born in England) and Rachel Morris (born in Wales), and died 23 January 1908, in Mount Vernon, NY (New York State death certificate). She was the sister of Helen Allgood, the wife of HPL's paternal grandfather George Lovecraft.

2. HPL originally copied the chart lent by his great-aunt Sarah Allgood in 1905, and made a new copy c. 1927 at the urging of his correspondent Wilfred Blanch Talman, an ardent family historian (see *SL* 2.179). HPL's copies are not found among his papers in the Special Collections of the Brown University Library in Providence, RI, but at least one copy reportedly survives in the hands of maternal relatives.

Prior Research

R. Alain Everts published the first account of the Lovecraft family in America (apart from Howard Lovecraft's own accounts in *Selected Letters*) in a periodical in 1975. Twenty years later, Necronomicon Press published *Stern Fathers 'neath the Mould: The Lovecraft Family in Rochester*, a book-length monograph covering the fortunes of the descendants of Joseph(1) and Mary Lovecraft in America written by Richard D. Squires, a librarian in Rochester, N.Y. More recently, Steven Sneyd published an account of his own search for Lovecraft's ancestors in Devonshire. Sneyd was the first to cite in print the heavy concentration of Lovecraft marriages and baptisms in Broadhempston parish in the LDS International Genealogical Index. Messrs. Squires and Sneyd have been kind enough to share information from their research with the authors; the authors benefitted particularly from a parish map of the "Lovecraft country" in south Devon traced by Mr. Sneyd from Humphrey-Smith (1999).

The Allgood Chart and Its Claims

Introduction

The Allgood chart claims that Thomas(A), the father of the emigrant Joseph, was born in 1745 and died in 1826, that he married Letitia Edgecombe, sister of the wife of Rev. Francis Fulford, in 1766, and that the couple's sixth child was the emigrant Joseph(1). According to the chart, Thomas(A) lost the family property of Minster Hall near Newton-Abbot in Devonshire to debt in 1823 (*SL* 2.183; *MWM* 293–94).

Lovecraft's account of the early origins of his family in Devonshire in his 5 April 1931 letter to Maurice W. Moe is particularly interesting and worth quoting:

In direct male line, I can't get back to the Conquest at all; the family of Lovecroft (early spelling) first appearing in Devonshire, in the valley of the Teign, circa 1450. I can't push my own lineal stem back of 1560 plus or minus, when John Lovecraft (present spelling) of Minster Hall near Newton-Abbot bore the present arms of the family: a chevron, engrailed, Or, between three foxes' heads, erased, or, on a field Vert. (*MWM* 293)[3]

The Lovecraft Family Arms

The Lovecraft family arms described by Howard Lovecraft have been blazoned by Henry L. P. Beckwith (see frontispiece). Beckwith believes that the arms originally depicted wolves', rather than foxes', heads, and constitute a "punning coat" based on *louve* (French for wolf bitch) + "croft" meaning place, farm, field, lair, cave, den. Beckwith believes that Lovecraft may represent a later form of the name, possibly borne by families whose living included wolf-hunting.[4]

---

3. In another letter (*SL* 2.182), HPL refers to this individual as "John Lovecroft (note spelling)." HPL provides the Latin motto accompanying the coat of arms in his letter to Richard F. Searight dated 14 November 1934: *Quae amamus tuemur* ("we defend the things we love") (*EHP* 335).

4. See Beckwith, *Lovecraft's Providence* 94–95 and "The Lovecraft Family Arns." In a letter to co-author Faig dated 4 April 1997, Beckwith noted that there were wolves in the Exmoor area until about 1200. For a scholarly discussion of the Love- and -craft/-croft surnames, refer to Hanks and Hodges. The authors note that OE *croft* refers to an arable enclosure, normally adjoining a house. The -croft surnames are thus habitation names deriving from the dwelling places of the bearers of the name. OE *croeft* refers to a craft, skill, machine, engine or mill. Under their entry for "Love," Hanks and Hodges offer the following discussion: "English and Scots: nickname from ANF *louve* female wolf (a fem. Form of *lou* cf. Low 3). This nickname was fairly commonly used for men, in an approving sense. It may have been bestowed on a staunch soldier, with reference to the ferocity with which the she-wolf defends her young."

The Lovecraft family arms are enrolled as number 645 of the roll of arms of the New England Historic Genealogical Society.[5] Because of their style and coloration, Beckwith believes the arms to be of considerable antiquity. As noted by R. P. Graham-Vivian, M.V.C., M.C. (Norroy & Ulster King of Arms) in a letter to Beckwith dated 19 June 1969, the arms "vert a chevron between three towers or" occur under different tinctures in the 1620 Visitation of Cornwall, but only as quartering to Elliott and to Boscawen.[6] Graham-Vivian wrote of the arms: "The fact that it appears only as an ancient Quartering by the time of the Visitations means that whatever it was, and it was unnamed, was extinct in the male line, and even the name lost sight of."

Boscawen

Boscawen is an ancient Cornish name, deriving from *bos, bod* (dwelling) and *scawen* (elder tree). According to Hanks and Hodges, it arose as a habitation name for two families dwelling near St. Buryan and one dwelling near Helston, both in Cornwall.[7] According to *Burke's Peerage*,[8] the family held the manor of Boscawen Rose in Cornwall as early as the reign of King John and were created Barons of Boscawen Ros by royal writ in 1264. John de Boscawen Ros (son of Henry) of St. Buryan parish married the heiress Johan [Joan] de Tregothnan (daughter of John) in 1335 and moved his home from the Penzance area to

---

5. NEHGS 11. There was also a registration (#638, p. 10) of the Fulford arms to Mary (Fulford) Lovecraft, since canceled.
6. *Burke's Peerage* records that the Eliot family (subsequently Earls of St. Germans) had a shield with twelve quarterings when its pedigree was entered in the 1620 Visitation of Cornwall.
7. St. Buryan is about midway between Land's End and Penzance. Helston is about midway between Penzance and Falmouth.
8. See entry for the Viscounts of Falmouth.

Tregothnan in the parish of St. Michael Penkivel. His descendant Edward Boscawen (1628–1685) of Tregothnan served as M.P. for Truro for more than twenty years. Edward's son Hugh Boscawen (1680?–1734) of Tregothnan was created Baron of Boscawen Rose and 1st Viscount Falmouth by King George I on 9 June 1720. Hugh's second son Admiral Edward Boscawen (1711–1761) distinguished the family with his naval career in the eighteenth century and is buried in St. Michael Penkivel church, which contains many other Boscawen family memorials.[9]

Edward Boscawen (1787–1841), 4th Viscount, was created Earl of Falmouth by King George IV on 14 July 1821. The earldom became extinct with the death of Edward's son George Henry Boscawen (1811–1852), 5th Viscount and 2nd Earl, but he was succeeded as 6th Viscount by his cousin Evelyn Boscawen (1819–1889). The holder of the title in 1995 was George Hugh Boscawen, 9th Viscount, born 31 October 1919. Burke's *The General Armory of England, Scotland, Ireland and Wales* (1884) provides two sets of arms for the family. For the Viscounts Falmouth: arms, ermine a rose gules barbed and seeded proper; crest, a falcon close proper belled or; supporters, two sea lions erect on tails argent gutee delarmes. For Boscawen (of Cornwall): arms, ermine a rose gules barbed vert; original crest, a falcon close proper; subsequent crest, a bear pass gules armed and membered. The motto is *patience passe science* (patience surpasses knowledge).

Elliott (Eliot)

There are several accounts of the Elliott (Eliot) family name. According to some authorities, the name represents a diminutive

---

9. Admiral Boscawen is stated to have ordered the lowering of the original church tower so that it could not be used as a landmark by enemies. The church was completely rebuilt in 1862–66 on the site of the old one.

form of Ellis or of the French Elias (Elijah). Hanks and Hodges trace the English-Scottish name to the OE given names *Adelgeat* (male) and *Adelgyd* (female) and the Scottish name to the Gaelic topographical names *Elloch* and *Eloth* and *eileach* (dam, mound, bank). The Scots clan removed from the vicinity of the river and village of Elot in Forfarshire to Lidderdale under a grant of lands from Robert the Bruce (r. 1306–29). The clan head built a tower on the bank overlooking Hermitage Water, near the junction with the Liddle, and was thereafter known as Robert Ellot of Redheugh; several successive generations of Ellot clan heads bore the title captain of Hermitage Castle. In 1995 the head of the Scots-English Eliott clan was Sir Charles Joseph Alexander Eliott of Stobs, 12th Baronet, born 9 January 1937, who succeeded to the title on the death of his father in 1989. This Eliott family traces its lineage as far back as Robert Elwald (d. 3 May 1497) of Redheugh, squire to the Earl of Angus. The Eliotts of Stobs descend directly from Gilbert Ellot of Stobs (son of Robert Ellot of Redheugh) and his wife Jean Scott, who bought the Stobs estates in 1607. His grandson, Sir Gilbert Eliott of Stobs, 1st Baronet, was knighted by King Charles II at Largo Sands on 14 February 1651, and created a baronet of Nova Scotia on 3 December 1666. The Earls of Minto (baronets of Scotland, 1700; earls of the United Kingdom, 1813) also descend from this Stobs line.

John Eliot (1604–1690), the famous "Indian Apostle," was the first of the family in the New World, arriving in Boston in 1631, but many American Eliots descend from Andrew Eliot, of East Coker in Sussex, who emigrated to Boston in 1670. A charming rhyme reflects the many branches of the Eliot family, who tried to distinguish themselves by the various spellings of the family name:

> The double L and single T
> Descend from Minto and Wolflee,
> The double T and single L
> Mark the old race in Stobs that dwell,
> The single L and single T
> The Eliots of St. Germains be,
> But the double T and double L
> Who they are nobody can tell.[10]

However, according to Tom Paterson's "Elliot—History of the Surname" (see note 10), the antiquary Willis stated that an Eliot family was seated in Devonshire as early as the time of King John; there were also Eliot families in Suffolk and Surrey. A Walter Eliot was recorded among the gentry of Cornwall as early as 1433. John Eliot acquired the former priory of St. Germans in Cornwall from the Champernowne family in 1540. The priory had fallen to the Champernownes following the dissolution of the monasteries under King Henry VIII. This John Eliot was of Devon descent, being the son of Edward Eliot of Coteland, Devon and Alice, daughter of Robert Guye. He traded some or all of his inherited property in Coteland, Devon (worth five hundred pounds) for the St. Germans estate in Cornwall. John's grandfather was John Eliot, who married Joan, the daughter of Ralph Bonville of Chute, Devon.

The parish of St. Germans in Cornwall (located just west of Plymouth) is named for the missionary St. Germanus of Auxerre

---

10. This rhyme may be found in Tom Paterson's "Elliot—History of the Surname" (q.v., web.ukonline.co.uk/members/tom.paterson/surnames/nelliot.htm) and in Allen Wade Mount, Sr.'s "Our Bobbitt Family" (q.v., www.thegenealogists. com/ourbobbittfamily/9.3.2_Dir/9.3.2.Page1.htm) (both consulted 14 November 2003). In the online transcription of the 1891 UK census of Cornwall (q.v., www.ancestry.com) (consulted 15 November 2003), the distribution of the variant surnames was as follows: Elliott, 234 individuals; Elliot, 25; Eliott, 11; and Eliot, 5.

(378–448), who traveled to England in 429 and 447 to oppose the Pelagian heresy. St. Germans in Cornwall was the seat of a bishopric (and an Anglo-Saxon cathedral) until the see was moved to Exeter in 1046.[11] A Norman church was erected on the site of the former cathedral in 1261. The St. Germans priory had been established as early as 986, and after the acquisition by the Eliot family in 1540, the property was renamed Port Elyut in 1573 and later Port Eliot. The most famous scion of the St. Germans Eliot family was probably Sir John Eliot (1590–1632), a notable M.P. and statesman, who married Rhadagund, daughter of Richard Gedie of Trebursye in Cornwall and had by her five sons and four daughters. His descendant Edward Eliot of Craggs (1727–1804) was created 1st Baron Eliot by King George III on 30 January 1784.

Edward's son John Eliot (1761–1823) was responsible for the extensive remodeling of Port Eliot in 1792, and was created 1st Earl of St. Germans by the Prince Regent (later King George IV) on 28 November 1815. Both the title and the property remain in the possession of his descendants, the present incumbent being Peregrine Nicholas Eliot, 10th Earl of St. Germans, born 2 January 1941, who succeeded his father in 1988. The family arms are argent, a fesse gules, between double cotisses wavy azure; the crest, an elephant's head argent, plain collared gules; the supporters, two eagles reguardant, wings displayed and inverted proper, each charged on the breast with an ermine spot sable. The motto is *praecedentibus insta* (press close upon those who take the lead). In 2002, the Eliot family and estate papers were donated to the Cornish Record Office in lieu of payment of taxes. The estate papers deal with property in Cornwall, Devon and Gloucestershire and date from the thirteenth through the nineteenth centuries.

---

11. Burhwold held the bishopric until his death in 1027. St. Germans was restored as a suffragan bishopric of Truro in 1905.

Could There Be a Lovecraft Connection?

While the Allgood chart as described by H. P. Lovecraft makes claims of eighteenth-century alliances with the illustrious Fulford and Edgecombe families of Devon, Lovecraft makes no mention of the Boscawen family of Tregothnan or the Eliot family of Port Eliot. The fact that quarterings of the claimed Lovecraft family arms do appear on the shields of the Boscawen and Eliot families with their pedigrees in the 1620 visitation of Cornwall, albeit with different tinctures, may perhaps be more significant for the stature of the family than the claimed eighteenth-century alliances. The family name Loccroft may be found as early as the 1332 lay subsidy (see below), and it is certainly not beyond belief that some members of the Devon branch of the family rose to some prominence in the early Norman period. Daughters of the Lovecroft or Loccroft family of Devon may well have married into the Boscawen family of Cornwall and the Eliot family of Devon and Cornwall. Today the memory of these early family members may be preserved only in the quarterings of the Boscawen and Eliot family shields in the 1620 Visitation of Cornwall.

One may however argue that the same family genealogist who concocted the eighteenth-century alliances with the Fulford and Edgecombe families chose the unidentified quarterings in the Boscawen and Eliot shields and altered the tincture in order to create a viable coat of arms for a family which in reality never bore arms. The Allgood chart as described by Lovecraft contains a great deal of information, subject to verification. The fact that the chart also contains demonstrably false claims leads one to approach its unverified claims with caution. It is interesting to note that two family members, Joshua Elliott Lovecraft (1844–1898) and his son George Elliott Lovecraft (1866/67–1932), son and grandson of Joseph Lovecraft, Jr., bore Elliott as a middle name despite the lack of Elliotts among their immediate ancestors. It is not impossible that their middle names reflect a family tradition of an ancient connection with the Elliott (Eliot) family.

Minster Hall

The claim of the Allgood chart that John Lovecroft was in 1560 proprietor of "Minster Hall" has probably been the greatest source of puzzlement regarding the armorial claims of the Lovecraft family. There appears to be no record of any such estate or property. The claim that the Lovecrafts were a landed family from the sixteenth century until 1823 remains unproven and dubious. On the other hand, there is good reason to believe that the family arms are ancient and may constitute a "punning coat" for a surname connected with the French *louve* for wolf bitch.[12] Knowledge of their origin seems lost, the only remaining records being two different-tinctured quarterings in the Boscawen and Eliot shields in the 1620 Visitation of Cornwall.

"Minster" derives from OE *mynster* meaning a monastery or Christian religious house, the church of a monastery or more generally any large church especially a collegiate or cathedral church. OED cites the following reference from Arthur F. Leach, ed., *Memorials of Beverley Minster: The Chapter Act Books of the Collegiate Church of S. John of Beverley 1286–1347* (Surtees Society, 1898, 1903): "The word minster itself is peculiarly one used not of monasteries but of secular churches—York, Beverley, Ripon, Southwell, Lincoln, Lichfield, Wimborne, these are the churches to which the title of minster has clung . . . and they were one and all churches of secular canons." Minster Lovell Hall in Minster Lovell, Oxfordshire, is the ruins of a fifteenth-century house with a surviving medieval dovecote. Cardiff, Wales, had in the twentieth century a Minster Hall used as a meeting place by the Christian Brethren and Lichfield, Stafford-

---

12. Beckwith, "The Lovecraft Family Arms" 2–3.

shire, has a Minster Hall Youth Centre. Parishes including Minster in their names include Minster (1676), Cornwall; Minster (1557), Kent; Minster in Sheppy (1703), Kent; Minster Lovell (1754), Oxford; and South Minster (1702), Essex.

The existence of Minster parish on the north Cornwall coast is interesting because of the connection of the Lovecraft arms with the Cornwall families of Boscawen and Eliot. Historically, the river Jordan divided the town of Boscastle (named for Bottreaux Castle) into the parishes of Forrabury (1710) and Minster (1676); the two parishes were united by Act of Parliament in 1779. The Minster parish church dedicated to St. Merteriana [Merthiana] was preceded on its site by Talkarne priory, confiscated by Parliament in 1407.[13] Talkarne priory was a dependency of the alien abbey of St. Sergius of Angers. This fact probably accounts for the fact that it was seized more than a century before the general dissolution of the English monasteries under Henry VIII.

Most of the church dates to the late fifteenth century, but the chancel is earlier (thirteenth century) and has a blocked doorway formerly leading to the monastic buildings of the priory. A porphyry baptismal font may date to the twelfth century. The church was restored in 1871 under the supervision of J. P. St. Aubyn and the patronage of Miss Hillyer. The church contains many seventeenth-century memorials to the Hender family of Bottreaux, but the carved bench ends and the carved oak chancel screen have been removed. The rectory house (possibly the original priory cell) was destroyed in 1765. William de Bottreaux was patron of the church in the twelfth century and deeded to it the tithes of Woolston in Poundstock and the lordship of the manor of Polyphant, which latter office still belongs to the rec-

---

13. Minster parish was undoubtedly named for the monastic establishment which once occupied the site of the parish church.

tor. Merthiana was a virgin who reputedly lived in the secluded vicinity later occupied by the priory; many miracles were attributed to her intercession.[14] Perhaps the monks of Talkarne priory adopted a local figure as patron of their church in order to win the adherence of the local population. *A Handbook for Travellers in Devon and* Cornwall (London: John Murray, 1865 [6th edition]) noted that the church was situated in "a striking and picturesque nook among the hills" and that a 150-foot waterfall was also close at hand.[15]

Today, the ecclesiastical parish of Boscastle with Davidstow embraces Davidstow (St. David), Forrabury (St. Symphorian), St. Julliot (St. Julitta),[16] Lesnewth (St. Michael and All Angels), Minster (St. Merteriana), Otterham (St. Denis), and Trevalga (St. Petroc). Lovecraft would have loved the legend connected with the missing bells of St. Symphorian in Forrabury. Three bells ordered by William, Lord of Bottreaux Castle, to ward off the

---

14. Most of this information concerning the Church of St. Merteriana [Merthiana] derives from Phil Ellery's Cornish website: freepages.genealogy.rootsweb.com/~cornwall/cornishfile/337.htm (consulted 15 November 2003). A naturalist website (www.wildcornwall.org.uk/autm98/a98/a98spec1.htm) (consulted 13 November 2003) notes that the church and its secluded neighborhood in the Valency river valley are one of the few habitats where the great horseshoe bat survives in the United Kingdom. The website reports that the Minster maternity roost, the largest known in Cornwall, has maintained a stable population of about two hundred over the last decade.

15. The authors are indebted to Richard M. Rogers for this reference. Beautiful color photographs of the church may be found on the Internet at www.caerkief.demon.co.uk/Minster.htm and www.bude.co.uk/church-trails/Boscastle/Minster.htm (both consulted 13 November 2003).

16. The British novelist Thomas Hardy, commissioned to restore St. Julitta Church in 1870, fell in love with and married the rector's sister-in-law Emma Gifford. His first published novel, *A Pair of Blue Eyes* (1873), is set in St. Julliot and is believed to be based on his own romance.

plague were lost when a sudden storm arose in the nearby harbor. The lord and his wife duly perished of the plague, but even today residents of Boscastle say that the ghostly peal of the lost bells can be heard whenever a storm is brewing.[17] A transcription of the 1841 UK census for Forrabury-Minster does not contain any instances of the Lovecraft family name or variants.[18] Despite the suggestiveness of the name of this beautiful Cornwall parish, it is well to remember that the Allgood chart specifically claims that Minster Hall was "near Newton Abbot" in Devonshire.[19]

It is possible that the Lovecraft family retained a tradition of the name of its family seat and simply translated its location to the known eighteenth-century center of the family near Newton Abbot in the absence of knowledge of the actual location. Minster parish is not far removed from Exmoor, where wolves still ranged during the reign of King John. The Love- names like Lovecroft and Loccroft derive from the brave attributes of soldiers and hunters who attended to their duties with the ferocity of the wolf bitch (French *louve*) in defense of her young. This explanation of the origin of the surname is the basis for the claim that the Lovecraft family arms are a punning coat. If Lovecroft or Loccroft daughters married into the Boscawen and Eliot families at some point following the Norman conquest, it is not impossible that they came from a family seat, now forgotten, located near a monastic establishment, perhaps Talkarne priory in what later became Minster parish in Cornwall. If so, their fami-

---

17. See cranstar.co.uk/church.htm (consulted 13 November 2003) for a retelling of the legend of Boscastle's bells.
18. freepages.genealogy.rootsweb.com/~kayhin/140169.html (consulted 13 November 2003).
19. *MWM* 293. The authors are particularly indebted to Richard M. Rogers for bringing Cornwall's Minster parish to their attention.

lies were forgotten and their family seats obliterated through the ravages of time.

The Church House Inn

A better Devon connection may be the "church house"—a house belonging to the (or a) church, or used for church purposes; formerly, a house adjoining the church, where church-ales, etc. were held; a "parish room" (OED). Quite a few former church houses have been leased or converted for secular use; there are at least twenty-six English pubs whose names contain the words "Church House," including sixteen in Devon, three in Cheshire, three in Wales, two in Wiltshire, and one each in Cumbria and West Yorkshire. Most notable for our purposes is the Church House Inn in Broadhempston, now operated as "The Monk's Retreat." According to Rev. H. R. Evans's parish history,[20] the proprietor of the Church House Inn in Broadhempston between 1774 and 1810 was Joshua Lovecraft (1739–1811), who married Sarah Ashweek (1740–1808) in Denbury on 20 October 1769.[21] Their daughter Ann Lovecraft (1771–1846), christened in Broadhempston on 17 November 1771, married William Hooper (1762–1841) in Broadhempston on 26 June 1806; Hooper succeeded his father-in-law Joshua Lovecraft as proprietor of the Church House Inn between 1810 and 1832.[22] It is possible that "Minster Hall" as contained in Allgood chart repre-

---

20. Evans, "Broadhempston" 116.
21. George Ashweek had been proprietor of the Church House Inn in 1764 (see Evans, "Broadhempston" 111), so perhaps Joshua Lovecraft succeeded his father-in-law as proprietor.
22. White's 1850 directory shows Thomas Williams as proprietor of the Church House. Morris and Company's 1870 directory shows William Hollett as proprietor of the Church House. By 1870, the village had another inn, "New Inn," operated by Henry John Harris. This is presumably the inn now operated as the Coppa Dolla.

sents a recollection of Joshua Lovecraft's proprietorship of the Church House Inn in Broadhempston. Nearby Torbryan also has a noted Old Church House Inn.[23]

Summary

The Allgood chart led Lovecraft to believe that his English ancestry consisted primarily of "small gentry" and Anglican clergy, until the decline caused by Thomas(A)'s debt caused his son Joseph(1) Lovecraft and his family to emigrate (*SL* 2.182). Of these families, the Fulford and Edgecombe families were surely the most illustrious. The Allgood chart also claimed alliances with the Washington family (there is no proven linkage to the family of U.S. President George Washington) (*SL* 2.180–81; *MWM* 293) and the Lovecroft family.[24]

The Fulford Ancestry Claim Disproved

The authors have attempted to verify some of the claims of the Allgood chart. Based upon a reference provided by Henry L. P. Beckwith, the authors obtained through the LDS Library a copy of the last will and testament of Rev. Francis Fulford (1734–1772), Vicar of Dunsford.[25] Mary Lovecraft, wife of emigrant Joseph(1), is buried in Mt. Hope Cemetery in Rochester, N.Y.; her tombstone[26] indicates that she died on 14 August 1864, aged

---

23. The authors are indebted to Richard McWilliams and Steven Sneyd for their discussions of "Minster Hall" and "Church House Inn."
24. *SL* 2.182. The Allgood chart claimed that HPL's ancestor George (D) married Hester Lovecroft, daughter of the late Richard Lovecroft (d. 1642), in 1649.
25. Records of the Prerogative Court of Canterbury, vol. 983 (1772) folio 441, LDS film number 92955.
26. Depicted along with the tombstone of her husband Joseph Lovecraft in Squires 13.

eighty-two years, having thus been born between 15 August 1781 and 14 August 1782. Thus, Rev. Francis Fulford, whose will was made on 16 May 1772 and admitted to probate on 24 December 1772, could not have been her father. There is no mention of a wife Ellen Edgecombe in Rev. Fulford's will; in fact, he leaves his estate to his sister Ann Fulford and the notice regarding the admission of his estate to probate describes him as "Clerk [in holy orders] and Batchelor."[27]

Joseph(1) Lovecraft's Marriage—The Bride's Name Was Full, Not Fulford

The 1805 Marriage at Woodland

The next step was to attempt to verify identity of the bride Mary of emigrant Joseph(1) Lovecraft. No such marriage could be found in the LDS International Genealogical Index, which the authors were cautioned does not contain records from about one-third of Devon parishes. Here the marriage index maintained by the Devon Family History Society proved an invaluable help. In the small rural parish of Woodland, southeast of Ashburton, Joseph Lovecraft of the parish, bachelor, married Mary Full of Denbury, spinster, by banns on 26 September 1805.[28] The witnesses were William and Elizabeth Full, probably the bride's siblings (see below). So, the surname of Joseph(1) Lovecraft's bride was Full, not Fulford.[29]

---

27. For the complete text of the Fulford will and further discussion, see Faig.

28. The marriage ceremony was probably performed by Rev. John White (1758–1841), curate of Woodland parish from 1788 until his death (see Evans, "Woodland" 209–15).

29. The fact that Joseph and Mary Lovecraft named their first son John *Full* Lovecraft is also strong circumstantial evidence for the identification of Mary's maiden name as Full. The name was probably chosen in honor of Mary's brother John Full.

Ancestry of Mary Full

Mary Full, the daughter of Richard and Elizabeth Full, was baptized privately at Denbury on 10 September 1782 and publicly received into the church on 24 September 1782. Subsequent children of Richard and Elizabeth (Brusey) Full baptized at Denbury were:

> John Full, baptized 6 January 1784
> William Tapper Full, baptized 9 November 1786
> Eliza Full, baptized 8 January 1789
> Jemima Full, baptized 30 March 1794
> Thomas Full, baptized 9 June 1797

Richard Full of Denbury and Elizabeth Brusey of Torbryan had been married by banns in Torbryan on 15 August 1782, with James Brusey and William Hooper as witnesses. Richard had been baptized at Woodland on 18 June 1758, the son of Richard Full and Mary Tapper, who married in the same parish on 18 January 1756. Elizabeth Brusey had been baptized at Denbury on 24 May 1763, the daughter of John Brusey and Joan Knapman.

The Family of Joseph(1) and Mary (Full) Lovecraft

With the assistance of staff of the Devon Record Office, the authors looked for children of Joseph and Mary Lovecraft baptized in Woodland parish. They found the following:

> John Full Lovecraft,[30] baptized 7 September 1806
> William Lovecraft,[31] baptized 23 February 1808

---

30. Co-author Searles found a date of birth of 16 April 1806 based upon his research in American records.

31. Squires 52 provides a date of birth of 1 February 1808 for William Lovecraft, in good agreement with his baptismal date. Co-author Searles

Joseph Lovecraft,[32] baptized 22 November 1810
Mary Lovecraft, baptized 12 February 1813
George Lovecraft,[33] baptized 9 February 1815
Aaron Lovecraft,[34] baptized 6 November 1817
Eliza Lovecraft, baptized 11 August 1820

There is one relevant burial record for the family: Mary, the daughter of Joseph and Mary Lovecraft, buried 7 April 1813, aged two months. Rev. Nicholas Pearkes, Rector of Broadhempston-Woodland,[35] provided the authors with some additional information of interest from the original records in his possession. When the baptisms of Mary, George, Aaron, and Eliza were recorded in 1813–20, Joseph and Mary Lovecraft and their family were residents of the hamlet of Pulsford. During this period Joseph worked as a carpenter, doubtless supported by the farms surrounding the tiny hamlet. Beginning in 1813, Thomas Harris

---

found a date of birth of 31 March 1804 based upon his research in American records, which seems clearly inconsistent with the baptismal record. William's New York State death certificate indicates that he died on 26 September 1882, aged 74 years 6 months 26 days, from which his inferred date of birth is 29 February 1808, also inconsistent with his baptismal record.

32. Co-author Searles found a date of birth of 4 November 1811 based on his research in American records. It seems probable that Joseph's date of birth was misstated by one year in the American records.

33. George Lovecraft's New York State death certificate indicates that he died on 11 September 1895, aged eighty years, in good agreement with his baptismal record.

34. Co-author Searles found a date of birth of 18 October 1817 based on his research in American records. This date is in good agreement with the baptismal record for Aaron Lovecraft.

35. The benefices of Woodland and Broadhempston were united by act of the Crown on 28 July 1938 (see Evans, "Woodland" 231–32). Services are still held in both churches.

and Joseph Charter, Esq. of Dartmouth were the proprietors of the farmland surrounding Pulsford. William Harris succeeded Thomas Harris in 1824 and Thomas Charter succeeded Joseph Charter in 1827. During the period 1813–30, the Harrises were often occupants of both of the farm properties with the Charters as proprietors *in absentia*.[36]

The Carpenter Becomes a Worsted-Spinner—Joseph(1) Lovecraft Removes to Bickington, Becomes a Bankrupt, and Emigrates

Emigration—1831

Citing a family Bible record, Squires states that the emigrant Joseph(1) Lovecraft and his family left England for America on 4 May 1831.[37] His account of the emigrant's son Joseph Lovecraft, Jr. states that Joseph, Jr. arrived in Rochester NY on 24 May 1831.[38] By way of contrast, H. P. Lovecraft in his letters claims that the emigrant Joseph(1) Lovecraft first arrived in Ontario,

---

36. Woodland parish Property Tax Assessments 1780–1830, LDS film 1526151.

37. Squires 21.

38. Squires 24. The claimed arrival date seems inconsistent with a departure date of 4 May 1831. Pike 79 gives 47 days as an average travel time in the 1850s for the voyage from Torquay to Quebec, while indicating that bad weather could lengthen the voyage considerably. Travel times probably decreased between the 1830s and the 1850s on account of the advent of larger and faster ships. Thus, the assertion that the Lovecraft family's entire trip from Devonshire to Rochester, NY, took only twenty days in 1831 is difficult to credit. It is possible, however, that Joseph Lovecraft, Jr. went out as a "scout" in advance of the rest of his family and actually did arrive in Rochester on 24 May 1831, especially in light of the relatively advanced age of Joseph Lovecraft Sr. at the time of his emigration. Squires kindly communicated to co-author Faig that his source for the date of arrival of Joseph Lovecraft, Jr. in Rochester was a newspaper obituary.

Canada, in 1827 and shortly thereafter located in Rochester (*MWM* 294). Lovecraft's account may be prone to error, since he proceeds to claim that the emigrant Joseph Lovecraft died shortly after settling on an "experimental farm" in New York, whereas he actually survived until 28 March 1850, when he died at the age of seventy-five.[39] As far as the authors are aware, the ports of embarkation and debarkation and the ship that carried Joseph(1) Lovecraft and his family to America have not been identified. Their arrival is not among those recorded for the port of New York City between 1820 and 1832.[40]

Bickington and Bankruptcy—1828–31

We do not know when Joseph(1) Lovecraft and his family departed from Pulsford. However, Mary, the daughter of Joseph and Mary Lovecraft, was baptized in Bickington parish on 4 November 1828.[41] White's 1850 Directory describes Bickington as a scattered village on the banks of the Lemon rivulet, three

---

39. See the photograph of his tombstone in Mt. Hope Cemetery in Rochester, NY (Squires 13).

40. See the following works compiled by Elizabeth P. Bentley: *Passenger Arrivals at the Port of New York 1820–1829* (Baltimore MD: Genealogical Publishing Company, 1999) and *Passenger Arrivals at the Port of New York 1830–1832* (Baltimore MD: Genealogical Publishing Company, 2000). The authors suggest that Torquay was the probable place of embarkation and Quebec the probable place of debarkation, since this was the customary emigration route from Devonshire to North America at the time. *Trewman's Exeter Flying Post* or other local newspapers may be the best place to search for notice of the departure of the Lovecraft family.

41. The baptismal date is in good accord with the date of birth (11 October 1828) provided by Mary (Lovecraft) Brown's New York State death certificate. Mary married James Brown (1806–1889) on 2 March 1854, and died in Rochester, NY, on 24 February 1907. For an account of her family, see Squires 45–46, 57–58.

miles northeast of Ashburton, on the main road to Exeter. The Bickford family had held property in the locality for more than six hundred years. The 1828 baptismal record gives Joseph's occupation as worsted-spinner. It was apparently the failure of this business led Joseph Lovecraft and his family to emigrate.[42]

The following notice, discovered by co-author Docherty, was published in the *London Gazette* (no. 18,852) for Tuesday, 20 September 1831:

> WHEREAS a Commission of Bankrupt is awarded and issued forth against Joseph Lovecraft, of the Parish of Bickington, in the County of Devon, Worsted-Spinner, Dealer and Chapman, and he being declared a Bankrupt is hereby required to surrender himself to the Commissioners in the said Commission named, or the major part of them, on the 11th and 12th days of October next, at Twelve o'Clock at Noon, and on the 1st day of November following, at the Clifford Arms, in Chudleigh, and make a full discovery and disclosure of his estate and effects, when and where the Creditors are to come prepared to prove their debts, and at the second sitting to choose Assignees, and at the last sitting the said Bankrupt is required to finish his examination, and the Creditors are to assent or to dissent from the allowance of his certificate. All persons indebted to the said Bankrupt, or that have any of his effects, are not to pay or deliver the same but to whom the Commissioners shall appoint, but give notice to Mr. William Doidge Taunton, Solicitor, Totnes, or to Mr. Joseph Blake, Solicitor, 19, Essex-Street, Strand, London.

A somewhat shorter notice of Joseph Lovecraft's bankruptcy appeared the following day in the *Times* for 21 September 1831: "Joseph Lovecraft, Bickington, Devonshire, worsted-spinner,

---

42. White's 1850 directory indicates that a serge manufactory employing 150 hands was operating in the village in 1850. Richard Caunter was the proprietor. It seems probable that Joseph Lovecraft's worsted-spinning business was a smaller enterprise.

Oct. 11, 12, at 12 o-clock, Nov. 1, at the Clifford Arms, Chudleigh; solicitor, Mr. Blake, Essex-street, Strand."

If the family Bible record cited by Squires is correct, Joseph Lovecraft and his family departed England for America on 4 May 1831, 139 days prior to the publication of the first of these notices. Rather than being driven into exile by the loss of the family estate of Minster Hall to his father Thomas's gambling debts in 1823, it appears that Joseph Lovecraft's own business failure was the motivating factor for his family's emigration. Records of bankruptcy proceedings from this period are very fragmentary, and despite diligent effort co-author Docherty failed to find any further record of the bankruptcy proceedings of Joseph Lovecraft. If bankruptcy proceedings against Joseph were already looming when he and his family departed England on 4 May 1831, it is possible that the family traveled under an assumed name. This could explain the difficulty which researchers have encountered in trying to discover an emigration record for the family.

The Troubled Economy—Political and Social Unrest 1830–32

Joseph may have determined to leave his carpentry business in the hamlet of Pulsford because of the widespread unrest among agricultural workers in the wake of the Napoleonic wars. The riots of agricultural workers over wages in the late autumn of 1830, called the "Swing Riots" after a Captain Swing who put up the rioters, may possibly have been part of the reason for the emigration of the Lovecrafts. The riots were centered in Hampshire, Wiltshire, and Dorset rather than Devonshire. There were however a number of disturbances in Devonshire, centering in Torquay and Newton-Abbot in November–December 1830, including the burning of a threshing machine in Newton-Abbot on 28 December 1830.[43] Many of the rioters were tried and transported to

---

43. Hobsbawm and Rude 352.

Australia for penal servitude in 1831. As a carpenter turned worsted-spinner, dealer, and chapman, Joseph Lovecraft would probably have had greater resources at his command than the average agricultural laborer. The passage from Torquay to Quebec would probably have been beyond the means of most agricultural laborers. One reference cites the following fares from the 1850s: three pounds to three pounds ten shillings for adults and one pound ten shillings to two pounds for children under fourteen.[44]

The economic difficulties contributed to a crescendo of social and political unrest that even raised fears of revolution around the time Joseph(1) Lovecraft and his family left England. King George IV had died on 26 June 1830 and was succeeded by his brother as William IV. Within weeks of the death of George IV, Charles X of France abdicated his throne on 2 August 1830 and went into exile in England. In 1831 Lord Grey and his Whig administration introduced the first reform bill, abolishing the "rotten" boroughs and changing the requirements for the franchise, and it passed its second reading in the House of Commons on 1 March 1831 by a margin of just one vote. With defeat staring the administration in the face, William dissolved parliament on 22 April 1831 and ordered new elections. Even so, the House of Lords defeated a second reform bill on 31 October 1831. The administration introduced a third reform bill on 6 December 1831, and William eventually consented to the creation of enough new peers to assure its passage. The House of Lords finally passed the third reform bill on 4 June 1832, and William gave it royal assent on 7 June 1832. All these dramatic events transpired while Joseph(1) Lovecraft and his family were seeking refuge from business failure in America.

---

44. Pike 79.

Coombe Cellars—A Possible Stopping Point?

Co-author Searles and Sneyd cite a tradition that the emigrant Joseph Lovecraft worked in a cotton mill in "Coombersellar." Sneyd (9–10) suggests that "Coombersellar" may correspond to Coombe Cellars, a small habitation on the Teign estuary, west of Teignmouth. It is certainly true that cotton mills often employed carpenters to maintain their equipment. Coombe Cellars is in close proximity to Combeinteignhead parish, where Joseph Lovecraft's brother Joshua Lovecraft (1776–1850) resided for many years. Combe Cellars was a popular place of resort because of its scenic location on the Teign, well known for its inn and gardens. The Ferry Boat Inn was famed for its Devonshire cream and seafood. Coombe Cellars was the setting for Sabine Baring-Gould's novel *Kitty Alone*. It was also a center for smuggling in the early nineteenth century. However, there are not known to have been any mills or spinning establishments located in the hamlet. The tradition recorded by Searles and Sneyd may actually recollect Joseph Lovecraft's business as worsted-spinner in Bickington.

Eliza, the Missing Daughter of Joseph(1) Lovecraft, and His Nieces Elizabeth Lovecraft and Mary (Lovecraft) Taylor

Eliza Lovecraft

We are left to wonder what became of Joseph's and Mary's daughter Eliza, baptized at Woodland parish on 11 August 1820. The annals of the Lovecraft family in America, as described by Howard Lovecraft, R. Alain Everts and Richard D. Squires, contain no account of a daughter Eliza born in 1820. She may have died before the family emigrated, or have been left with relatives in England. It is also possible that Eliza emigrated with her parents and siblings but died young. Co-author Searles has Rochester burial records for a number of Lovecrafts whose relationship to Joseph(1) and Mary (Full) Lovecraft has not been established, including Arthur Lovecraft (died 3 October 1839), M. W. Lovecraft (died 14 September 1838) and "Mrs. Lovecraft's child" (died 14 April 1840). There is also a Nathan Lovecraft in the 1838 Rochester city directory. It seems unlikely that Eliza Lovecraft, baptized in 1820, would have been called a child if she had died in 1840.

Two Gaskin-Lovecraft Marriages—1806 and 1833

John Full Lovecraft, the eldest son of the emigrant, was a carpenter-joiner and opened his own lumber mill in Rochester in 1849.[45] He married Elinor Gaskin at St. Luke's Church in Rochester on 8 June 1833.[46] Joshua Lovecraft, brother of the emigrant Joseph(1) Lovecraft, and Eleanor Gasking [*sic*] had married at Torquay St. Marychurch parish on 12 June 1806. They had two daughters baptized at Stokeinteignhead parish: Mary, baptized on 11 November 1810, and Elizabeth (surname written Lucraft) baptized on 20 February 1812. Everts (7) indicates that John Full Lovecraft "apparently married his first cousin, Elinor Gaskin (Lovecraft) Lovecraft (1782–1872)." However, the St. Luke's church record gives the surname of the 1833 bride as Gaskin. It is difficult to credit the assertion that John Full Lovecraft married his aunt Elinor (Gaskin) Lovecraft (the Torquay St. Mary Church bride of 1806) in 1833. The marriage of John Full Lovecraft and Elinor (Gaskin) Lovecraft produced children between 1834 and 1845, well beyond the reproductive age of a woman born in 1782. While it is not impossible that Joshua and Elinor (Gaskin) Lovecraft had a daughter Elinor (born say 1808, two years after their marriage), one must

---

45. Squires 14–15.
46. Letter of Emily W. Owlett (secretary of the Church of St. Luke and St. Simon, Rochester NY) to co-author Faig, 16 March 1988.

ask why the 1833 marriage record of such a putative daughter would give her maiden name as Gaskin. Joshua Lovecraft is listed as a farmer in Combeinteignhead in the 1850 White's Devon directory, and the death of Joshua Lovecraft is recorded in the Newton-Abbot civil registration district for September 1850.[47] After the death of her husband, Joshua's widow Elinor (Gaskin) Lovecraft (1782–1872) joined her daughter Elizabeth and her son-in-law Joseph Lovecraft, Jr. in Rochester.[48]

Joseph(1)'s Niece Elizabeth Lovecraft Marries Her First Cousin Joseph Lovecraft, Jr.—1839

While more Lovecrafts than just Joseph(1) and his immediate family undoubtedly emigrated to the New World, intermarriage within the family probably contributed to its reproductive failure in the nineteenth century. Elizabeth Lovecraft, the daughter of Joshua and Elinor (Gaskin) Lovecraft, can probably be identified as the Elizabeth Lovecraft who married Joseph Lovecraft, son of Joseph(1), at "Mr. J. S. Lovecraft's" in Rochester on 10 October 1839.[49] Joseph Lovecraft's widow Elizabeth died in Rochester on 29 October 1896, aged eighty-four years, in good agreement with the baptismal date of Elizabeth, daughter of Joshua and Elinor (Gaskin) Lovecraft. The New York State death certificate of Joseph Lovecraft's widow Elizabeth gives her parents' names as Joshua Lovecraft and Elinor Lovecraft. (While usually the maiden

---

47. Joshua Lovecraft was buried at Stokeinteignhead parish on 8 September 1850.

48. Elinor (Gaskin) Lovecraft is buried with her daughter and son-in-law in the family lot (S 1/2 lot 66 Section R) in Mt. Hope Cemetery in Rochester (see letter of Carol O'Kell to co-author Faig, 9 June 1988). Squires 29 also mentions this fact.

49. Letter of Emily W. Owlett to co-author Faig, 16 March 1988, citing St. Paul's Church records.

name of the mother would have been given, the informant may not have known this information.) The death certificate states that Elizabeth had been in the United States fifty-nine or sixty years at the time of her death, which places her arrival in 1836 or 1837.

Joseph(1)'s Niece Mary (Lovecraft) Taylor and Her Family

Elizabeth's sister Mary Lovecraft married Joseph Taylor in Combeinteignhead parish, Devon on 16 February 1836; Elizabeth Lovecraft and her father Joshua Lovecraft acted as witnesses. John Lovecraft Taylor, son of Joseph (shoemaker) and Mary Taylor, was baptized at Combeinteignhead parish on 29 December 1836. According to Squires (55), George Lovecraft's adoptive daughter Augusta Charlotte Allgood (1842?-1884) (sister of his wife Helen Allgood) married one John Lovecraft Taylor (1836–1899) on 24 December 1862. This marriage produced a son George Lovecraft Taylor.[50] It seems very likely that John Lovecraft Taylor, baptized in Combeinteignhead on 29 December 1836, was also the groom of 24 December 1862.

John(A) and Mary (Tapper) Lovecraft— Probable Parents of Joseph(1)

Their Family

John Lovecraft (husbandman) and Mary Tapper (spinster), both of the parish, were married by banns in Woodland parish on 2 January 1768. The witnesses were John Tapper and Thomas Bowden. Both the bride and the groom made their marks in the parish register, indicating that they were probably illiterate. The following Woodland baptismal records probably record their children:

---

50. Born 6 October 1877, Rochester, NY; died 12 July 1900, Mt. Vernon, NY (New York State death certificate).

John, son of John and Mary, baptized 9 October 1768
Joseph, son of John and Mary, baptized 20 November 1774
Joshua,[51] son of John and Mary, baptized 15 September 1776

The natural presumption is that son Joseph may be identified with the 1805 Woodland groom and son Joshua with the 1806 Torquay St. Marychurch groom, and that the two grooms were thus brothers. Note that son Joseph's baptismal date is in good agreement with Joseph(1) Lovecraft's stated age of seventy-five at his death on 28 March 1850.

John Lovecraft Mariner Makes His Will

H. P. Lovecraft referred to his great-grandfather Joseph(1) Lovecraft as the "sixth child" of Thomas Lovecraft (*MWM* 294). There is another explanation than possible removal to another parish for the long gap between the births of John in 1768 and Joseph in 1774. On 22 March 1777, Joseph Lovecraft made his last will and testament while serving on HMS *Boyne* under Captain Herbert Sawyer. His will, probably made whilst at sea, reads as follows:[52]

> In the Name of God Amen—I John Lovecraft Mariner belonging to his Majesty's Ship Boyne Herbert Sawyer Esquire Commander being of sound and disposing mind and memory and considering the dangers of the Seas and uncertainties of this Transitory Life as for avoiding controversies after my Decease make publish and declare this my last Will and Testament in manner following (that is to say) first I recommend my soul to God that gave it and my Body to the Earth or Sea as it shall please God to order and as for my worldly Estate whatsoever as shall be any ways due or owing or be-

---

51. In the Woodland parish register, Joshua's surname is written as "Luckraft," struck through with a line and "Lovecraft" written above.
52. Records of the Prerogative Court of Canterbury, vol. 1072 folio 576, LDS film 0093044.

longing to me at this time of my decease I give devise and bequeath the same to my dearly beloved Wife Mary Lovecraft of Woodlan [*sic*] in the County of Devon and I do hereby nominate and appoint the said Mary Lovecraft to be Executor of this my last Will and Testament hereby revoking all former and other Wills Testaments and Deeds of Gifts by me at any time heretofore made and I do ordain and ratify these Presents to stand and be for my only last Will and Testament. In Witness whereof to this said Will I have set my hand and Seal the twenty second day of March in the seventeenth Year of the Reign of our Sovereign Lord George the Third over Great Britain ffrance and Ireland King Defender of the Faith and so forth and in this Year of our Lord one thousand seven hundred and seventy seven. John Lovecraft [LS] Signed Sealed and published in the presence of us Herbert Sawyer Captain—Rich. Saunders, 2d Lieut.

John's will was admitted to probate before the Prerogative Court of Canterbury on 30 December 1780, and administration granted to his widow Mary Lovecraft.

HMS Boyne *and Her Exploits*

Captain Sawyer, a longtime Navy veteran, took command of the *Boyne,* a warship carrying 520 men and 68 guns, in 1777. The *Boyne* was the second of three ships bearing this name and was launched at Plymouth Harbor on 31 May 1766. John Lovecraft is shown among the crew mustered for the *Boyne* on 1 July 1777.[53] The *Boyne* sailed for the West Indies on 19 November 1777 but returned to Spithead, Portsmouth, by 2 May 1778. She saw action against the French at St. Lucia on 13 November 1778 and off Grenada on 6 July 1779. In the latter action, the *Boyne* suffered the loss of 12 men killed and 30 men wounded.[54] John Lovecraft last appeared in the ship's musters for March and

---

53. Public Record Office, ADM 36/8011.
54. The *Boyne* saw further action in Martinique in 1780. She was broken up at Plymouth Dock in May 1783.

April 1779, and the presumption is that he fell ill before the engagement of 6 July 1779. John was probably returned by hospital ship to the naval hospital in Plymouth, England, from which he was discharged dead on 4 October 1780.[55] He can probably be identified with the John Lovecraft buried at Woodland parish on 7 October 1780.

John Lovecraft's great-great-grandson H. P. Lovecraft was an unapologetic Anglophile who always regretted the rebellion of the American colonies against England. He would doubtless have been very proud to find among his ancestors a mariner who fought against the French allies of the American rebels. The authors suspect he might have been prouder of the mariner John Lovecraft than he was of the minor country gentry and clergy who he believed to be his ancestors.

Mary Lovecraft Remarries

Widow Mary Lovecraft, of the parish, married bachelor Henry Priston, sojourner in the parish, by banns in Woodland parish on 23 May 1782. William Lovecraft and John Palk were witnesses. It seems likely that Mary was Mary (Tapper) Lovecraft, the widow of mariner John Lovecraft, who died at Plymouth Hospital on 4 October 1780. The death of her husband John had left Mary Lovecraft with at least three young children: John, barely twelve years old; Joseph, not yet six years old; and Joshua, four years old. Probably still only in her mid-thirties, she would have had strong motivation to remarry. Although Henry Priston [Preston] was only a sojourner in Woodland parish when he married Mary in 1782, he apparently remained in this parish, or at least returned to the parish to witness the marriage of John

---

55. Public Record Office, Naval Pay Book ADM 34/109. The discharge date was originally written as 12 October but "12" was struck out and replaced by "4."

Lovecraft and Mary Harris, both of the parish, on 29 September 1796. The authors have not as yet undertaken a search for Preston family records in Woodland parish.

John Lovecraft the mariner had two first cousins: William, the son of Jonah and Elizabeth (Ludgar) Lovecraft, baptized at Woodland on 4 June 1731, and William, the son of Joshua and Elizabeth (Willinge) Lovecraft, baptized at Broadhempston on 14 December 1734. William Lovecraft married Jane Full in Woodland parish on 13 July 1755, with John Tapper and William Gardner and witnesses. Joan Lovecraft, wife of William, was buried at Woodland parish on 13 July 1761. William Lovecraft (widower) married Elizabeth Garner in Woodland parish on 3 February 1777, with John Tapper and Jonah Lovecraft as witnesses. The authors suggest, based on the witnesses, that William Lovecraft, the 1755 and 1777 Woodland groom, was probably William the son of Jonah and Elizabeth (Ludgar) Lovecraft. The authors further suggest that he was probably the William Lovecraft who witnessed the marriage of Mary (Tapper) Lovecraft and Henry Priston at Woodland parish on 23 May 1782. It seems likely that he was the also William Lovecraft who held one of the Lake farms in tenancy from Robert Abraham in Woodland parish between 1780 and 1801.[56] He may be the William Lovecraft who was buried at Woodland parish on 11 September 1812. If John Lovecraft's sons did not accompany their mother Mary Lovecraft after her marriage to Henry Priston in 1782, William Lovecraft's Lake farm might have provided a place of refuge for them.

---

56. Woodland Parish Property Tax Assessments 1780–1830, LDS film 1526151. That William's nephew Joseph(1) Lovecraft established himself at Pulsford, close to the Lake farms, as a carpenter not later than 1813, may be some further support to these identifications.

Joseph(B) and Mary (Pitt) Lovecraft—Probable Grandparents of Joseph(1)

Attempting to climb the family tree another generation based on baptismal records is more speculative. The marriage of Joseph Lovecraft and Mary Pitt on 22 December 1728 is recorded in the bishop's transcripts for Woodland parish. The following children of Joseph and Mary Lovecraft baptized at Woodland parish may possibly include the groom John Lovecraft of 2 January 1768:

> Agnes, daughter of Joseph and Mary, baptized 11 October 1730
> Joseph, son of Joseph and Mary, baptized 25 August 1733
> Mary, daughter of Joseph and Mary, baptized 9 January 1734/35
> Joshua, son of Joseph and Mary, baptized 2 December 1739
> John, son of Joseph and Mary, baptized 14 November 1742

Joseph and Mary Lovecraft also had a son John Lovecraft, buried 28 September 1740 at Woodland parish. It is possible that Mary Lovecraft, buried at Woodland parish on 14 March 1771, and Joseph Lovecraft, buried at Woodland parish on 27 November 1781, were the bride and groom of 22 December 1728. Joseph may be identified with Joseph Lovecraft, son of William (weaver), baptized at Broadhempston on 13 June 1703.[57] If correct, this identification would make the emigrant Joseph(1) John(A) Joseph(B) William(C) rather than Joseph(1) Thomas(A) John(B) Joseph(C) George(D) William(E) Richard(F) John(G).

---

57. Kitty Turner's Broadhempston parish record extracts indicate that a Joseph Lovecraft was buried in the parish on 10 March 1717/18. However, it is not necessarily the case that the decedent of March 1717/18 was identical to the child baptized on 13 June 1703. The authors are indebted to Richard McWilliams for Kitty Turner's Broadhempston parish record extracts.

Will(C) Lovecraft (Weaver) of Broadhempston and His Family

The authors have not been able to identify the parents of Will (William) Lovecraft, weaver, of Broadhempston parish. Baptisms for some eighteen children of Will Lovecraft are recorded in Broadhempston parish between 1701 and 1736. Among these baptisms are those of sons Joseph (13 June 1703), Jonah (22 April 1705) and Joshua (21 October 1706).[58] Will Lovecraft and George [*sic*] Merifeild,[59] weavers, had been married in Broadhempston parish on 27 December 1699. However, not all the eighteen children of Will Lovecraft baptized in Broadhempston parish between 1701 and 1736 were children of this couple. One and only one of these baptismal records lists a mother's name: that of John, son of William and Alice, baptized 22 September 1724. There is also recorded the burial of Agnis Lovecraft, wife of Will, in Broadhempston parish on 28 January 1722/23. Also, William Lovecraft and Mary Cole were married in Broadhempston parish on 12 May 1724 and some of the later baptisms probably belong to this couple. According to Kitty Turner's Broadhempston parish record extracts, a William Lovecraft, son of John, was baptized in Broadhempston parish on 3 March 1694/95; perhaps he was the groom of 12 May 1724. It is possible that Will Lovecraft (weaver) married in succession George [*sic*] Merifeild (27 December 1699), Agnis —— (died 28 January 1722/23), and Alice —— (child baptized 22 September 1724), but other theories could also fit the known facts.

---

58. The baptisms of Jonah and Joshua were found only in Kitty Turner's Broadhempston parish record extracts. A review by the Devon Record Office did not confirm these records.

59. George is an unusual name for a female child, but not unknown. George Merrifield or Mirrifell was christened at Widdecombe in the Moor parish on 17 June 1677, but he was a male child, the son of George and Anne Merrifield.

Comparing the Allgood Chart with the Authors' Results

The Allgood chart makes William(E) the son of Richard(F) and the grandson of John(G). It may be noted that a Richard Lovecraft was buried in Broadhempston parish on 2 November 1711; it is possible that he was the father of Will. In addition, John Lovecraft, Jr. was buried in Broadhempston parish on May 28, 1696 and John Lovecraft (weaver) was buried in Broadhempston parish on 10 January 1705/06. If John Lovecraft (weaver) was the grandfather of Will, it is possible that three generations of Lovecrafts before Joseph (baptized 1703) were weavers. If one throws out Thomas(A) and George(D), it is remarkable to note the records consulted by the authors are consistent with the paternal ascent provided by the Allgood chart. On the other hand, the omission of two generations makes the chart's dating of John Lovecroft (fl.1560) impossible.

While the name Thomas Lovecraft occurs multiple times in seventeenth- and eighteenth-century parish records in Broadhempston, Woodland, and Torbryan, the same cannot be said for George Lovecraft. Apart from the 1815 Woodland baptism of Lovecraft's grandfather George, the only other parish record relating to George Lovecraft so far found by the authors relates to George Lovecraft, son of John, baptized in Broadhempston on 3 June 1821.[60] The authors suggest that George(D) might have been added to the paternal ascent in the Allgood

---

60. Another George Lovecraft may be found in the 1860 U.S. census of eleventh ward of New Orleans, Louisiana, where there then resided George Lovecraft, male aged 36, born New York, a laborer with personal estate of $100, with his wife Eliza Lovecraft, female aged 35, born New York, washerwoman, and their two daughters, Caroline, female aged 16, born New York, and Charlotte, female aged 13, born Louisiana. The authors do not know the ancestry or further history of this Louisiana Lovecraft family.

chart based on the 1699 Broadhempston marriage of Will [William(E) in the Allgood chart] Lovecraft to George Merifeild.

There can be no question that the 26 September 1805 Woodland parish marriage of Joseph Lovecraft and Mary Full is the marriage of the emigrants Joseph(1) and Mary (Full) Lovecraft. Whether Joseph(1) can be identified with Joseph, the son of John and Mary (Tapper) Lovecraft baptized at Woodland parish on 20 November 1774 is less certain but nevertheless very likely. The excellent agreement of the baptismal date with the stated age at death of the emigrant Joseph(1) Lovecraft and the existence of a brother Joshua Lovecraft are good supportive evidence for the claim that the Joseph Lovecraft, son of John and Mary (Tapper) Lovecraft, baptized at Woodland parish on 20 November 1774 was the emigrant Joseph(1) Lovecraft.

Searching for Thomas(A) Lovecraft

The Claims of Thomas(A) of the Allgood Chart

The authors believe that the identifications of John and Mary (Tapper) Lovecraft as parents, of Joseph and Mary (Pitt) Lovecraft as paternal grandparents, and of Will and George (Merifeild) Lovecraft, as paternal great-grandparents of the emigrant Joseph(1) Lovecraft, are tentative. One must surely give some weight to the identification of Joseph(1)'s father as Thomas(A) in the Allgood chart especially given the fairly copious account that H. P. Lovecraft provides of the life of Thomas(A) Lovecraft (1745–1826). Given the proven falsity of the claim that Ellen Edgecombe was the wife of Rev. Francis Fulford, however, it seems likely that the claimed 1766 marriage of Thomas(A) Lovecraft and her sister Letitia Edgecombe should be questioned. Just as a family historian may have substituted Fulford for Full in the family history, the same person may have "reached" for a link with the only slightly less illustrious Edgecombe family. Edgecombe family genealogist Alan Taylor stated in correspondence to co-author Faig that he could identify no sisters Ellen and Letitia Edgecome contemporary with Rev. Francis Fulford and Thomas(A) Lovecraft.[61]

*Jonah and Elizabeth (Ludgar) Lovecraft—
Parents of the Missing Thomas?*

Another large Woodland parish Lovecraft family contemporary with that of Joseph(B) and Mary (Pitt) Lovecraft was that of Jonah and Elizabeth (Ludgar) Lovecraft.[62] Kitty Turner found a 22 April 1705 baptismal record for Jonah Lovecraft, son of Will, in Broadhempston parish, from which one naturally infers that Joseph (baptized 1703) and Jonah (baptized 1705) were brothers. Jonah Lovecraft and Elizabeth Ludgar married in Woodland parish on 26 September 1728, according to the bishop's transcripts. The following Woodland baptisms are recorded for children of Jonah and Elizabeth Lovecraft:

---

61. Letter to co-author Faig, 12 April 1995. The name of Mary Anne Edgecombe Full, an illegitimate child born in Ugborough parish on 2 February 1811, and christened there on 21 February 1811, combines several names found in the Allgood chart. The Ugborough parish registers contain many records appertaining to the Full and Luscombe families. See Faig for some further discussion of the Ugborough records. The LDS Library has a Full family genealogy not seen by the authors: Frances Lane Harris, *Elura Morgan Full Lane: Her Descendants and Ancestors* (Vancouver BC: Published by the author, 1986).

62. Jonah Lovecraft signed the Woodland bishop's transcripts as church warden c. 1745. Perhaps Jonah Lovecraft's office as church warden was close as one of HPL's paternal ancestors got to clerical employment. However, it should also be noted that Broadhempston tailor William Lovecraft (1776–1855) was active in the parish church band (see Evans, "Broadhempston" 114, 119).

Joan Lovecraft, daughter of Jonah and Elizabeth, baptized 15 July 1729

William Lovecraft, son of Jonah and Elizabeth, baptized 4 June 1731

Elizabeth Lovecraft, daughter of Jonah and Elizabeth, baptized 18 August 1734

Thomas Lovecraft, son of Jonah and Elizabeth, baptized 22 November 1736

Jonah Lovecraft, son of Jonah and Elizabeth, baptized 10 October 1738

Joseph Lovecraft, son of Jonah and Elizabeth, baptized 13 November 1740

Agness Lovecraft, daughter of Jonah and Elizabeth, baptized 29 June 1746

Son Jonah was buried on 25 April 1741 at Woodland parish. It is possible that Elizabeth Lovecraft, buried on 23 August 1779 at Woodland parish, and Jonah Lovecraft, buried on 6 July 1780 at Woodland parish, were the bride and groom of 26 September 1728.

Thomas Lovecraft, the Torbryan Groom of 1772

There were certainly contemporary Thomas Lovecrafts in Devon who might have been the father of Joseph(1) Lovecraft. As indicated above, Jonah and Elizabeth Lovecraft had a son Thomas baptized at Woodland on 22 November 1736. In addition, Mary Lovecraft had a son Thomas baptized at Broadhempston exactly five years later on 22 November 1741; the name of the father is not given in the baptismal record. This is probably the same Thomas Lovecraft, son of Mary, buried at Broadhempston on 18 January 1742/43. A Thomas Lovecraft married Martha Hollock (or Hollett)[63] "with the consent of all parties" at nearby

---

63. The Devon Record Office notes that the incumbent entered the sur-

Torbryan parish on 4 August 1772; both were stated to be residents of the parish. The bride and groom made their marks in the baptismal record while witnesses —— [illegible] Hollett and Susanna Winsor signed their names. The staff of the Devon Record Office examined the baptismal records of Torbryan parish for the period 1772–80 for the authors but found no children recorded for Thomas and Martha Lovecraft.

Is Thomas the Name of a Family Patron?

Whether Thomas(A) may be identified with Jonah and Elizabeth Lovecraft's son Thomas Lovecraft baptized at Woodland on 22 November 1736 or Thomas Lovecraft married to Martha Hollock (or Hollett) at Torbryan parish on 4 August 1772 is questionable. If Thomas was a successful man, it is possible that Joseph(1) Lovecraft may have taken him as a patron or even as an adoptive parent. A legacy left by Thomas(A) Lovecraft (died 1826) might even have made possible the emigration of Joseph(1) Lovecraft and his family to America, which H. P. Lovecraft states to have occurred as early as 1827.[64] The authors suggest that the Allgood chart's 1827 date for the emigration of Joseph(1) Lovecraft and his family may actually recall their removal from Pulsford to Bickington. Perhaps money given or lent by a patron or an adoptive father Thomas Lovecraft may have

---

name of the bride in the register as Hallett.

64. The baptism of Mary Lovecraft, daughter of worsted-spinner Joseph Lovecraft, in Bickington parish on 4 November 1828 makes it extremely unlikely that her father emigrated to America as early as 1827. However, it must be remembered that there is at present no evidence to support HPL's assertion that Joseph(1) Lovecraft and his entire family traveled to America together. It is possible that some of Joseph Lovecraft's children preceded him to America, and that others followed him. It is known that Joseph Lovecraft's niece Elizabeth Lovecraft (who married his son Joseph Lovecraft, Jr.) arrived in the United States as late as 1836–37.

enabled Joseph(1) Lovecraft to establish himself as a worsted-spinner in Bickington.

It is also interesting to note that White's 1850 Devon directory listed one Thomas Maye Luscombe as a gentleman residing at Broadhempston Hall, the former Rowe dower house at Beaston.[65] The property had come to the Rowe family as the jointure of Mary Trevilyan, wife of Thomas Rowe.[66] According to Morris and Company's *Commercial Directory and Gazetteer* (1870), John Grant Luscombe, yeoman, was still in possession of Oakhill Farm, Beaston in that year.[67] The Rowe family lost possession of their greater property of Kingston House by 1778.[68] Kingston House was owned by the Rendell family between 1816 and 1936.[69] Whether the Luscombe family of the South Hams had any connection with the emigrant Joseph Lovecraft and his family is a matter for speculation in the absence of additional evidence.[70]

The widow Mary Lovecraft and her three young boys would

---

65. Evans, "Broadhempston" 117–18, 122. Figure 7 (p. 74) depicts the Georgian house erected by Austin Rowe at Beaston, connected to the older house by a later erection.

66. Evans, "Broadhempston" 107.

67. Found at freepages.genealogy.rootsweb.com/~valhender/dirtrans/mort1870/broad.htm. Beaston is currently in the possession of dentist Dr. John Hunt (see fdiworldental.org/about/abcov.htm).

68. Evans, "Broadhempston" 109.

69. See www.kingston-estate.net (consulted 5 April 2001) for photographs and history of the Kingston Estate, currently operated as a guesthouse and special events facility.

70. This family should not be confused with the Hoare banking family, baronets of Luscombe. Charles Hoare (1767–1851) contracted with architect John Nash (1752–1835) to build Luscombe Castle near Dawlish in 1800. There is also a Devon village named Luscombe, located about two miles south of Totnes.

certainly have needed support after the death of her husband John(A) Lovecraft at Plymouth Hospital in 1780. Whether the boys remained with Mary and her new husband Henry Priston after Mary's remarriage in 1782 is not known to the authors. As they grew up, they may have been employed by their father's cousin William Lovecraft on his Lake farm in Woodland parish. There is also the possibility that Joseph(1) Lovecraft received patronage from another member of the family named Thomas Lovecraft.

The Lovecraft Family of Devon— Sixteenth through Eighteenth Centuries

Frequency and Geographical Distribution of Marriages

Stepping back from the questions relating to the immediate ancestors of the emigrant Joseph(1) Lovecraft, it is pleasant to contemplate the conformity of surviving records with the broader history of the Devon Lovecraft family as given by H. P. Lovecraft based on the Allgood chart. The authors have found seven Lovecraft/Lovecroft marriages in Devon before 1600, commencing with the marriage of Steven Lovecraft and Joane Wakeham in Loddiswell parish on 3 June 1567.[71] The eighteen seventeenth-century Devon Lovecraft/Lovecroft marriages found by the authors are distributed by parish as follows: Broadhempston, six; Torbryan, five; Loddiswell, five; Ashburton and Littlehempston, one each.[72]

---

71. The earliest marriage record for the Lovecroft surname variant found by the authors is the marriage of Margaret Lovecroft and Vincent Cutmore in Stokeinteignhead parish on 2 July 1576.

72. If we admit Lucraft/Luccraft marriages in parishes where the Lovecraft/Lovecroft name is known to have flourished, we add twelve additional seventeenth-century (1601–1700) marriages: nine in Loddiswell and three in Woodland.

By the eighteenth century, adjoining Broadhempston and Woodland parishes had clearly become the center for the Lovecraft family name. Of the forty-four eighteenth-century Devon Lovecraft marriages contained in the index maintained by the Devon Family History Society, more than seventy percent occurred in Broadhempston or Woodland parishes: Broadhempston, sixteen; Woodland, fifteen; Denbury, two; Torbryan, two; Staverton, two; and Chagford, Ashburton, Cornworthy, Widdecombe in the Moor, St. Peter Exeter, Plymouth Charles, and Rockbeare, one each.

The Protestation Returns (1641) and the Muster Roll (1569)

There is other evidence for the early preeminence of the Lovecraft surname in Broadhempston and Woodland parishes. The Devon Protestation Returns of 1641[73] contain only four occurrences of the Lovecraft family name: one (Henry) in Cornwood parish, Ermington Hundred and three (John, Samuel and Thomas) in Broadhempston parish, Haytor Hundred. By way of contrast, there are some twenty-one occurrences of the more common Luc(k)raft surnames and variants. The Luc(k)raft surnames and variants are actually rare in Broadhempston and Woodland, where the Lovecraft surname predominates. Even earlier, the Devon muster roll for 1569[74] listed but three occurrences of all these related surnames: pikeman Luke Luckrafte in Revelstock parish, Plympton Hundred; archer William Lockroste in Littlehempston parish, Haytor Hundred; and billman John Lovecroft, South Milton parish, Stanborough Hundred. It is interesting that H. P. Lovecraft records Lovecroft as an early

---

73. See A. J. Howard, *The Devon Protestation Returns 1641* (n.p.: Privately published, 1973).
74. See A. J. Howard and T. L. Stoate, *The Devon Muster Roll for 1569* (Bristol, UK: T. L. Stoate, 1977).

version of the family name, and that South Milton parish had a John Lovecroft in 1569 and Stokeinteignhead parish a Margaret Lovecroft in 1576.

Earlier Records and the Relationship with the Lucraft Family Name

Common Origins?

The relationship of the Lovecraft/Lovecroft family and the Luc(k)raft family[75] might be the subject of long discussion. The Lovecrafts, centering in Broadhempston, Woodland, and surrounding parishes, appear to be well distinguished by the eighteenth century. Nevertheless, it seems likely that the two family names have a remote common origin. In a presentation entitled "Devon Origins in the South Hams" given before the Luc(k)raft Family Conference in Exeter in May 1999,[76] Ian Lucraft identified Richard de Loccroft, assessed for 18 pence in Essewater (Ashwater) parish of Black Torrington, north of Okehampton, in the 1332 lay subsidy.[77] In the same presentation, he identified the following individuals in the 1524 lay subsidy:

---

75. Ian Lucraft of Sheffield, UK, has done extensive research on the Luc(k)raft family documented in the twenty volumes of his Luc(k)raft One Name Study intended for eventual deposit with the Society of Genealogists. He is publisher of the *Luc(k)raft Newsletter* and sponsored a successful family conference held in Exeter in May 1999. The website of the Luc(k)raft One Name Study is www.lucraft.org.

76. Published in the *Luc(k)raft Newsletter* No. 7 (December 1999).

77. In their discussion of the Lucraft surname, Hanks and Hodges (335) indicate that the name is in fact a habitation name deriving from Luckcroft in Ashwater, Devon, whose name derives from OE *loca* (enclosure) + OE *croft* (paddock). Hanks and Hodges indicate that the Luckraft variant is first found c. 1554 at Stoke Gabriel. The earliest Lovecraft/Lovecroft parish records thus far found by the authors date from 1560 (burial of Agnise

William Lovecrofte (G5), Loddiswell parish
John Lovecroft (G4), Loddiswell parish
John Lovecroft (G3), Loddiswell parish
William Lowcrofte (W1), Harberton parish
Richard Lowcrofte (W1), Harberton parish
William Lomecrofte (G8), Bridford parish
John Lowcroffthe (G3), Exeter St. Sidwell parish

It is certainly interesting to find two John Lovecrofts in early sixteenth-century records. The most remote direct ancestor claimed by H. P. Lovecraft was John Lovecroft (fl. 1560) (*SL* 2.182). Everything that the authors have found concerning the origins of the Lovecraft/Lovecroft family name supports the general accuracy of the account given by Lovecraft based upon the Allgood chart. A number of members of the Luc(k)raft family have submitted to DNA testing in the effort to establish the closeness of their relationship.[78] The difficulty with respect to the Lovecraft/Lovecroft family will be to find a living member in the male line to submit to such testing.

Lovecraft Into Luccraft—A Case Study in Loddiswell Parish

The authors have found only rare occurrences of the Luc(k)raft surname changing to Lovecra(o)ft. The reverse transformation is easier to find. Loddiswell parish was an early center for the Lovecraft family name from 1560 forward. However, once we reach the second quarter of the seventeenth century, the Love-

---

Lovecraft at Loddiswell) and 1576 (marriage of Margaret Lovecroft at Stokeinteignhead), respectively.
78. For DNA testing, see Ian Lucraft's *Luc(k)raft Newsletter* No. 6 (December 1998): [1]; No. 7 (December 1999): [5]; No. 8 (January 2001): [4]; No. 9 (January 2002): [3]. No. 9 also includes a supplement with the title "The DNA Study and Our American Family Groups."

craft family name in Loddiswell has begun to change to the Luccraft family name. The last Lovecraft baptism in Loddiswell is 17 December 1628; the last marriage, 1 November 1617; the last burial, 5 May 1624. Thereafter, the name is recorded as Luccraft, Luccrafte, or Lucraft in the Loddiswell parish records, the sole exception being the burial of John Luccraft on 8 December 1735—in this record alone "Luccraft" has been struck out and replaced by "Lovecraft." The Luc(k)raft surname eventually was borne by many more persons than the Lovecra(o)ft surname, and perhaps there was natural tendency to yield to the more popular name, especially considering the lack of uniformity in spelling during these centuries.

The Lovecraft Family Name Dies Out in the Nineteenth and Twentieth Centuries

Contemporary Lovecrafts?

It is quite possible that the Lovecraft and Lovecroft surnames originating in South Devon are now extinct. Although he wrote of a grandson of Joseph Lovecraft "who went west in the 1880's and dropped from sight,"[79] it seems probable that H. P. Lovecraft was the last person in North America to bear his surname. Gordon Lovecraft Brown, Sr. (1901–1975) and Gordon Lovecraft Brown, Jr. (1927–2003), grandson and great-grandson of Mary (Lovecraft) Brown and James Brown, proudly bore Lovecraft as their middle names. A number of United States residents listed in current electronic telephone directories use the Lovecraft family name. How many, if any, of these persons actually descend from the Devon Lovecraft family remains to be verified.

---

79. *MWM* 294. The reference is to George Elliott Lovecraft, son of Joshua Elliott Lovecraft. See the essay on him in this book.

Lovecrafts in England through the Mid-Nineteenth Century

The Lovecraft/Lovecroft surname also became rarer and rarer in England as the nineteenth century progressed. John Lovecraft, buried on 4 December 1844 at the age of seventy-one, is the last Lovecraft to appear in the Woodland parish records.[80] John Lovecroft (so spelled), master of the schooner *Gleaner* of Torquay, Devon, died while his ship was in the port of Tynemouth, Northumberland, and was buried there on 29 July 1844.[81] William Lovecraft (died 14 February 1855, aged 79; buried 20 February 1855) and his wife Elizabeth (died 7 February 1835, aged 55; buried 10 February 1835) have monuments in Broadhempston parish churchyard.[82]

William was baptized at Broadhempston parish on 6 February 1776, the son of Joshua and Sarah (Ashweek) Lovecraft; Ann (Lovecraft) Hooper was his sister. William Lovecraft and Elizabeth Bennett married in Broadhempston parish on 3 December 1799 and had a family of twelve children, baptized in Broadhempston between 1800 and 1823. William, a tailor, played a prominent role in early nineteenth-century Broadhempston parish affairs, well recorded in Rev. H. R. Evans's parish history,[83] until his removal to London following the death of his wife to conduct his business in Threadneedle Street in 1835. William Lovecraft must have been successful in his tailoring

---

80. The authors thank Rev. Nicholas Pearkes, Rector of Broadhemptson-Woodland, for this information. Despite the discrepancy in age, it is possible that this John Lovecraft, was the same as John Lovecraft, son of John(A) and Mary (Tapper) Lovecraft, baptized at Woodland parish on 9 October 1768. If so, he was the brother of the emigrant Joseph(1) Lovecraft.

81. The authors thank the Devon Family History Society for this information.

82. The authors thank Bob Nield for this information.

83. Evans, "Broadhempston" 114, 119, 122, 123.

business in London, for he retired to Broadhempston in 1850 and built for his family the handsome home "Greenhill," now called "Sneydhurst."[84] It seems probable that William Lovecraft (1776–1855) was the grandson of Joshua Lovecraft (baptized 1706) and Elizabeth Willinge, married in Broadhempston parish on 19 November 1731. If Joseph (baptized 1703) and Joshua (baptized 1706) were both sons of William (weaver) of Broadhempston, this relationship would make William Lovecraft (1776–1855) the tailor and Joseph(1) Lovecraft (1774–1850) the carpenter, worsted-spinner and emigrant second cousins.

Marriages

Witnessing the decline of the surname, the LDS International Genealogical Index records but seventeen Lovecraft/Lovecroft marriages in England in the nineteenth century. Interestingly, the very last such record (the marriage of John Daniel Radick and Elizabeth Anne Lovecroft on 10 June 1878 in St. James's Church, Westminster, London[85]) was for the less common Lovecroft variant of the surname. Given the simultaneous decline of the surname in America, it is possible that Winfield Scott Lovecraft and Sarah Susan Phillips (St. Paul's Cathedral, Boston, MA, 12 June 1889), George Elliott Lovecraft and Celia L. Marchand (Racine, Wis., 20 November 1890), George Elliott

---

84. The authors are indebted to Steven Sneyd for information concerning William Lovecraft.

85. The bride, Elizabeth Anne Lovecroft, was a widow, residing at St. James Clerkenwell at the time of the marriage. She was the daughter of William Thorne, linen draper, deceased. The groom, John Daniel Radick, was a bachelor, employed as a tailor, residing at 54a Marshall Street at the time of the marriage. He was the son of Daniel Radick, carriage builder, deceased. Freidrich [sic] William Rother and Filsey Louisa Rother were witnesses to the marriage.

Lovecraft and Norma Hanlon (New York City, 7 August 1905), and Howard Phillips Lovecraft and Sonia Haft Greene (St. Paul's Chapel, New York, N.Y., 3 March 1924) were the only Lovecraft family marriages after the 1878 marriage in London.

1881 UK Census—Six Lovecrafts Remain

By the time of the 1881 census, there were but six persons bearing the name Lovecraft remaining in the United Kingdom.[86] William Lovecraft, aged 77 years, born in Broadhempston, Devon, and his wife Elizabeth Whithear Lovecraft, aged 71, born in Deptford, Kent, were living at 69 South Hill Park in Hampstead, London, in a household also including three servants. William, a retired farmer, can probably be identified with the son William of William and Elizabeth (Bennett) Lovecraft baptized at Broadhempston parish on 19 July 1803. William Lovecraft, gentleman of Broadhempston parish, had married Elizabeth Whithear Knowles, spinster of Greenwich, daughter of the late Samuel Posgate Knowles, at St. Alphenge parish, Greenwich, on 4 September 1862. William Lovecraft died in Q1/1883, aged 79, in Hampstead, London and his widow Elizabeth Lovecraft in Q3/1893, aged 84, in Lambeth, London.

Also recorded in 1881 was Sarah Lovecraft, aged 80 years, unmarried, born in Broadhempston, Devon, living in the household of her brother-in-law Bernard J. Muller, aged 65, fur manufacturer at 158 Highbury NP in Islington, London. She can probably be identified with the daughter Sarah of William and Elizabeth (Bennett) Lovecraft baptized at Broadhempston parish on 14 November 1800. She was thus the sister of William Lovecraft of 69 South Hill Park. Sarah Lovecraft died in Q1/1889,

---

86. The authors are indebted to the Devon Family History Society and Bob Nield for information concerning Lovecraft family members in the 1881 UK census.

aged 88, in Islington, London. Also in the Muller household in 1881 were two daughters and four servants. Mr. Muller had married Sarah's younger sister Jane Lovecraft[87] at Old Church, St. Pancras, London, on 31 March 1844.

Elizabeth Lovecraft, a nurse aged 70 years, born in Chudleigh, Devon, widow, was recorded as head of household at 1 Hill View, Warren Road, Tormohun, Devon in the 1881 census. It seems probable that she may be identified with the Elizabeth Bickley who married John Lovecraft at Tormohun on 13 July 1835. Also in Elizabeth Lovecraft's Tormohun household in 1881 were Margaret Gooding, aged 38, born Kingswear, Devon, married with a husband at sea, and five of her children born in Torquay between 1873 and 1880. Elizabeth Lovecraft died in Q2/1884, aged 73, in Newton Abbot, Devon.

Rounding out the Lovecraft population of England in 1881 were two younger persons. John Lovecraft, a farm servant aged 44 years, born Lydford, Devon, unmarried, was living in the household of John Hannaford in Widdecombe, Devon. Head of household Elizabeth Lovecraft, a dressmaker aged 31 years, born Shoreditch parish, London, unmarried, was living at 19 Gerrard Street, Islington, London.

1901 UK Census—One Lovecraft or Three?

Apparently, only John Lovecraft remained when the 1901 census was enumerated. In 1901, John was recorded as a single male age last birthday 61, retired farm laborer, residing as an inmate in the Exminster Lunatic Asylum in Devon. Civil records

---

87. Jane Lovecraft had been baptized on 16 November 1823 in Broadhempston parish. She had a double wedding with her sister Elizabeth Lovecraft (baptized on 26 September 1819 in Broadhempston parish), who was married to George Kerby in the same church on the same day.

reveal that John Lovecraft died at the age of 71 in Q1/1911.[88] It seems tragic that the last person to bear the Lovecraft name in England died in such circumstances. The English family was not alone in suffering such misfortunes. Joshua Elliott Lovecraft (1844–1898) and Winfield Scott Lovecraft (1853–1898), grandsons of the emigrant Joseph(1) Lovecraft (sons of Joseph, Jr. and George, respectively), ended their lives in mental institutions, and another grandson, Frederick Aaron Lovecraft (1850–1893), son of Aaron, committed suicide.[89]

The online transcription of the 1901 UK census lists sisters Ellen Lovecroft (single female age last birthday seventy-one) and Henrietta Lovecroft (single female age last birthday sixty-six), both born in Stourbridge, Worcestershire, residing at The Naples, Wigginton, Lichfield, Staffordshire, living on their own means. However, co-author Docherty found the same two sisters enumerated in the 1881 census in Tamworth, Staffordshire, as Ellen Laverock, age 51, and Hetty Laverock, age 46, both born in Stourbridge, Worcestershire. The International Genealogical Index lists Old Swinford, Worcestershire, baptisms of Helen Loverock, 11 February 1830, and Henrietta Loverock, 1 October 1834, both daughters of Robert and Catherine Loverock. The au-

---

88. John Lovecraft was also the only individual with surname Lovecraft or Lovecroft enumerated in the 1891 UK census (q.v., www.ancestry.com, consulted 15 November 2003). On 5 April 1891, he was enumerated as a pauper in the Exminster Lunatic Asylum in Woolborough, Devon (just south of Newton Abbot). He was a single male, aged fifty years, a former agricultural laborer, born in Princetown, Devon. By way of contrast, 53 individuals with the Lucraft surname and 93 individuals with the Luckraft surname were enumerated in the 1891 UK census.

89. Squires 26–29 (Joshua Elliott Lovecraft), 32–33 (Winfield Scott Lovecraft), 38–44 (Frederick Aaron Lovecraft).

thors believe that the Lovecroft sisters listed in the 1901 census transcription actually bore the surname Loverock or Laverock.

The possibility exists, of course, that the two Loverock or Laverock sisters chose to claim relationship with the Lovecraft family by the time the 1901 census was enumerated. H. P. Lovecraft's account of a Lovecraft estate in chancery in 1911 (*MWM* 294–95) suggests that there may have existed monetary motivations to assume the Lovecraft family name in the early twentieth century. It is interesting to note that the sisters' city of residence, Lichfield, Staffordshire, has one of those cathedral churches associated with the ancient name "minster," and that a Minster Pool, Minster Restaurant, and Minster Hall Youth Centre all figure in the city landscape today. One wonders if "Minster Hall" might have entered the Allgood chart through correspondence between Sarah Allgood and these two sisters of Lichfield.

The Lovecraft Family of Broadhempston-Woodland: From Eighteenth-Century Weavers to a Nineteenth-Century Gentleman Tailor

Seventeenth-Century Ashburton Baptisms

The thinning ranks of the Lovecraft family in the nineteenth century may be compared with the prolific family centered in Broadhempston and Woodland parishes in the eighteenth century. The LDS International Genealogical Index records four Lovecraft baptisms in nearby Ashburton between 1665 and 1677. John Lovacraft, son of Nicholas, was baptized on 5 February 1665; Mary Lovercroft, daughter of Nicholas, was baptized on 8 October 1667; Elizabeth Lovecraft, daughter of William, on 13 April 1669; and Joane Lovcraft, daughter of William, on 2 March 1677. Here we note the surname struggling toward its final preferred form Lovecraft.

Broadhempston Baptisms

The first Broadhempston baptism is that of Agnes Lucrafte, daughter of Thomas, on 26 December 1613; the first Woodland baptism, that of Mary Luccraft, daughter of Edward and Elizabeth on 23 October 1692. In some of the early Broadhempston baptisms we also see the surname struggling toward its final form: Honour Louckerart, daughter of John, baptized 19 August 1683, and Richard Luckerart, son of Thomas, baptized 29 April 1684. Some of the early Broadhempston baptisms provide indications of the occupations of some of the early Lovecrafts in this parish: Joane, daughter of John (weaver), baptized 20 March 1697; Agnis, daughter of Thomas (weaver), baptized 13 July 1699; Joseph, son of William (weaver), baptized 13 June 1703. Some later Broadhempston Lovecrafts were stone masons.

Family Burials

The earliest Lovecraft family burial discovered to date by the authors is that of Agnise Lovecraft, who was buried 30 August 1560 in Loddiswell parish. A Caterina Lucrafte was buried in Torbryan parish as early as 7 April 1600. The early Broadhempston parish Lovecraft family burials make an interesting succession of records:[90] Joane Lovecraft, wife of Samuell, 2 January 1671/72; Thomas Lovecrafte, 2 March 1671/72; Thomas, son of Samuel, 17 August 1681; Thomas, son of Thomas, 19 September 1685; Susanna[*], wife of John, 20 April 1690; Samuel Ye Elder, 1 January 1690/91; Elizabeth[*], 29 December 1691; Joan[*], daughter of John, 16 July 1692; Thomas, son of John, 30 April 1696; John Junior, 28 May 1696; Joan Lovcraft, 6

---

90. The records marked with an asterisk are from Kitty Turner's Broadhempston parish record extracts and were not confirmed in a recent review of these records undertaken for the authors by the Devon Record Office.

June 1696; Dorithy Lovcraft, wife of John, 12 November 1696; Elizabeth[*], daughter of John, 22 March 1696/97; John (weaver), 10 January 1705/06; Mary, "a poor child," 12 May 1706; Edward Louckraft, servant of Thos. Lovcraft, 30 June 1708; Thomas, Sr., 2 February 1711; Richard, 2 November 1711; Benjamin[*], son of William, 13 December 1711; Joan, 24 November 1712; Elizabeth, 13 July 1714; Joan Lovecraft, wife of Edward, 22 July 1717; Edward, 30 January 1717/18; Joseph[*],10 March 1717/18; Jonathan Lovcraft, 15 September 1721; Agnis, wife of Will, 28 January 1722/23; Susannah, widow, 12 December 1724; John, 26 February 1724/25; Edward[*], 8 January 1731/32; Elizabth Lovecrafte, daughter of Will, 21 February 1731/32; Elizabth Lovecrafte, 26 April 1735.

A reconstruction of seventeenth- and early eighteenth-century Broadhempston parish Lovecraft family groups poses many challenges. However, it is interesting to note how given names like John, Thomas, and Richard, included in H. P. Lovecraft's version of his line of descent, recur in the early Broadhempston records. John Lovecraft, son of Joseph and Mary Lovecraft, buried 28 September 1740, is the first Lovecraft burial in the Woodland parish records.

Family Occupations

That a number of the early eighteenth-century Lovecraft residents of Broadhempston and Woodland parishes were weavers is not surprising. In his Woodland parish history, Rev. H. R. Evans notes that Devonshire was a major exporter of wool cloth by the fifteenth century and that "Woodland lent itself to sheep pasture" ("Woodland" 169). In fact, the ancient Culling farmhouse at Higher Woodland[91] contains a "wool chamber" whose floor "is even now slippery from wool grease." Evans writes further: "The

---

91. Depicted in Evans, "Woodland" 168.

streams, from which three farms took the name Lake (OE *lacu* = stream) were admirable for washing short wool, the water afterwards being diverted to enrich the pasturage and hay meadows."[92]

That the Lovecrafts of Broadhempston and Woodland parishes were primarily yeomen and associated tradesmen (e.g., weavers, carpenters, and masons) seems an inescapable conclusion.[93] The major property-owning families or "gentry" of Woodland parish, as given by parish historian Rev. H. R. Evans ("Broadhempston" 195–96) were Cullings, Dyers, Neyles, Pinsents, and Abrahams. The authors examined the property tax records of Woodland parish for the period 1780–1830 on LDS microfilm[94] and found one tenant William Lovecraft of land owned by Robert Abraham between 1780 and 1801, but no property owners with surname Lovecraft.

However, the entrepreneurship exhibited by the descendants of Joseph(1) Lovecraft and Mary (Full) Lovecraft in North America, amply described in Squires, certainly indicates that some of the members of the family in England may have risen to comfortable circumstances, even if they were not strictly speaking members of the landed gentry. William Lovecraft, aged 77, and his sister Sarah Lovecraft, aged 80, both children of the tailor William Lovecraft (1776–1855), seem to have been living in comfortable circumstances in London in 1881, with multiple servants in their households.

---

92. Evans, "Woodland" 196. The "Lake" farms are located close to the hamlet of Pulsford where Joseph(1) Lovecraft and his family resided in 1813–20.

93. It is also possible that John(A) Lovecraft was not the only one of his family to pursue a career as a mariner. Devon men were very active in the Newfoundland fishery business.

94. Woodland Parish Property Tax Assessments 1780–1830, LDS film number 1526151.

Howard Phillips Lovecraft and His Paternal Ancestry—Myth and Reality

Ancestral Sites

H. P. Lovecraft expressed the wish that he might be able to search for living and deceased relatives in the vicinity of Newton-Abbot if he were ever able to visit Devon (*MWM* 294). Had he hit upon the monuments to William and Elizabeth Lovecraft in Broadhempston churchyard, the authors believe he would have been close to the point of his origins. A walk of only a few miles would have taken him to Woodland Church, where his great-grandparents Joseph(1) Lovecraft (1774–1850) and Mary (Full) Lovecraft (1782–1864) were married in 1805. In these parishes the family name flourished in the eighteenth century and then died out in the nineteenth.

Denbury Hill Fort

Lovecraft, a great walker, would doubtless have enjoyed surveying the local scenery of Woodland parish. Only a modest hike from his great-grandfather's carpentry workshop in the hamlet of Pulsford stands Denbury Hill Fort, believed to have been constructed by the Welsh Dumnonii about 300–100 B.C., which would doubtless have stirred the author's thoughts of the later Roman occupation of Britain. Woodland parish originally appertained to Ipplepen, originally the possession of a Celt named Ipla. Goda was in possession at the time of the Norman conquest, but lost his possession to the Breton Ralph de Fougeres.[95]

---

95. The foregoing early history of Woodland parish may be found in Evans, "Woodland" 159–161. See also *Domesday Book: A Complete Translation* (Penguin Books, 2002), 324.

A Seventeenth-Century Meteorite and a Thirteenth-Century Theobald

In his 1886 work *A History of Devonshire*, R. N. Worth, F.G.S., recorded several colorful traditions concerning Woodland parish:

> Woodland is noteworthy for the fact that the last male of that ilk, Sir Walter de Woodland, was a follower and attendant of the Black Prince.[96] The tradition is yet current in the parish, of the fall, near Strachleigh, in 1623, of a meteoric stone weighing 23 lb. (243)

Lovecraft, whose famous story "The Colour out of Space" (1927), concerned the fall of a mysterious meteor, would doubtless have found the tradition of a meteor fall in Woodland parish fascinating. Had he encountered Worth's work, he would have been even more delighted by its account (305–10) of the nearby market towns of Newton Abbot and Newton Bushell. In 1246 the manor of Teignweek, ancestor of Newton Bushell, was given to one Theobald de Englishville, and from him it passed to his foster child and kinsman Robert Bushell. Lovecraft's own favorite pseudonym was "Lewis Theobald."[97]

Of Woods and Wolves

In his work *A View of Devonshire in MDCXXX*, dedicated to Baldwin Fulford, Thomas Westcote, Gent., remarked upon the abundance of woods in the parish (404), doubtless the origin of the local surnames Woodley and Woodland. If the Lovecrafts were indeed ancient inhabitants of Woodland and the surrounding parishes, some of the heads of household may well have followed the profession of hunter or woodsman. It is not difficult to imagine wolves ranging from their domain in Exmoor to wooded area in Devon in medieval times. So the abundant

---

96. Edward (1330–1376), Prince of Wales, son of King Edward III.
97. HPL was an aficionado of the eighteenth century and took his pseudonym from playwright and essayist Lewis Theobald (1688–1744).

woods of early Woodland parish may provide further circumstantial support for the Lovecraft family arms as blazoned by Henry L. P. Beckwith. H. P. Lovecraft would doubtless have cherished a blazoning of the family arms such as the one by Mr. Beckwith that accompanies this article.

Summary: Devon Ancestors of H. P. Lovecraft

By 1881, there were only six persons bearing the surname Lovecraft left in the United Kingdom and probably not many more than that in North America. The authors hope that they may be proven wrong in their supposition that the Lovecraft and Lovecroft family names originating in Devon are now extinct in the male line. That the Devon Lovecrafts and Lovecrofts were ancient but hardly illustrious families seems apparent. This fact, however, does not reduce the interest of the family's Devon origins for the many thousands of readers who admire the work of Howard Phillips Lovecraft.

Authors' Acknowledgments

The authors wish to thank for their assistance: the staff of the Devon Record Office; Henry L. P. Beckwith; Rev. Nicholas Pearkes, Rector of Broadhempston-Woodland; Ian Guthrig and John Glanville, administrators of the Devon Family History Society's marriage indexes; Richard McWilliams; Richard D. Squires; Steven Sneyd; Gary Sumpter; Ian Lucraft; Bob Nield; Mary Bula-Alvarez; Rev. Norman Clarke, retired Vicar of Dunsford; Emily W. Owlett; Carol O'Kell; Richard M. Rogers; Stephen Walker; and Alan Taylor. However, the authors remain solely responsible for any errors or opinions expressed in this article. The authors plan to progress to a full genealogy of the Lovecraft and Lovecroft families and welcome correspondence from interested persons.

Suggested Paternal Ancestry of Howard Phillips Lovecraft

HUSBAND	WIFE
Howard Phillips Lovecraft born 20 August 1890, Providence RI USA died 15 March 1937, Providence RI USA	Sonia Haft Greene married 3 March 1924, New York NY USA born 16 March 1883, Ukraine, Russia died 26 December 1972, Sunland CA USA
Winfield Scott Lovecraft born 26 October 1853, Rochester NY USA died 19 July 1898, Providence RI USA	Sarah Susan Phillips married 12 June 1889, Boston MA USA born 17 October 1857, Foster RI USA died 24 May 1921, Providence RI USA
George Lovecraft baptized 9 February 1815, Woodland Devon died 11 September 1895, Mt. Vernon NY USA	Helen Allgood married 1839, Rochester NY USA born 1820 Northumberland UK died 3 December 1881, Mount Vernon NY USA
Joseph Lovecraft baptized 20 November 1774, Woodland Devon died 28 March 1850, Rochester NY USA	Mary Full married (1) September 1805, Woodland Devon baptized 10 September 1782, Denbury Devon died 14 August 1864, Rochester NY USA
John Lovecraft baptized 14 November 1742, Woodland Devon buried 7 October 1780, Woodland Devon	Mary Tapper married (1) 2 January 1768, Woodland, Devon married (2) Henry Priston, 23 May 1782, Woodland Devon
Joseph Lovecraft baptized 13 June 1703 Broadhempston Devon buried 27 November 1781, Woodland Devon	Mary Pitt married 22 December 1728, Woodland Devon buried 14 March 1771, Woodland Devon
Will [William] Lovecraft (weaver)	George [sic] Merifeild (weaver) married 27 December 1699 Broadhempston Devon

Bibliography

Published Sources

Beckwith, Henry L. P. "The Lovecraft Family Arms." *Moshassuck Review* (February 1998): 2–3.

———. *Lovecraft's Providence and Adjacent Parts*. West Kingston RI: Donald M. Grant, 1986.

Evans, Rev. H. R. "Broadhempston." *Transactions of the Devonshire Association* 90 (1958): 62–126.

———. "Woodland." *Transactions of the Devonshire Association* 92 (1960): 158–232.

Everts, R. Alain. "The Lovecraft Family in America," *Xenophile* 2, No. 6 (October 1975): 7, 16.

Faig, Kenneth W., Jr. "The Impact of the Fulford Will on Lovecraft's Claims of Fulford Ancestry." *Moshassuck Review* (August 1996): 1–3. Includes a reproduction and transcription of the 1772 Prerogative Court of Canterbury will.

Hanks, Patrick, and Flavia Hodges. *A Dictionary of Surnames*. Oxford: Oxford University Press, 1988.

Hobsbawm, Eric, and George Rude. *Captain Swing*. 1969. London: Phoenix Press, 2001.

Humphrey-Smith, Cecil. *The Phillimore Atlas and Index of Parish Registers*. 1984. 2nd ed. 1995.

NEHGS (1960). *Ninth Part of a Roll of Arms Registered by the Committee on Heraldry of the New England Historic Genealogical Society*. Boston: NEHGS Committee on Heraldry, 1960.

Pike, John. *Tall Ships in Torbay*. Bradford on Avon, UK: Ex Libris Press, 1986.

Sneyd, Steven. "Hunting for Lovecraft's Ancestors." *Ibid* No. 106 (January–March 1999).

Squires, Richard D. *Stern Fathers 'neath the Mould: The Lovecraft Family in Rochester*. West Warwick RI: Necronomicon Press, 1995.

Westcote, Thomas, Gent. *A View of Devonshire in MDCXXX, with a Pedigree of Most of Its Gentry*. Exeter, UK: William Roberts, 1845.

Worth, R. N., F.G.S. *A History of Devonshire*. London: Elliot Stock, 1886.

Internet Sources

www.old-maps.co.uk. Reproductions of 19th-century ordnance survey maps, with full gazetteer.

www.genuki.org. Parish-by-parish historical and genealogical information for UK and Ireland.

www.familysearch.org. Free genealogical database maintained by LDS church with links to many other resources.

www.ancestry.com. Proprietary genealogical database maintained by Ancestry, Inc. with some limited free access.

www.devon-cc.gov.uk/library/locstudy. Library resources for historical and genealogical research in Devon.

Edward Francis Gamwell and His Family

In Memory of Phillips Gamwell 1898–1916
Marion Roby Gamwell 1900–1900
The Children of Edward Francis Gamwell and
Annie Emeline Phillips Gamwell

Without the unstinting support and guidance I received from Beverly Downing Schroder this study of Edward Francis Gamwell and his family could never have been written. Her assistance has been an inspiration ever since I first decided to undertake a study of Howard Phillips Lovecraft's Gamwell in-laws. Mrs. Schroder also generously loaned me portraits of members of the Gamwell family.

Doris Gamwell Wendell was equally generous in sharing with me the results of her genealogical research on the Gamwell family. Before Mrs. Wendell generously shared her work with me, I was ignorant of the family background of Edward Francis Gamwell's grandfather Samuel Gamwell.

Both Mrs. Schroder and Mrs. Wendell generously read my manuscript and offered comments. They saved me from numerous errors and helped me add additional insights to the paper through this process. Needless to say, responsibility for any remaining errors of fact and for all the opinions expressed in the paper remains with me.

I have cited letters from Mrs. Schroder and Mrs. Wendell by their initials (BDS and DGW, respectively) and the dates of the letters.

Martha Mitchell of the Brown University Archives launched me on the search for Lovecraft's Gamwell in-laws with her generous assistance during a half-day of research in the Archives following the H. P. Lovecraft Centennial Symposium at Brown University in August 1990. John White Gamwell, a fourth-generation graduate of Brown University, first put me in touch with his cousin Mrs. Schroder.

Needless to say, I found the story of the Gamwell family a fascinating one. I hope the readers of this paper will find the story interesting as well.

Quotations from the journal of Irving Henry Gamwell (1871–1963) by permission of Doris Gamwell Wendell

Quotations from the journal of John Milton Gamwell (1825–1863) by permission of Beverly Downing Schroder.

Quotations from the letters of Doris Gamwell Wendell and of Beverly Downing Schroder by permission of the authors.

Edward Francis Gamwell, the husband of Lovecraft's aunt Annie Emeline Phillips Gamwell, is mentioned only four times in Lovecraft's letters. The two most substantial mentions occur in Lovecraft's long autobiographical letter to Rheinhart Kleiner dated 16 November 1916 and are worth quoting in full:

> I extracted not a little celebrity & egotism from my mimicry of various types of callers; particularly of one Edward F. Gamwell, who next to my grandfather was my ideal male. I was infinitely delighted when this individual (then a Brown student) decided upon a lasting affiliation with the family. The engagement of my aunt & Mr. Gamwell, & the customary levity of the younger set in their good-natured raillery of the two, imparted to me a curiously worldly cynicism regarding sentimental matters, & forever turned my Muse from the field which you so gracefully adorn. (*RK* 64)

> My other uncle-in-law, Mr. Gamwell, was a Cambridge man, hence my converse with him was less frequent; but I made the most of every opportunity. He had taught me to rattle off the Greek alphabet when I was six years old; a feat which made Greek much easier for me in high school. In 1903 he was owner & editor of the Cambridge Tribune, & stimulated my editorial tendencies to such an extent that I founded the Rhode Island Journal of Astronomy, to replace the almost defunct Scientific Gazette (I conducted both simultaneously in 1903–1904.) (*RK* 72)

The other two references to Edward F. Gamwell in both occur in his long autobiographical letter to Maurice w. Moe dated 1 January 1915, and are briefer. The first identifies his younger aunt as "Anna [*sic*], now wife of Mr. Edward Gamwell, Associate Editor of The Boston Budget and Beacon" [*sic;* actually, *Budget* and *American Cultivator* (two separate publications)] (*MWM* 43). The second reference in this letter is just a bit longer:

> My two uncles-in-law, Dr. Clark and Mr. Gamwell, both Brown University men, stimulated my intellectual activities immensely. Dr. Clark is a physician and student of the highest type, whose articles have had a wide circulation in medical journals, whilst Mr. Gamwell is an editor and all-around literary man of very thorough scholarship. (*MWM* 46)

While Dr. Franklin Chase Clark, M.D., the husband of Lovecraft's elder aunt Lillian D. Phillips, who died before Lovecraft attained his twenty-fifth birthday, continues to be mentioned infrequently in published letters through the end of the author's life, there is complete silence in the published letters concerning Edward F. Gamwell after 1916. Yet Mr. Gamwell, whom Lovecraft described in his 1916 letter to Kleiner as the second most important role model in his life, after his grandfather, survived Dr. Clark by more than twenty years. His obituary appeared in the *Brown Alumni Monthly* (37:52) for July 1936:

1894, Edward Francis Gamwell, writer, b. South Weymouth, Mass. May 22, 1869, son of Franklin v. [*sic*] Gamwell '60 & Clarissa V. (Maxwell) Gamwell, d. Boston, May 10, 1936. He taught English at Brown after graduation & had been in newspaper & advertising work for many years.

He entered Brown from Holliston, Mass. High School & was an eager & able student. His major study was English. After a year as instructor in English & two years as managing editor of the Atlantic Medical Weekly, he served from 1896 to 1915 on the editorial staffs on the Cambridge, Mass. Chronicle, the Cambridge Tribune, of which he was also the owner; the Budget, & the American Cultivator, Boston. Since 1915 he had been in advertising, with freelance writing as his chief occupation in recent years.

He was editor of "Historic Guide to Cambridge" & author of articles in many publications. He had served as secretary of the Class & was a member of Phi Beta Kappa. He was married June 3, 1897 to Annie E. Phillips & there was a son, Phillips Gamwell. His brother is Irving H. Gamwell '96 of Pittsfield, Mass.

Who was Edward F. Gamwell and what was his background? Why did he disappear so completely from his nephew's life and letters after 1916? These are some of the questions I sought to answer when I began to look into the matter of Edward F. Gamwell and his family. While I failed to develop any definitive answers to the questions that started me on my research, I did manage to develop a fair amount of family background that sheds light on Gamwell's life and his connection with the Phillips family.

The first American Gamwell was Samuel Gamwell, who was born c. 1704 in what is now Northern Ireland. He emigrated to Massachusetts from Londonderry, c. 1718. He died in Northborough, Mass., on 25 January 1788. The first Samuel Gamwell was married three times. By his first wife Margaret (surname unknown) he had two daughters, Margaret and Mary, the first of whom became the wife of William Brown of Groton, Mass., and the second of whom became the wife of John Mahan of

Worcester, Mass. On 11 March 1735, Samuel Gamwell married Ann Montgomery, the widow of Patrick Hambleton. By this marriage he had three children: Abigail Gamwell, who married John Kennedy; Samuel Gamwell, Jr., who married Jane Crooks; and John Gamwell, who was the ancestor of Edward Francis Gamwell. Samuel Gamwell's second wife Ann died before 1756 in Westboro, Mass., and he subsequently married Eunice Sawyer, the widow of Mr. Dunsmore. By his third wife Samuel Gamwell had an additional two children: Anne Gamwell, who married William Moore of Bolton, Mass., and James Gamwell, who had eight children by his first wife Mary (surname not known) and an additional eight children by his second wife Polly Kingston.

The third child of the marriage of Samuel Gamwell and Ann Montgomery was John Gamwell, born in Westboro on 8 September 1742. He was twice married and died in Chester, Mass., on 10 April 1813. By his first marriage to Elizabeth Elder he had four children: Rebecca Gamwell; John Gamwell, Jr.; Samuel Gamwell, M.D.; and Elizabeth Gamwell. After the death of his first wife, he married Jane Hamilton on 11 November 1779. Jane was the daughter of James and Margaret Hamilton of Worcester and was born there on 25 November 1753. Jane died a few weeks before her husband in Chester on 18 February 1813. The marriage of John Gamwell and Jane Hamilton produced ten children, the first six born in Northborough and the last four in Chester:

1. Betsey Gamwell, born 5 November 1780, who did not marry;
2. Deacon Moses Gamwell, born 19 May 1782, who married Martha Bell on 4 March 1805 and died on 19 July 1865;

3. Samuel Gamwell, born 20 January 1784, who was the ancestor of Edward Francis Gamwell;
4. Bille Gamwell, born November 1785, who died young;
5. William Gamwell, born 5 September 1786, who died 13 August 1802;
6. James Gamwell, born 26 August 1789, who married Sally Chapin on 18 November 1809 and died in 1862 in Springfield Center, Oneida County, New York;
7. Jane Gamwell, born 19 June 1790, who married Moses Ayers of Pittsfield, Mass. (intention dated 24 March 1815);
8. Anne Gamwell, born 11 January 1792, who married Howard Chapin of Sheffield, Mass., on 1 April 1811;
9. Sewell Gamwell, born 30 October 1793, who married Amanda;
10. Cheney and died in 1870;
11. Aaron Gamwell, born 17 April 1796, who married Lydia Matthews (1800–1855), daughter of Samuel Matthews and his wife Lydia Bixby, on 13 February 1820 in Hinsdale, Mass., and died 5 October 1832 in Washington, Mass.

Of the children of John Gamwell (1742–1813) and his second wife Jane Hamilton (1753–1813) our attention focuses on the third child and second son Samuel Gamwell, born in Northborough on 20 January 1784. Samuel lived the biblically allotted seventy years, dying in Chester on 3 April 1854. He married first Ann Quigley, on 19 December 1805, in Chester. However, his first wife Ann died less than a year later, on 13 November 1806, in the same town. On 19 September 1810, in Northborough, Samuel Gamwell married his second wife Clarissa A. Moor, the daughter of William Moor and Abigail Shepard

(1763–1800) of New Marlborough, Mass. Clarissa was born 18 June 1790, in New Marlborough and died in Providence, R.I., on 2 May 1868. Samuel's father John Gamwell sired fourteen children by his two wives and Samuel himself sired ten children, all by his second wife Clarissa A. Moor:

1. William Gamwell, born 10 February 1812, who married Sarah Conant Willard (1822–1892) on 20 May 1841 and died on 5 February 1855;
2. Abigail Vianne Gamwell, born 24 October 1814, who married Chauncey G. Varney and died on 2 December 1877;
3. Albert Augustus Gamwell, born 29 October 1816 in Peru, Mass., who married first Susan Easterbrooks and second (on 6 August 1861) Phoebe Greene (1834–1924) and died 18 December 1871 in Providence, R.I.;
4. Amanda Gamwell, born 12 November 1818, who died unmarried on 4 November 1835;
5. Sarepta Gamwell, born 17 January 1821 in Washington, Mass., who married Peres Munn Bagg on 30 January 1840 and died on 26 August 1906;
6. Ariel Moore Gamwell, born 20 May 1823, who died on 24 February 1870, in Rennselaer, N.Y.;
7. John Milton Gamwell, born 29 December 1825 in Tyringham, Mass., who married Betsey Ann Reed (1827–1893) on 27 March 1851 and was killed in action serving with the Union forces during the Civil War at Port Hudson, Louisiana, on 27 May 1863;
8. Franklin Bert Gamwell, born 29 July 1829 in New Marlborough, Mass., who married Victoria Clarissa Maxwell (1843–1920) on 29 November 1866 and died on 24 March 1904 in Holliston, Mass.;

9. Andrew Henry Gamwell, born 2 November 1831, who died unmarried on 17 November 1860;
10. Dexter Jones Gamwell, born 2 August 1834, who died unmarried on 15 February 1893.

It was the eighth child and fifth son of Samuel Gamwell (1784–1854) and his wife Clarissa A. Moor (1790–1868), Franklin Bert Gamwell, who became the father of Edward Francis Gamwell.

Franklin Bert Gamwell followed his elder brother Albert Augustus Gamwell in attending Brown University, from which he graduated in 1860. Perhaps his entry among the members of the class of 1860 in the *Historical Catalogue of Brown University 1764–1904* (Providence, RI: Brown University, 1905), published shortly after his death in 1904, offers as succinct a review of his life as any:

> GAMWELL, FRANKLIN BERT, A.M. Principal high school, Marlboro, Mass., 1860; usher Latin school, Boston, Mass., 1860–61; principal Conn. literary institution, Suffield, Conn., 1861–65; South high school, Weymouth, Mass., 1866–73; Golden Gate academy, Oakland, Cal., 1873–74; superintendent of schools, Weymouth, 1875–77; principal high school, Rock Island, Ill., 1881–82; instructor English, German-American academy, Chicago, Ill., 1882–87; superintendent of schools, Holliston, Mass., 1889–91; resident Holliston 1891–1904. Author numerous school reports. Born New Marlboro, Mass., July 29, 1829; died Holliston, Mass., March 26, 1904. P., Nee., 1904 (p. 259).

Franklin's alumnus file in the Brown University Archives adds a few details to his life story as told by the foregoing. In a survey form for the *Historical Catalogue* that he signed and dated on 24 November 1903, only a few months before his death, Franklin listed his wife, Victoria Clarissa Maxwell, whom he married on 29 November 1866, and his three children Edward Francis, Irving Henry, and Helen Sears. He indicated that he was born in New Marlboro, Mass., on 29 July 1829 and was educated at the Phillips Academy before coming to Brown. He indicated that he had been a member of Phi Beta Kappa at Brown. He indicated that his wife was a graduate of Mt. Holyoke College, which had been founded by his uncle Ariel Moor's sister-in-law Mary Lyon. He gave the date of her class as 1864, but a note on his wife's obituary in the *Baptist* gives the date as 1867. He listed his occupation as that of a retired invalid. (It is notable that his son Irving Henry Gamwell suffered serious circulation problems in his legs as a sexagenarian and that among Irving Henry Gamwell's four grandchildren two suffered from early onset diabetes. Mrs. Schroder feels these circumstances may offer some explanation of Franklin Bert Gamwell's ill health in his later years [BDS, 6/18/1991].) Within months of completing the survey form, Franklin Bert Gamwell was dead. A newspaper cutting in his Brown University Archives files gives his date of death as 26 March 1904, and provided the only reference to the name of his father, Samuel Gamwell, that I possessed before I had the benefit of Doris Gamwell Wendell's forty years of family research.

The first of the three children born to the marriage of Franklin Bert Gamwell and Victoria Clarissa Maxwell was their son Edward Francis Gamwell, born in South Weymouth, Mass., on 22 May 1869. Edward's entry in the *Historical Catalogue of Brown University 1764–1934* (Providence, RI: Brown University, [1936]) was the final one reviewed by him during his lifetime and offers as succinct a biographical summary as any:

CLASS OF 1894

    Gamwell, Edward Francis, A.B. Instructor in English, Brown Univ., 1894–95; managing editor, Providence Atlantic Medical Weekly, 1894–96; city editor, Cambridge Chronicle, 1896–1901; editor and proprietor, Cambridge Tribune, 1901–12; associate editor, Budget and American Cultivator, Boston, 1913–15; advertising agent, 1915– Phi Beta Kappa. 48 South Russell St., Boston, Mass. (364)

Edward's entry in the *Historical Catalogue of Brown university 1764–1904* gave his address as 438 Broadway, Cambridge, and mentioned him as "author various articles in newspapers and magazines." His entry in the *Historical Catalogue of Brown University* (1950 edition) is brief, providing his dates of birth and death and his profession as that of "adv & wrt," that is, advertising and writing. Edward served as secretary for the Brown's graduating class of 1894, and his alumnus file in the Brown University Archives contains correspondence between him and Harry Lyman Koopman, the successor of Reuben Aldridge Guild as University Librarian concerning class matters. (Koopman served in that position from 1893 until his retirement in 1930; together, he and his predecessor Guild served for some 82 years.) Edward was active as an editor of the *Brown Daily Herald* during his years at Brown University and the 1893 edition of *Liber Brunensis* contains a photograph of the editorial staff (opposite p. 184) in which Edward appears, standing, at the far right-hand side. His expression is certainly that of a serious young man; in the quotations attributed to various members of the class of 1894 printed on pages 231–33, Edward's (p. 233) reads as follows: "Men who undertake considerable things, even in a regular way, ought to give us ground to presume ability."

As might be expected from his family background, Edward is found listed in *Liber Brunensis* as a member of the Brown University Young Men's Christian Association (YMCA); he is listed on page 174 as a member of the Employment committee of this organization.

However, by far the richest resource regarding Edward among those connected with Brown University is his alumnus file in the University Archives. Over the years Edward (or possibly his brother Irving in some cases) sent to the university a number of newspaper cuttings regarding Edward's life that are of considerable interest. The file closes with Irving's postcard, postmarked 6 June 1936, notifying the Associated Alumni office of the death of his brother Edward in Boston on 10 May 1936. One of the most intriguing newspaper cuttings in the file is the following, which presumably dates from Edward's high school years in Holliston, Mass.:

> The Amateur Journal
> A Monthly Amateur Paper
> F. Gamwell, Publisher
> Holliston, Mass.
> P.O. Box 354

This cutting would appear to be strong evidence that Edward was involved in the amateur press association movement of his time. While the surname Gamwell does not occur in the Index (The Fossils, 1959) to Truman J. Spencer's *History of Amateur Journalism* (The Fossils, 1957), this work does not purport to mention the names of all persons who were active in the amateur journalism movement. If Edward Francis Gamwell was active as an amateur journalist, it is extraordinary that his nephew Howard Phillips Lovecraft, who was deeply involved in amateur journalism from 1914 until his death in 1937, never mentioned his uncle's connection with the hobby. Knowing of his uncle's interest in literary matters in general, it seems unlikely that Lovecraft, who was close friends with amateurs such as Ernest A. Edkins and Edith May Dowe Miniter, who were active in the 1880s, would have missed this connection. One can only speculate that the separation of Edward Francis Gamwell and his wife Annie Emeline Phillips Gamwell may have occurred at an early point during Lovecraft's involvement in amateur journalism and that Lovecraft missed the connection through failing to mention his uncle's name to fellow amateur journalists. However, one does find Edward Francis Gamwell mentioned affectionately in Lovecraft's 1916 letters (cited earlier) to fellow amateur journalists Maurice W. Moe and Rheinhart Kleiner, so the matter is certainly debatable. Another possibility is that Edward's *Amateur Journal* was never issued or survived for only a few numbers.

Edward's listing among the members of the Junior Class in *Liber Brunensis* for 1893 (112) gives his campus address as Hope, 13. In *Liber Brunensis* for 1896 (the year his brother Irving graduated from Brown University as president of his class) Edward is listed as a candidate for the degree of Master of Arts residing at 159 Benefit Street (104). He had served as an instructor in English and rhetoric in 1894–95. It does not appear that Edward ever took his A.M. degree from Brown University. A postcard dated 4 March 1896, addressed to Harry Lyman Koopman, shows his business address as the Atlantic Medical Weekly, 49 Westminster Street, Providence, R.I. In his response to a questionnaire for the university's forthcoming general catalogue (perhaps the one eventually realized as the *Historical Catalogue of Brown University 1764–1904*), Edward gave his position as managing editor, Atlantic Medical Weekly, 49 Westminster Street, room 516, Providence, Rhode Island, and his home address as 159 Benefit Street, Providence. His questionnaire response also mentions that he was active on the editorial staff of the *Brown Daily Herald* from December 1891 until June 1894, that is, for the larger portion of his entire career as Brown undergraduate (1890–94).

Edward probably decided to abandon his studies for the master's degree when he decided to become city editor of the *Cambridge* [Mass.] *Chronicle* in 1896. A postcard addressed to Harry

Lyman Koopman during this period (2 December 1896) gives Edward's business address as 573 Massachusetts Avenue, Cambridge, and his residence address as 371 Harvard Street, Cambridge. Doubtless, however, he kept close ties with Providence; during this period he must have begun his courting of Annie E. Phillips, whom he married in Providence on 3 June 1897. A letter written by Edward to Harry Lyman Koopman on 14 February 1898, on the stationery of the *Cambridge Chronicle*, gives Edward's residence address as 65 Ellery Street, Cambridge. Edward's and Annie's only son Phillips Gamwell was born in Cambridge a few months later, on 23 April 1898, and by the next time Edward wrote to Professor Koopman (14 November 1898) he was residing at 438 Broadway, Cambridge, where he would remain at least until 3 July 1913, when he completed a Brown University questionnaire from that address. A diary entry made by Edward's brother Irving H. Gamwell after the death of Edward's son Phillips Gamwell on 31 December 1916 indicates that Edward was then living at 65 Hancock Street, Boston. By the time he completed another Brown University questionnaire on 4 December 1923, he was living at 48 South Russell Street, Boston, where he apparently continued until his death. His 1923 questionnaire response gave his profession as advertising and mentioned his authorship of the *Historic Guide to Cambridge*. Writing to the Alumni Office from 48 South Russell Street in Boston for a final time on 3 April 1934, Edward requested that his profession be listed as writing rather than advertising in the forthcoming historical catalogue. Edward's wishes were not followed for the 1934 [1936] edition of the *Historical Catalogue,* but for the 1950 edition the editors listed both advertising and writing as his profession.

Perhaps the most telling newspaper cuttings in Edward Gamwell's Brown University alumnus file are those concerning his high school years in Holliston, Mass., beginning with the notable indication of his affiliation with amateur journalism during that period mentioned above. The cuttings bespeak the early promise of both Edward and his younger brother Irving and Edward's especial interest in literary and dramatic matters. A cutting from the *Weymouth* [Mass.] *Gazette* dating to 19 June 1877 indicates that Franklin Bert Gamwell, formerly superintendent of South Weymouth schools, had removed to Holliston and purchased a farm of 140 acres after eight years in South Weymouth, where his elder son Edward had been born on 22 May 1869. Franklin Bert's résumé in the 1904 edition of the *Historical Catalogue* contains a gap for the years 1877 to 1881, and we may presume that he was engaged in farming in Holliston during these years. Undoubtedly he shared the love of the soil with his eldest brother Albert Augustus Gamwell, a love that was passed to both of them from their father Samuel Gamwell and his yeoman farmer forbears. Albert Augustus Gamwell's son Roland Greene Gamwell was later a noted floriculturist, and Mrs. Schroder remembers that her grandfather Franklin Bert Gamwell's son Irving Henry Gamwell always kept a garden, buried his garbage, and "raised & dispatched chickens much to my consternation" (BDS, 6/18/1991). It is unclear whether Franklin Bert Gamwell's family followed him when he took up the position of principal in the Rock Island, Illinois, schools in 1881; a cutting from the *Rock Island Daily Argus* dated 19 July 1881, preserved in his son Edward's alumnus file, records Franklin Bert's assumption of the principalship, which had been made vacant by the election of the incumbent, a Mr. Kemble, to the superintendency of schools on 18 July 1881. In any case, the Franklin Bert's position in Rock Island was short-lived and from 1882 until 1887, when he returned to Holliston as superintendent of schools, Franklin Bert served as an English instructor in the German-American Academy in Chicago, Illinois.

The cuttings in Edward Gamwell's alumnus file make clear that Edward and his brother Irving were attending high school in Holliston during part of their father's Illinois sojourn. A cutting from the *Mt. Hollis Targum,* published from Holliston in April 1885, lists the participants in the closing exercises of the winter term at Holliston High School, among them Irving Gamwell presenting "Aspirations of Youth" and his brother Edward presenting an original essay on Washington and Lincoln. A cutting from the *Framingham Tribune* of 12 June 1885 mentions repairs being made to Miss Gamwell's grammar school in that town. (Miss Gamwell was Mary Elizabeth "Libby" Gamwell, the daughter of Edward's late uncle William Gamwell.) A cutting from the *Holliston Transcript* of 27 November 1885 records that Edward Gamwell won honorable mention in a declamation contest "last Friday evening." The same newspaper on 29 January 1886 mentioned Edward as vice president of the high school Shakespeare Club. A note of 14 May 1886 mentions a meeting of this club, addressed by "J. H. Gamwell," whose identity escapes me, unless it represents a misprinting of the initials of Edward's brother Irving Henry Gamwell. Edward graduated from Holliston high school in the spring of 1886; the *Transcript* of 2 April 1886 mentioned him as taker of second honors after Edward O. Parker. The same issue of the *Transcript* recorded the details of a supper and accompanying entertainment offered at the high school the prior Wednesday evening, evidently in conjunction with the forthcoming graduation exercises. Supper was served by seniors and guests, after which Edward's brother Irving H. Gamwell unveiled a bust of Homer. There followed a presentation of the tent scene from Shakespeare's *Julius Caesar,* in which Edward F. Gamwell played the role of Brutus.

Edward Francis Gamwell (1869–1936), from 1894

But Edward's high school days were over. A cutting from the *Milford* [Mass.] *Gazette* of 25 June 1886 recorded that his cousin (once removed) Lorenzo Gamwell, a lawyer in Pittsfield, Mass., had been elected a Massachusetts state representative. Edward himself was not long in beginning a career of his own. The *Transcript* of 6 August 1886 reported that Edward would enter the employ of D. Lothrop & Company in Boston on 16 August 1886. "We're sorry to have him leave our town," the editors of the *Transcript* opined. On 3 September 1886, the *Transcript* reported Edward as "much pleased" with his new position in Boston. On 22 October 1886, the *Transcript* published an article by

Edward, describing the first reunion of the Holliston high school class of 1886, which took place at the home of Edward O. Parker in East Holliston on Friday, 15 October 1886.

The notices regarding Edward Gamwell's subsequent career, as reflected in his Brown University alumnus file, are few and far between after this period and apart from his 1896–1900 correspondence with Harry Lyman Koopman consist mostly of his responses to alumni questionnaires. A brief notice in the *Brown Alumni Monthly* for November 1900 mentioned Edward as associate manager of the *Cambridge Chronicle;* his position is listed as that of city editor in the *Historical Catalogue* entries that he himself reviewed. The year 1900 had brought sadness to the lives of Edward Gamwell and his wife Annie E. Phillips Gamwell; on 9 February 1900, in Cambridge, Annie gave birth to their second child, a daughter Marion Roby, who lived only five days.

Professionally, the high point of Edward's career undoubtedly came with his acquisition of an ownership interest in the *Cambridge Tribune* in 1901. His response to the questionnaire for the 1904 *Historical Catalogue* dated 7 February 1904, from his residence at 438 Broadway in Cambridge, gave the business address of the *Tribune* as 36 Boylston Street in the same city. Mrs. Schroder has preserved some tearsheets from the issue of the *Cambridge Tribune* published on Saturday, 2 March 1907. The masthead indicates that the *Tribune* was then published every Saturday from 36 Boylston Street in Cambridge and that Edward F. Gamwell and J. Lee Robinson were editors and proprietors. The cost of a single copy was five cents and of an annual subscript $2.50. A long article on the celebration of the centenary of Henry Wadsworth Longfellow in this issue probably reflects Edward Gamwell's own literary interests.

While Edward undoubtedly remained connected with the newspaper business for the remainder of his life, as an advertising man and writer, his last editorial association was with *Budget* and the *American Cultivator,* both published from Boston, in 1913–15. Thereafter, he worked a freelance writer and independent advertising agent. I have not seen a copy of the *Historic Guide to Cambridge,* the only publication specifically cited in his biographical notices. The great sorrows of the later years of Edward's life were undoubtedly the breakdown of his marriage with Annie E. Phillips Gamwell and the death of their son Phillips Gamwell of pulmonary tuberculosis on the last day of 1916. The Gamwells had separated sometime previous to the death of their son. Edward's brother Irving H. Gamwell recorded the death of their son Phillips in his diary:

> Edward Francis Gamwell, son of Franklin B. Gamwell, p. 41. His son Phillips *died* in Colorado Sunday, Dec. 31, 1916, at 2 A.M. Brief services were held at undertaker's chapel at 4 P.M. [Dec. 31, 1916]. Annie (his mother) started east same day. Her address: care of Edwin E. Phillips, 874 Chalkstone Ave., Providence. E. F. G. [Edward Francis Gamwell] was then living at 65 Hancock St., Boston. He was married at Providence, R.I. to *Annie* Emeline Phillips on June 3, 1897. He was the father of two children: Marion Rhoby, who was born in Cambridge, Mass., February 9 or 14, 1900, and lived only five days; Phillips, who died at the age of 18 years, 8 months, and 8 days. (Born, Cambridge, Mass., Apr. 23, 1898). *Annie,* E. F. G.'s widow, *died* January 29, 1941. Ralph w. Greenlaw, C.T.A., was administrator.

Irving H. Gamwell's attention to detail can be seen throughout his voluminous journals; when I obtained a copy of Phillips Gamwell's Colorado death certificate with the permission of Mrs. Schroder, I found that Phillips had indeed died of pulmonary tuberculosis on 31 December 1916, at 1:45 A.M., a time his mother may well have stated as 2 A.M. in telegrams to family. Phillips and his mother had resided in Colorado since 7 October 1916. Phillips died in the town of Roswell, in El Paso county, outside of Colorado Springs. Presumably, he and his mother came to Colorado in the search for a last-ditch cure of his illness. According to Mrs. Schroder, Edward F. Gamwell's maternal uncle George Maxwell, the brother of Victoria C. Maxwell, lived in Colorado Springs with his daughters Doroty and Ruth (BDS, 1/26/1990) and another brother (BDS, 10/16/1990). So perhaps Annie and her desperately ill boy stayed with their Maxwell in-laws during their brief stay in Colorado. The only real inaccuracy in Irving H. Gamwell's entire account of his nephew's life is his hesitancy concerning the date of birth of his niece Marion Rhoby Gamwell; in actuality, she was born on February 9 and died on 14 February 1900.

Edward's son Phillips Gamwell was a promising youth. His first cousin Howard Phillips Lovecraft published a poetic tribute to the recently deceased youth, "An Elegy on Phillips Gamwell, Esq." in the *Providence Evening News* for 5 January 1917. It was Phillips Gamwell who launched his cousin Lovecraft's voluminous career as a letter-writer, witness Lovecraft's own letter to Maurice W. Moe dated 5 April 1931:

> Not until I was twenty years old did I write any letters worthy of the name—and my beginning then was due to the fact that my well-beloved little cousin Phillips Gamwell (died 1916) had reached the age of twelve and blossomed out as a piquant letter-writer eager to discuss the various literary and scientific topics broached during our occasional personal conversations. Four or five years of Johnsonese periods loosed upon this youthful and encouraging audience form'd the preparation for the verbal deluges which you first sampled in the 1914–15 season. (*MWM* 303)

In his letter to J. Vernon Shea dated 4 February 1934, Lovecraft recalled his cousin Phillips in conjunction with a discussion of some of the popular ballads of his youth:

> In this wholly innocuous form "Bedelia" was a veritable knockout—a stampede—lasting well into 1904. I remember my little cousin Phillips Gamwell (now dead—his mother [Annie E. Phillips Gamwell] is the aunt now heading my household) singing it at the age of six. (*JVS* 230)

In an earlier letter to James Ferdinand Morton, Jr. dated 24 June 1923, Lovecraft recalled a hobby shared with his young cousin and the family's grief at his passing:

> That old [stamp] collection of mine hasn't been mine since 1916, when I gave it to my cousin Phillips Gamwell. He died on the last day of that same year—from other causes—and the collection is now stored among his mother's things in some obscure place—either in Providence or Cambridge. She treasures his effects so much, that I'm damned if I know whether it would be in good taste to ask for the things back again—one must be aesthetic, even if cynical and unsentimental—so I couldn't possibly predict the future of these varicolour'd scraps of paper. But if I do get hold of 'em—look for a windfall! My cousin was a great kid—a Belknap and Alfredus rolled into one. They remind me of him—he was my best and earliest grandson! I can still see myself training him when he was three and I was eleven! . . . (*JFM* 49)

Of Phillips Gamwell Mrs. Schroder wrote to me:

> My mother [Constance Gamwell Downing, daughter of Irving H. Gamwell] is 87 now and quite lucid and of course Phillips was also her first cousin . . . It is her recollection that Phillips was at Harvard when he died. That would be easy to verify and she may be wrong. At any rate, it has always been my understanding that he held great promise and was quite a remarkable young man. I have his silverware (knife and fork) so his memory comes to mind from time to time. (BDS, 10/16/1990)

I followed Mrs. Schroder's suggestions and inquired at Harvard University about Phillips Gamwell. On 29 October 1990, Rebecca J. Bates of the Harvard University Archives replied to me that the University had no record of Phillips as either graduate or student. At this remove in time, it seems most likely that Phillips and his family may have intended that he pursue his studies at Harvard University and that his declining health interfered with that intention; Mrs. Downing remains convinced that it was his intention to matriculate there (BDS, 1/9/1991). It seems doubtful whether his failing health even permitted him to graduate from high school, which he would ordinarily have done in the spring of 1916. Poor health also interfered with the education of Phillips's cousin Lovecraft, who never obtained any high school diploma of his own despite statements to the contrary. R. Alain Everts published a photograph of Phillips Gamwell, dating to 1909, in *Nyctalops* for April 1973; he obtained it, not through Mrs. Schroder, but from relatives of Annie Gamwell's close friend and co-heir, Edna W. Lewis.

Of Edward Gamwell's life following the death of his son and his earlier separation from his wife Annie there is little to tell. Of his separation from his wife and later life Mrs. Schroder wrote to me:

> I do know that the [Gamwell] family was very fond of his mother [Annie E. Phillips Gamwell] and were quite close to her and visited her even after the separation. We all know that the loss of children takes a heavy toll in a marriage. The other reasons I can only surmise—although I know my grandfather took care of the funeral [of Edward F. Gamwell] and worked out all the details and that Edward did not leave a will. My feeling is that he felt estranged and isolated and may have been depressed. Somewhere, there's some record about the exact cause of death. If I am able to find it, I'll let you know. My grandfather [Irving H. Gamwell] kept a journal all his life, starting at the age of about 17 and I have most of them. There are many references to Edward, especially when they were in their late teens and I do not detect any great problem in their relationship. (BDS, 10/16/1990)

Mrs. Schroder later found the record of her grandfather's journal entry concerning the death of his brother Edward F. Gamwell and wrote me concerning it:

> My grandfather was notified by a state police officer (by telephone) and he IHG [Irving Henry Gamwell] had to go to Boston to claim the body [of Edward F. Gamwell] from the morgue. He [Irving Henry Gamwell] writes that "he [EFG] died from natural causes and suddenly"; he died of "chronic valvular heart trouble." He was brought to the hospital at 9:20 A.M. [May 10, 1936] and died at 10:50 A.M. My hunch is that the two brothers were not terribly close and that Edward was in some sense quite alone. He attended the Jacoby Club at 16 Dartmouth Street and evidently a Mr. Charles Carter, assistant to David McPheton, the executive secretary [of the club], told my grandfather much about Edward. He said he learned that he also belonged to the Wells Memorial at 985 Washington Street [Boston]. I have no knowledge about either one of these organizations. (BDS, 1/9/1991)

Earlier, Mrs. Schroder had sent to me a brief newspaper cutting concerning Edward's death and burial:

FUNERAL SERVICES FOR EDWARD GAMWELL

> Funeral services for Edward F. Gamwell of Boston were held yesterday afternoon [May 12, 1936] at the Maxwell homestead on Mechanic Street with burial in the family lot in Arms cemetery. Rev. C. H. Patrick, pastor of the Baptist church, conducted the services and the bearers were Henry Ware, Herbert Ware, Frank S. Field, and Frank E. Swan.
>
> Mr. Gamwell was the son of the late Victoria Maxwell Gamwell and grandson of Deacon Benjamin Maxwell of this place. He is survived by a sister, Miss Helen S. Gamwell of this place and Irving H. Gamwell of Pittsfield. He was a graduate of Brown University and had always been engaged in newspaper work. In his youth he was a frequent visitor at the family homestead on Mechanic Street.

This cutting is dated in Irving H. Gamwell's hand to 13 May 1936 and presumably derives from the local newspaper of Shelburne Falls, Mass., the home of Deacon Benjamin Maxwell (1804–1892) and his family. Edward was buried in the Arms Cemetery at Shelburne Falls, alongside his beloved mother Victoria C. Maxwell, the daughter of Deacon Benjamin Maxwell, and his father Franklin B. Gamwell. The obituary contains no mention of Edward's deceased children nor of his surviving widow Annie E. Phillips Gamwell.

At some point in time following the death of his brother Edward F. Gamwell, the Brown Alumni office must have queried Irving H. Gamwell concerning survivors. He replied succinctly in a letter dated 20 November 1936, addressed to Alfred H. Gurney, Alumni Secretary, at Faunce House. He stated that Edward was also survived by his sister Helen S. Gamwell of Shelburne Falls. Edward's son, Irving Gamwell replied, had died more than twenty years ago, a slight misstatement (Phillips Gamwell had then been dead for slightly less than twenty years) uncharacteristic of the writer. His brother's former wife, Irving Gamwell stated, was still living. Between the few words of his communication to the Alumni Secretary can be read the strain and sorrow which Edward's and Annie's separation and the early loss of their son had created. While Irving Gamwell referred to Annie as Edward's "former wife" in this communication, there is no evidence to support the assertion that they were divorced. Annie's obituaries refer to her as the widow of Edward F. Gamwell. It is perhaps more likely that they were legally separated, but I have made no effort to verify this supposition in the Massachusetts or Rhode Island courts.

As evidence of the affection which Annie E. Phillips Gamwell continued to bear toward her adopted family, even after her separation from her husband, Mrs. Schroder sent me a copy of a letter which Annie addressed to her, in her characteristic hand, upon the birth of her brother in 1928. I shall quote it in full:

> Cake Grove Hotel
> Boothbay Harbor
> On the Coast of Maine
>
> Dear "Miss Beverly Bryer Downing"
> I am delighted to hear of the arrival of your brother.
> To mother—I think your announcement is delightful—the fact is fine & putting it in Beverly's name is new & charming to me.
> I most sincerely congratulate you all—I am a devout lover of families! I hope you are well Constance as well as little brother & big sister & husband.
> It must be very interesting to live in old New Orleans.
> I have been here at Boothbay a month & in a few days am going to Ogunquit Maine till after Labor Day. I am spending the summer with Miss Ripley hence this luxurious way of doing it. When we go back to Providence I am going to have a tiny apartment of my own for a bit & my friend with whom I have lived for four years is also going into an apartment.
> I am just craving a little spot all my own even if for a short time & be it ever so humble.
> I wish I might sometime have a snapshot of you all.
> Lovingly—
> Annie E. P. Gamwell

July 22, 1928

Constance Downing had sent the announcement of the birth of her son under the name of her daughter from their then home in New Orleans, Louisiana.

Of all the members of the Gamwell family, it is only Lovecraft's aunt Annie Emeline Phillips Gamwell who is consistently mentioned over the years in the author's published letters. Born 10 July 1866, in Coventry, Rhode Island, Annie was the last-born of five children—four girls and one boy—of Whipple Van

Buren Phillips (1833–1904) and his wife Robie Alzada Place Phillips (1827–1896). Annie took her middle name from her elder sister Emeline Estella Phillips (1859–1865), who had died away at school in East Greenwich, Rhode Island on 15 April 1865, aged only five years and nine months. Annie was educated in the Providence schools (R. Alain Everts once told me Miss Wheeler's School) and did not attend the Wheaton Seminary in Norton, Mass., as did her elder sisters Lillian Delora and Sarah Susan. In 1881, Whipple Phillips moved into the home at the corner of Angell Street and Elmgrove Avenue on the East Side of Providence, where his daughter Annie was to reside until her marriage to Edward Francis Gamwell on 3 June 1897. Both Annie Gamwell and her nephew Howard Phillips Lovecraft were deeply attached to this home and bemoaned each change to its premises after the family lost possession in 1904. Alone at home, Annie received news of the bursting of the Owyhee Land and Irrigation Company's first Bruneau River dam on 5 March 1890.

While neither Whipple Phillips nor his only son Edwin Everett Phillips ever affiliated with the First Baptist Church of Providence, all the surviving female members of the household did so in 1883. Whipple's wife Robie Alzada Place Phillips was admitted on the basis of her experience on 26 April 1883. Annie and her elder sister Sarah Susan were admitted by baptism on 29 April 1883, in the same class as Olive Wells Gamwell Weeden, the daughter of Albert Augustus Gamwell and his second wife Phoebe Greene Gamwell. The eldest Phillips sister, Lillian Delora, was admitted by letter on 2 May 1883. The Baptist religious affiliations of the Phillips family became a perfect setting for the romance and marriage of Annie and Edward Francis Gamwell. Lovecraft relates that Annie was part of a lively social circle that brightened the Phillips household during the otherwise dark days of the institutionalization of Winfield Scott Lovecraft, the illness and death of Robie Alzada Place Phillips, and the financial decline of the Owyhee Land and Irrigation Company. One supposes that the romance of Annie and Edward F. Gamwell commenced while the latter was a student (1890–94) and then an instructor (1894–95) at Brown University. Edward's appointment to a managerial job with the *Cambridge Chronicle* in 1896 was probably an important factor in their decision to marry. While I do not know the place of their marriage on 3 June 1897, it was registered in Rhode Island and therefore the First Baptist Church is a natural supposition.

The narrative of the Gamwell family has told much of the subsequent story of Annie and Edward F. Gamwell, insofar as it is known. The year 1898 brought two happy events to their new household: the birth of a son Phillips Gamwell on April 23 and the marriage of Edward's younger brother Irving Henry Gamwell to Sarah Wilson Bryer (born exactly three years after Annie Gamwell) in Bristol, R.I., on 9 August 1898. These happy events in the life of her younger sister hopefully helped dull the pain of the long-expected widowhood that came to Sarah Susan Phillips Lovecraft with the death of her husband Winfield Scott Lovecraft, hospitalized since 1893, on July 19 of that year. But sadness was not long in coming into the household of Annie and Edward F. Gamwell, for their daughter Marion Roby Gamwell, born on 9 February 1900 in Cambridge, lived only five days, dying there on February 14 of the same year. Mrs. Schroder speculates, undoubtedly correctly, that the loss of both of Annie and Edward Gamwell's children before they reached adulthood played a principal role in the effective dissolution of their marriage.

I've not been able to pinpoint the date of Annie and Edward Gamwell's separation. The fact that Edward F. Gamwell's Brown University alumnus file locates him at 438 Broadway in Cambridge between 14 November 1899 and 3 July 1913 adds credibility to the speculation that the marriage endured for at least this period. The fact that Edward sold his ownership interest in the *Cambridge Tribune* in 1912 may possibly be indicative of financial difficulties; his next position was an editorial one with *Budget* and the *American Cultivator*, both of Boston, which he held from 1913 until 1915. Thereafter, he was engaged in independent advertising work and writing. Lovecraft's letter to Rheinhart Kleiner dated 9 November 1919 (*RK* 145–47) records his attendance, with fellow amateurs; at a lecture delivered by Lord Dunsany at the Copley Plaza Hotel in Boston. Therein he mentions: "I had not been in Boston before since Jan. 1916—and not in Cambridge since 1910." I don't think, however, that we ought to conclude on the basis of this casual remark that Annie and Edward Gamwell separated as early as in 1910. In the first place, Boston would have been a natural meeting place for relatives located in Providence and Cambridge, respectively. Secondly, Lovecraft's published letters do not record any visits to Boston in conjunction with amateur matters as early as 1916. (His first overnight stay was apparently in 1921.)

My own speculation is that the final separation of Annie and Edward Gamwell did not occur until 1915–16. By this time their son Phillips must have been failing and perhaps the parents disagreed over some aspect of his medical care. Edward Gamwell may well have been loath to give up his many connections with the Boston area in the face of a medical recommendation that his son seek another climate for his health. In any case, the holiday season would have been a natural time for tensions to come to a head and January 1916 a logical time for Annie's relatives to visit her in Boston if in fact a separation had ensued during this period. It is likely that Lovecraft himself was accompanied by several members of the prior Phillips generation. If indeed the family visit was made under difficult circumstances, I suspect that

Lovecraft and his mother would have been accompanied either by his aunt Lillian Delora Phillips Clark, widowed in 1915 by the death of her husband Dr. Franklin C. Clark, or by his uncle Edwin Everett Phillips.

If Lovecraft's letters make only sparse mention of Edward F. Gamwell, they are nearly entirely silent concerning his uncle Edwin Everett Phillips, the fourth of the five Phillips children, born 4 February 1864 in Coventry, R.I. (I believe Edwin's date of birth is given as 14 February on the Phillips monument in Swan Point Cemetery in Providence, but I am using here the date of birth implied by the age at death given in his death certificate.) Edwin and his sister Annie were the "babies" of the family and were probably closer to each other than they were to their elder sisters Lillian Delora (born 1856) and Sarah Susan (born 1857), who shared the common bond of the remembered loss of their middle sister Emeline Estella in 1865. Edwin was associated with his father in his business endeavors for most of his life and was manager of the Owyhee Land and Irrigation Company's hotel in Grand View, Idaho, in 1887–88. On 30 July 1894, Edwin married Martha Helen Mathews, the daughter of Joseph G. and Jennie E. Mathews, in Providence. Subsequently, Edwin quarreled with his father and divorced his wife. However, father and son reconciled before the death of Whipple Phillips in March 1904, and Whipple's will dated July 1903 left his son a residual share of his estate, after his surviving daughters had been provided for. Furthermore, Edwin Phillips remarried his former wife Martha Helen Mathews in Providence on 23 March 1903—indeed, perhaps this remarriage enabled the reconciliation between father and son.

Edwin never enjoyed the business success of his father and spent most of his later years as a loan broker and rent collector. Over the years, he also served as a manufacturer's representative and coin dealer. Edwin is identified as an uncle in several of Lovecraft's letters, but the only substantive mention in the published letters occurs in Lovecraft's long autobiographical letter to Maurice W. Moe dated 5 April 1931, wherein he mentions that "an uncle lost a lot of dough for my mother and me in 1911" (*MWM* 301). While this reference could conceivably be to Franklin C. Clark, Edward F. Gamwell, or Edwin E. Phillips, Lovecraft's almost total silence concerning Edwin E. Phillips in his published letters makes the identification of this uncle with Edwin plausible. Although Whipple Phillips's old friend and business associate Clarke H. Johnson served as the executor of his estate, Edwin Phillips, having been involved in Whipple's business endeavors, would have been a natural choice to act as manager of his widowed sister's remaining investments. Lovecraft remarks dissatisfaction with the winding up of Whipple Phillips's Idaho business interests, so that friction between sister and brother over finances may have begun early. Fear and anxiety concerning her financial affairs dogged Sarah Susan Phillips's later years and eventually drove her into Butler Hospital in the spring of 1919. It would be natural for tension to exist between her and her brother, if he remained as her principal financial adviser. As a practical business man, Edwin Phillips very likely had little patience with Sarah Susan's non-productive son; and if he urged Sarah Susan to force her son to find employment, these pressures may have been the origin of tension not only between brother and sister but between uncle and nephew.

The Phillips family crisis of the winter of 1915–16 was soon compounded by the death of Edwin's wife, Martha Helen Mathews Phillips, aged only forty-seven years, of pneumonia at the couple's home at 874 Chalkstone Avenue in Providence on 9 February 1916. If indeed Martha Phillips accompanied her husband on a visit to her sister-in-law and nephew in Boston in January 1916, her fatal illness followed only shortly thereafter. If in fact the death of Martha Helen Mathews Phillips coincided nearly with the separation of Annie and Edward F. Gamwell, it would only have been natural for Edwin Phillips to invite his sister to join his now-empty household. (The marriage of Edwin E. Phillips and Martha Helen Mathews was childless.) With plans probably already in the works to seek medical treatment for Phillips Gamwell in the West, Annie may have found the offer of lodging with her brother in Providence more attractive than rented quarters in Providence.

By the summer of 1916 Annie and her son were probably living with her brother at his home at 874 Chalkstone Avenue in Providence. Sometime in 1916, Lovecraft made the donation of his stamp collection to his gravely ill cousin—a point he mentions in his letters to James Ferdinand Morton, Jr. dated 24 June 1923 (*JFM* 48–50). Perhaps further medical consultations concerning Phillips Gamwell's health were taken during this period. By 7 October 1916, however, he and his mother had removed to Colorado, where they would live with Annie's Maxwell in-laws (brothers of Victoria Clarissa Maxwell) in Roswell, near Colorado Springs, until the death of Phillips of pulmonary tuberculosis on 31 December 1916. After a brief undertaker's service later that day, Annie departed immediately for Providence with the body of her son. There she registered her son's death and buried him in her father's lot in Swan Point Cemetery. (Annie's daughter Marion Roby is also buried with her there; the date of removal of Marion Roby's remains, which I do not know, may be a further clue, with regard to the date when Annie and Edward Gamwell separated. I suspect, however, that Marion Roby's body was only removed to Providence after the death of her brother Phillips.)

While Annie Phillips Gamwell cannot be found in Providence

city directories until 1932, when she appears at 61 Slater Avenue, I suspect she continued to live with her brother Edwin E. Phillips for some time after her return to Providence following the death of her son Phillips Gamwell. She was soon, however, to lose her only brother to the same disease that had killed her son, for on 14 November 1918 Edwin E. Phillips expired of pulmonary and general tuberculosis in the Providence City Hospital, aged fifty-four years nine months and ten days. It is natural to speculate whether, in fact, Edwin Phillips may have contracted the disease from his young nephew during the period when the latter resided in his home.

The loss of the last remaining male family member, apart from her own son, apparently removed Sarah Susan Phillips's last hold on mental stability; from these dark days of the winter of 1918–19 must date Clara L. Hess's recollection of a confused Mrs. Lovecraft on the Butler Avenue car. It evidently became necessary to separate mother and son and during the early weeks of 1919. Sarah Susan tried living with her elder sister Lillian Delora while Annie, very probably, managed house for her nephew at 598 Angell Street, where Sarah Susan and her son had lived since their removal from 454 Angell Street in 1904, following the death of Whipple Phillips. Sarah Susan could no longer adapt to home life, however, and on 13 March 1919 she was admitted to Butler Hospital, there to remain until her death on 24 May 1921. During this period, 1919–24, Lillian Delora and Annie were joint housekeepers for their nephew at 598 Angell Street. Annie, with more connections among Providence society, often summered elsewhere in New England, but was probably at 598 Angell Street most of this time. Annie's 1928 letter to Beverly Bryer Downing [Beverly D. Schroder] indicates that she shared an apartment in Providence with a friend (perhaps the Miss Edna W. Lewis mentioned in Annie's will) in 1924–28.

When her nephew returned to Providence in 1926, he and his elder aunt Lillian Delora both found rooms at 10 Barnes Street. Sometime after Mrs. Clark died there on 3 July 1932, Lovecraft and his surviving aunt Mrs. Gamwell determined to seek common quarters, an endeavor in which they succeeded in May 1933 with the renting of the upstairs flat at 66 College Street, located in a semi-hidden gardenlike surrounding just behind Brown University's John Hay Library.

This happy combinations of households allowed the resurrection of many long-stored relics from 454 Angell Street and formed the basis for Lovecraft's own most fulfilling years in Providence. Unfortunately, they were marred by his own and his aunt's increasing ill health. Soon after their arrival, Annie suffered a painful fracture on the stairs that necessitated many weeks of nursing on the part of her nephew. Then in the early spring of 1936 Annie was diagnosed with breast cancer and underwent a radical mastectomy to remove her cancerous right breast. When Edward F. Gamwell died in Boston on 10 May 1936, Annie was still recovering from her own operation. She never fully recovered, for her cancer unfortunately metastasized and she died of cancer at Jane Brown Memorial on 29 January 1941. After the loss of her own children, the most severe loss of Annie's later years was undoubtedly the loss of her beloved nephew in March 1937. Her closest remaining relatives were second cousins, grandchildren of her father's brother James Wheaton Phillips (1830–1901) and his wife Jane Ann Place Phillips (1829–1900), among them Esther M. Phillips Morrish (1888–1987).

Both Annie and Edward Gamwell were fortunate to have support systems to fall back upon after their tragic separation. Annie had her many social friends and acquaintances, dearest among them Edna W. Lewis. Apart from the occasions when medical requirements dictated otherwise, she and her nephew lived very independent lives at their common home of 66 College Street. Lovecraft would occasionally appear to greet his aunt's callers and vice versa; but while Annie continued to be active in Providence society, her nephew remained known only in fantasy and science fiction circles, maintaining the deliberate reserve he had kept since returning to his native city after the failure of his own marriage in 1926. Annie also had the benefit of a loving kindness on the part of her Gamwell in-laws which extended to keeping up correspondence and acquaintance. For himself, Edward Gamwell undoubtedly found solace in his business and club associates in Cambridge and Boston.

The years have obliterated the closely guarded secrets of the tragic separation of Annie and Edward Gamwell. Lovecraft's lifelong militance against alcohol makes one wonder whether Edward Gamwell might have been a victim of this tragic addiction. If so, alcohol would indeed have worked a tragedy in Lovecraft's own immediate family circle. Given Edward Gamwell's strict religious upbringing and the reproductive success of Edward and Annie's marriage, an addictive problem of some kind seems a likelier contributing factor to the separation than infidelity. Whatever the cause or causes, it seems that even Edward Gamwell's own family placed the principal responsibility on his shoulders. Compounded with the death of his son at the end of 1916, it must have been a difficult burden to bear, even with the help of business and social friends. With a lawyer's innate discretion, Irving Henry Gamwell omitted to record in his diary what he learned of his brother's final years from Edward's club associate Charles Carter.

Over many decades now they have rested separately. Annie Emeline Phillips Gamwell and her children Phillips Gamwell and Marion Roby Gamwell have been united since 1941 in the burial lot of Annie's father Whipple Phillips in Swan Point Cemetery in Providence. All the descendants of Whipple Phillips and his wife Robie Alzada Place Phillips are buried there, with the sole exception of Lillian Delora Phillips, who lies with her husband Dr. Franklin C. Clark iri a nearby lot of the same cemetery. Miles away, in the Arms Cemetery at Shelburne Falls, Mass., Annie's husband Edward Francis Gamwell rests with his. closest relatives, including his mother Victoria Clarissa Maxwell, his sister Helen Sears Gamwell, and his father Franklin Bert Gamwell. His brother Irving Henry Gamwell and his wives and son are buried in Irving's adopted home of Pittsfield, Mass. His Maxwell grandparents, Deacon Benjamin Maxwell and his wife Clarissa Munson Maxwell, are buried in Heath, Mass., a few miles away. His Gamwell grandparents, Samuel Gamwell and his wife Clarissa A. Moor, are buried in the Huntington Street Cemetery in Chester, in the western Massachusetts region where the Gamwells first settled in the eighteenth century. Similarly, the generation of Phillipses before Whipple Phillips rest in graves close to their western Rhode Island region where their ancestors settled in the eighteenth century.

The two families, Phillipses and Gamwells, united in Annie and Edward, shared many common threads: humble but proud origins from old English stock; an agrarian background; a respect for learning and education; deep religious convictions; ambition for self-betterment; strength in the face of adversity. Few parents endure more than the death of both children during their own lifetimes, compounded by the tragedy of separation. Fortunately, each spouse had a support system in the friends and associates of a lifetime. Annie had the love of her own family and her Gamwell in-laws as well. Edward endured the same pain—perhaps more if he was generally considered to be the party responsible for the separation—and seemingly more isolation.

Together, however, they and their son Phillips all touched the life of Howard Phillips Lovecraft, who wrote of them all with concern for the tragedies that visited their lives. While he himself accepted none of the religious beliefs that had guided the Phillipses and Gamwells through their generations, Lovecraft appreciated the necessity for a high standard of ethical and moral conduct in civilized society. Tragedy beset the marriages both of his mother and of his aunt Annie. But alongside those tragedies Lovecraft perceived many examples of high moral standards and conduct: his maternal grandfather's steadfast honesty through the many ups and downs of his business fortunes, the devotion to learning of Franklin Bert Gamwell and his family, the agrarian background and old English stock of both the Phillips and the Gamwell lines.

I hope I have filled in a small part of the family life of the Gamwells and of the Phillipses that touched the life of Howard Phillips Lovecraft. I think it was not an unimportant part. Lovecraft was fortunate to have as in-laws a family whose respect for their country's educational, political, and religious institutions was as strong as that of the Berkshire, Massachusetts, Gamwells. In the achievements of his Gamwell in-laws Lovecraft saw much which he himself failed to accomplish. Yet the strong moral sense which their lives and the lives of his own Phillips forbears ingrained in his being helped him to become and to continue to be remembered as one of the great gentlemen of letters of all time. For many lonely souls Lovecraft's correspondence was as much a charity as the more formal charities of his religious forbears. Indeed, his charity was unconventional, but I have no doubt that it would have been recognized as nothing less than charity by his more conventional relatives and in-laws. Lovecraft could never have been happy in the white-painted farmhouses of western Rhode Island and Massachusetts, where his Phillips and

Gamwell ancestors tilled the soil. He could not share the lives of these ancestors, which were centered upon religion and weather, as he remarked in his own poem "Waste Paper." Nevertheless, he could appreciate his heritage and he considered cultural continuity one of the highest values of a civilization. That Lovecraft partook of a certain degree of snobbishness concerning his ancestry cannot be doubted. However, his real heritage is not his purported connections with armigers—if in fact such connections can be proven—but his connection by blood and marriage with the hard-working, honest English stock we see in both the Phillipses and Gamwells. He could not have wished for better.

George Elliott Lovecraft: Lost Scion of the House of Lovecraft

H. P. Lovecraft believed that he was the last person to bear his surname on the North American continent. Writing to Maurice W. Moe on 5 April 1931, Lovecraft qualified his belief only as follows: "Joseph had a grandson who went west in the 1880's and dropped from sight [. . .] unless this lost western grandson of Joe Junior managed to keep alive amidst the wild and woolly—you behold in Old Theobald the Last of a Dynasty" (*MWM* 294). Lovecraft refers here to Joseph Lovecraft, Jr. (1810–1879), the son of Joseph Lovecraft, Sr. (1774–1850), the original 1831 emigrant from Devonshire, England, to Rochester, New York. A full account of the American careers of the emigrant Joseph Lovecraft, Sr. and his five sons (John, William, Joseph Jr., George, Aaron) and daughter Mary (Lovecraft) Brown may be found in Richard D. Squires's work *Stern Fathers 'neath the Mould* (Necronomicon Press, 1995).

The emigrant Joseph Lovecraft and his wife Mary (Full) Lovecraft (1782–1864) have living descendants in female lines, many of them traced by Squires in his work. However, as stated above, H. P. Lovecraft believed in 1931 that the Lovecraft name, at least in North America, would die with him. The last person to bear the Lovecraft name in England was John Lovecraft, who died at age 70 in St. Thomas, Devonshire, in the first quarter of 1911. An Australian family branch came to an end in the male line when William John Lovecraft, aged 25, died in the Bankstown, West Liverpool suburb of Sydney, New South Wales, Australia, in September 1867. Setting aside the question of persons who have subsequently adopted the Lovecraft family name in honor of H. P. Lovecraft, it appears that Lovecraft was actually the last person in the world to bear his surname, subject to the doubt he expressed concerning the survival of a grandson of Joseph Lovecraft, Jr. who "went west" and disappeared.

That grandson was George Elliott Lovecraft, born to Joseph, Jr.'s son Joshua Elliott Lovecraft (1844–1898) and his wife Libbie M. (Vandervort) Lovecraft (1847–1873) in Rochester, N.Y., sometime between 20 August 1866 and 11 June 1867.[1] Joseph Lovecraft, Jr. had founded his barrel head manufacturing business in Rochester in 1856, and his son Joshua Elliott Lovecraft was early associated with the enterprise as a bookkeeper. After a brief period in Indianapolis and Chicago around the year 1870, Joseph Lovecraft, Jr. and his family returned to Rochester to refocus their energies on the barrel head manufacturing business. Two of Joseph Jr.'s brothers were involved with allied businesses: John F. and his son Sidney J. with a planing mill, and William, with the manufacture of hoops and staves. By the late 1870s, Joshua Elliott Lovecraft was fully involved in the management of the family business, and the death of his father in 1879 left Joshua Elliott and his mother Elizabeth Lovecraft (1812–1896) in charge of the business. After completing his education, Joshua Elliott's son George became involved in the family business in the mid-1880s, working first as a bookkeeper just as his father had done.

George was not content to labor on as a bookkeeper in his father's business. About the year 1890, he became involved in a manufacturing enterprise in Chicago—whether his father had acquired a barrel head manufacturer in that city or George ac-

---

1. This date range is inferred from George's stated ages in the 1870 (age 3 as of 19 August 1870) and 1880 (age 13 as of 11 June 1880) U.S. censuses. George clearly misstated his age in his 7 August 1905 marriage record and in the 1910 U.S. census.

quired or founded a business of his own, is unknown. The Chicago directories for 1889–1890–1891 did not capture George Lovecraft, and the 1890 U.S. census has been forever lost to us. The only tangible record we have remaining from George's Chicago sojourn is his marriage on 20 November 1890 in Racine, Wisconsin, to a Rochester girl, Celia Marchand,[2] daughter of the late Jacob and Frances Marchand. French-born Jacob Marchand had operated a soda water manufacturing business in Rochester in partnership with Frank Damotte. William F. Peck's *Landmarks of Monroe County New York* (1895) (part III, pp. 293–94) records a few facts about Jacob Marchand and his family. Jacob was born in Besançon, France, in 1827 and resided in Detroit, Michigan, and Buffalo, New York, before settling in Rochester. He married Frances Perriard, also born in France. Jacob, age 43, died by drowning in September 1871.[3] His widow Frances died in Rochester of inflammation of the bowels in July 1888. Thus, Celia Marchand was an orphan at the time of her marriage to George Elliott Lovecraft in November 1890. According to Peck, Jacob and Frances Marchand had children: Josephine (m. 1876 Joseph A. Man); Eugenie; Mary (d. 28 June 1873, age 19 years 4 months); Frederick; Louis;[4] Cecilie; and two infants.

---

2. There is some variation in Celia's given name, both Celia and Cecilia occurring. It seems likely that her given name (in French) was Cecilie.

3. George Elliott Lovecraft's mother Libbie M. (Vandervort) Lovecraft died by drowning in Lake Ontario on 16 September 1873. Thus, George Elliott Lovecraft and his wife Celia (Marchand) Lovecraft both lost a parent by drowning.

4. Louis J. Marchand and his wife Fanny were living at 180 Albermarle in Rochester NY when the 1928 city directory was compiled . He was then president of the Igrad Condenser & Manufacturing Company at 26 Avenue D.

Just how long George and his new bride remained in Chicago, is unknown; but the 1892–93 New York City directory recorded George as a clerk residing at 2200 8th Avenue—the first of four Manhattan addresses that we have for George, dating to 1892–93, 1893, 1910, and 1933–34. Throughout his years in New York City, George resided consistently on the city's Upper West Side, not too far removed from the northern city suburbs like Mt. Vernon, Eastchester, and Pelham where other family scions, mostly descendants of Joseph, Jr.'s brother George Lovecraft (1815–1895), resided. Since the family tradition in H. P. Lovecraft's line was that George Elliott Lovecraft had disappeared in the West (probably based upon his residence in Chicago c. 1890), it seems unlikely that George Elliott became reacquainted with his great-uncle George while the younger man resided in New York City in 1892–94. Nor does it seem likely that the younger George knew the elder George's children Emily Jane (Lovecraft) Hill (1849–1925), Winfield Scott Lovecraft (1853–1898), or Mary (Lovecraft) Mellon (1855–1916). Squires (p. 26) records that young George Lovecraft worked for Frederick A. Lovecraft (1850–1893), son of Joseph Jr.'s brother Aaron Lovecraft, in his early years in New York City.

Tragedy was not long in seeking out George Lovecraft. His young wife Celia (Marchand) Lovecraft, aged only 22 years, died on 12 July 1893, at their then home at 316 West 119th Street after suffering from general peritonitis for three days.[5]

---

5. The fact that Celia (Marchand) Lovecraft (d. 1893), her sister Mary Marchand (d. 1873), and her mother Frances (Perriard) Marchand (d. 1888) all died of bowel disease suggests the possibility of either (1) a common hereditary bias or (2) some common environmental exposure. Mary and Frances are stated to have died of inflammatory bowel disease. Celia died of acute peritonitis of three days' duration after suffering from stenosis of the rectum and the resulting retention of fecal matter.

Their marriage was apparently childless—at least, no child was recorded for them in New York City in 1892 and 1893. George suffered yet a further loss with the suicide of his employer Frederick A. Lovecraft on 26 October 1893, and would later (12 March 1894) testify in court as to the mental condition of Frederick, who left a contested will. The bereaved George, however, soon refocused on the family businesses, for his father Joshua Elliott Lovecraft had acquired two new mills, in Olean, N.Y., and Salamanca, N.Y., in the same year that Celia (Marchand) Lovecraft died. In 1895–98, George lived at the Olean House in Olean, and managed the mills in Olean and Salamanca.

A newspaper sketch of George Elliott Lovecraft made during his attendance at the 1894 contest of the will of his former employer Frederick A. Lovecraft. Courtesy Richard D. Squires.

George soon faced more challenges. His father Joshua Elliott Lovecraft, began to exhibit increasing signs of madness, caused by paresis, and had to be institutionalized at Rochester State Hospital on 10 April 1896. (Winfield S. Lovecraft, son of George Lovecraft, had been admitted to Butler Hospital in Providence, R.I., with a similar diagnosis on 15 April 1893.) George's aged grandmother Elizabeth Lovecraft died on 31 October 1896, after having made her will, witnessed by Robert B. Brown and E. Della Brown of Rochester on 15 April 1896—just five days after her son Joshua Elliott Lovecraft had been admitted to Rochester State Hospital.[6] Petition to admit Elizabeth's will to probate was filed on 2 December 1896, and granted on 12 December 1896 by George A. Benton, Surrogate. Elizabeth's will left the entirety of her estate, real and personal, to her grandson George Elliott Lovecraft and also named him as executor. The general index of the Surrogate's Court records shows that Elizabeth's estate was estimated at $6,000 personal property and $83,000 real property. Amazingly enough, the inventory filed on 8 June 1897 showed the value of the estate as $411.40.[7]

The Surrogate's Court appointed George Elliott Lovecraft as committee for the estate of his incompetent father Joshua Elliott Lovecraft. In this matter, interested parties included not only Joshua Elliott Lovecraft but also his second wife Alice D. (Ward) Lovecraft. Joshua Elliott Lovecraft had made his will on 17 October 1890, with Charles M. Williams and David Bruce, Jr. of Rochester, N.Y., as witnesses.[8] Therein, he left all his

---

6. Will Book 57, pp. 514–17. Monroe County (NY) Surrogate's Court. LDS film 1004341.

7. The general index for vols. 12–13 (LDS film 833809) references Will Book 57 (p. 514), Order Book 63 (p. 245), Letter Book 13 (p. 253), and Special Guardian 15 (p. 431). Of these records, the author examined only Will Book 57 on LDS film 1004341. The real estate which George E. Lovecraft inherited from his grandmother Elizabeth Lovecraft in 1896 was eventually sold at sheriff's auction in 1898 to satisfy claims of the National Bank of Olean, NY, against George.

8. Will Book 60, pp. 61–63. Monroe County Surrogate's Court. LDS film 1004344.

household furniture "useful and ornamental" to his wife Alice D. Lovecraft, as well "horse, harness and carriage," his residence at 25 Reynolds Street in Rochester, and his life insurance proceeds. Income on the residue of his estate he left to his wife during her lifetime and upon her death to his son George E. Lovecraft. He directed his executors to shut down his businesses as soon as possible after his death and to invest the sale proceeds in "good and safe securities." Joshua Elliott Lovecraft was to outlive his mother Elizabeth Lovecraft; in his 1890 will he made no specific provision for her, but expressed the wish that she continue to reside with his wife. He named his wife Alice D. Lovecraft and his friend George Hyck as executors, and gave his executors authority to "sell, mortgage or lease" his real estate.

Even before the death of Joshua Elliott Lovecraft at Rochester State Hospital on 7 November 1898, George E. Lovecraft, as committee for the estate of his incompetent father, encountered severe problems in the Surrogate's Court. He failed to file any inventory of his father's assets and was arrested for contempt by order of the court. John F. Brayer was appointed as the new committee for the estate of the incompetent Joshua Elliott Lovecraft. To secure his release from jail, George Elliott Lovecraft had to post assets satisfactory to the court and secure bondsmen. The former committee George E. Lovecraft maintained that his father's estate was indebted to him in the amount of $5,000, while the new committee John F. Brayer estimated that George E. Lovecraft was indebted to his father's estate in the amount of $7,000 or $8,000—a net amount in dispute of $12,000 to $13,000. Some forty-eight hearings were held at a cost of $720 to try to sort out the financial disputes. The new committee John F. Brayer maintained that the assets of Joshua Elliott Lovecraft had amounted to $24,000 when George E. Lovecraft was appointed committee. After Joshua Elliott Lovecraft died, however, his widow and executor Alice D. Lovecraft and George E. Lovecraft obtained a court decree determining that George was not indebted to his father's estate, thereby releasing the property which George had assigned to secure his release from arrest.

The entire situation seems quite convoluted and it appears that Alice D. Lovecraft as executor then maintained that committee John F. Brayer's expenses during the incompetency of her late husband were excessive and had not been authorized by her. However, Justice Sutherland of the Monroe County Court ruled in favor of committee John F. Brayer on 20 April 1899. The Surrogate's Court general index indicates that an inventory of Joshua's estate in the amount of $2,063.34 was filed on 6 March 1899. (The original estimated amount of the estate was $2,000 personal property and $20,000 real property—close to committee Brayer's estimate.) During the year 1899, the Olean mill was sold to pay debts and the Salamanca mill was seized by the village for back taxes (Squires 28).

On 15 December 1900, John F. Brayer filed a claim of $3,106.87 with interest from 1 May 1899 against the estate of Joshua Elliott Lovecraft. However, the petitioner indicated his willingness to accept $2,300 in full and final settlement of his claims.[9] Joshua's widow Alice D. Lovecraft had remarried on 25 September 1900 and was now Mrs. William Williams. Brayer's claim was allowed and the estate of Joshua Elliott Lovecraft was finally closed in January 1901.[10] According to Squires (28), Al-

---

9. Brayer's claim may be found at pp. 306–07 of LDS film 1004353 (miscellaneous records 1900–1901).

10. The Surrogate Court's general index for vol. 12–13 (LDS film 833809), in addition to Will Book 60 (p. 61), references Order Book 67 (p. 533), Letter Book 14 (p. 233), Settlement Book 14 (p. 248), and Box No. 1081. The author has not seen these additional references and wonders if Box No. 1081 might contain some of the original papers relating to

ice D. Williams ultimately realized only $134.17 from the estate of Joshua Elliott Lovecraft. I wonder if executor Alice D. Lovecraft and former committee George E. Lovecraft (her stepson) might have reached some private agreement regarding the disposition of property then in possession of George E. Lovecraft, before filing for the court decree that George was not indebted to his father's estate and before filing the $2,063.34 inventory of Joshua Lovecraft's estate on 6 March 1899. The amount of the 6 March 1899 inventory was just $236.66 short of the amount which finally settled committee John F. Brayer's claim against the estate of Joshua Elliott Lovecraft in January 1901.

If George Lovecraft, the dismissed committee, remained in Rochester, he apparently lay low or used a pseudonym when the 1900 U.S. census was taken. I have failed to find him in the 1900, 1920, and 1930 U.S. censuses. Only in the 1910 U.S. census did Gary Sumpter of Burlington, Ontario, find not George, but Eliot Lovecraft, living with a wife Norma at 1743 Amsterdam Avenue on the Upper West Side of New York City.[11] Eliot was then working as an editor for the A.M. Press Association. How can we be sure that this Eliot Lovecraft was in fact the same person as George Lovecraft? New York City records of the marriage of "Eliot George Lovecraft" and Norma Hanlon at St. Mary's [Protestant Episcopal] Church in Manhattan on 7

---

the estate of Joshua Elliott Lovecraft.

11. I am grateful to Mr. Sumpter for communicating this information to me. Mr. Sumpter also found George Lovecraft (1815–1895) and his family in the 1880 U.S. census in Eastchester, Westchester County, NY. Son Winfield Scott Lovecraft, last noted working as a blacksmith in the 1871–74 Rochester city directories, was recorded in the 1880 U.S. census as working in a "tap wines" business. At the time of his marriage to Sarah Susan Phillips in Boston on 12 June 1889, he was a resident of New York City, working as a traveling salesman for Gorham Silversmiths of Providence, RI.

August 1905 give the names of the groom's parents as Joshua Lovecraft and Libbie Vandervort, clinching the identification. At the time of his marriage in 1905, George (or Eliot) stated his place of residence as Rochester. He claimed to be twenty-eight years old but was in fact thirty-eight or thirty-nine; he claimed to be single and marrying for the first time, but was in fact a widower marrying for the second time. It is interesting to note that both George Lovecraft and Howard Lovecraft—the two survivors of the surname in North America—chose to be married in Episcopal churches in New York City. H. P. Lovecraft married Sonia (Haft) Greene at St. Paul's Chapel in Manhattan on 3 March 1924.

Fresh tragedy awaited George Lovecraft in the spring of 1910. His young wife Norma (Hanlon) Lovecraft had been hospitalized at Seton Hospital in the Spuyten Duyvil section of the borough of the Bronx for treatment of pulmonary tuberculosis on 16 February 1910. She died there at the age of 25 years[12] at 4.30 A.M. on 27 May 1910, and was buried at Calvary Cemetery in the Woodside section of the borough of Queens on 30 May 1910. George was once again alone.

After the death of Norma (Hanlon) Lovecraft, I lose the trail of George Elliott Lovecraft for a dozen years. Then, as Steve Walker has discovered, on 15 September 1922 E. G. Lovecraft, D. E. Lovecraft, and S. W. Ferzon incorporated the Lovecraft Safety Pocket Corporation in Manhattan as a New York corporation with capital of $10,000. A safety pocket was an anti-pickpocket device. Today, the New York Corporations Division has no record of this inactive corporation. It is as if it has vanished into thin air—if the *New York Times* had not published a

---

12. Nora Hanlon's date of birth of May 1880 as recorded in the 1900 U.S. census makes it more likely that she was actually thirty years of age at the time of her death on 27 May 1910.

listing of its incorporation in its 16 September 1922 issue we would know nothing of it. Surely E. G. Lovecraft can be no one other than our own "Eliot George Lovecraft." Who was D. E. Lovecraft? George and his first wife Celia (Marchand) Lovecraft do not appear to have had any children. Any child of George and his second wife Norma (Hanlon) Lovecraft would have been too young to act as an incorporator in 1922. The author's assumption is that D. E. Lovecraft is most likely a third wife of George Lovecraft. H. P. Lovecraft had been in New York City in the spring of 1922 as the guest of his future wife Sonia (Haft) Greene, but there is no record of his meeting George Lovecraft at any time. As far as H. P. Lovecraft was concerned, George Lovecraft was "lost."

Then another gap of nearly a dozen years—from 1922 to the compilation period of R. H. Polk's 1933–34 New York City directory. There on page 2078 we find:

Lovecraft Geo. A. elev opr r. 232 E. 84th St.

Aged about 67, George was making his living at this time as an elevator operator. While he is not living as far north on Manhattan as he lived in 1892–93 (2200 8th Avenue, 316 West 119th St.) and 1910 (1743 Amsterdam Avenue), he is still north of Central Park in what we would still call the "Upper West Side." There, as far as we know, he had lived since marrying for the second time in 1905. Did he become the last surviving person bearing the Lovecraft surname with the death of H. P. Lovecraft in Providence on 15 March 1937? Or did he predecease his younger cousin?

With the great migration of genealogical records to electronic media, we may learn more of the life of George Elliott Lovecraft in the future. If he was hiding under a pseudonym for certain periods of his life, however, there will likely remain gaps in our knowledge. Joseph Lovecraft Jr.'s branch of the family was unlikely to have made much noise after the disarray of the family fortunes in 1896–1901—events in which George Elliott Lovecraft played a principal, and controversial, role. My own presumption is that George Elliott Lovecraft probably lived out most of the remainder of his life not in the wild "West," but on the Upper West Side of Manhattan, from 1905 onward.[13]

We can imagine that H. P. Lovecraft, on one of his holiday visits to New York City in the mid-1930s, encountered his family name in the R. H. Polk & Co. city directory of 1933–34.[14] Perhaps Lovecraft would have invited his friend Frank Belknap Long to accompany him on a mission to 232 East 84th Street. What sort of welcome Lovecraft might have received, it is difficult to imagine. Given his compelling correspondence habit, it seems highly unlikely that such an adventure would have gone unrecorded, unless he had uncovered very degrading circumstances indeed. If George Lovecraft was once more a widower by the mid-1930s, one hopes that he was at least making ends meet by working as an elevator operator in his old age. He had finally been bold enough to report himself under his own name in this directory after many years of absence. (I have found him in no New York City directory between 1892–93 and 1933–34.) Perhaps he would have had many family memories to share with his second cousin Howard Phillips Lovecraft.[15] Perhaps he might even have discussed how the Lovecraft coat of arms could be

---

13. In 2019, R. Alain Everts discovered that George Elliott Lovecraft died in Manhattan on 27 December 1932.
14. The 1933–34 New York City directory was the last published.
15, George Elliott Lovecraft and HPL shared a common set of great-grandparents (Joseph Lovecraft, Sr. and Mary (Fulford) Lovecraft) and were thus second cousins rather than first cousins. First cousins share a common set of grandparents.

found as a quartering in the arms of the Elliott family, accounting for the middle name which he and his father shared. Perhaps he might have recalled such memories as he had of Lovecraft's father Winfield S. Lovecraft (1853–1898) and grandfather George Lovecraft (1815– 1895)—although these would probably have been early memories from time spent in Rochester, New York. We will never know. Except in fantasy, it is highly unlikely any such mid-1930s meeting between H. P. Lovecraft and George Elliott Lovecraft ever transpired.

Bibliography

Docherty, Christopher J.; Searles, A. Langley; and Faig, Kenneth W., Jr. *Devonshire Ancestry of Howard Phillips Lovecraft*. Glenview IL: Moshassuck Press, 2003.

Monroe County (NY) Surrogate's Court Records.
General Index K–M. LDS film 833795.
General Index v. 12–13 (1896–1904). LDS film 833809.
Will Book v. 57 [Elizabeth Lovecraft will]. LDS film 1004341.
Will Book v. 60 [Joshua Elliott Lovecraft will]. LDS film 1004344.
Miscellaneous Records v. 26 (1900–1901) [John F. Brayer claim]. LDS film 1004353.

Mount Hope Cemetery [Rochester NY] Interment Records. www.lib. rochester.edu/index.cfm?page=3310
[Input first two letters of surname and then select desired date range.]

Squires, Richard D. *Stern Fathers 'neath the Mould: The Lovecraft Family in Rochester*. West Warwick, RI: Necronomicon Press, 1995.

Sumpter, Gary. Correspondence with the author, February 2002 and August 2004.

Walker, Steve. *The Limbonaut* No. 5, originally published as *The Criticaster* in Esoteric Order of Dagon mailing 120 (Hallowmas 2002). Now available at library.ucmo.edu/faculty/walker /]jmbonau t_5.html
[testimony of George A. Lovecraft of Olean, NY, in the estate of Frederick A. Lovecraft (1894); claim of T. H. Babcock against George Lovecraft (1898); Lovecraft Safety Pocket Corporation (1922).

———. *The Limbonaut* No. 6, originally published as *The Criticaster* in Esoteric Order of Dagon mailing 121 (Candlemas 2003). Now available at library.ucmo.edu/faculty/walker/limbonaut_6.html
[Monroe County court ruling relating to George E. Lovecraft (1899)]

Lovecraft Was Our Neighbor: The People of The Arsdale

In Memory of Lovecraft's Fellow Ailurophiles: Marian F. Bonner and Evelyn M. Staples

Introduction

There is little doubt that H. P. Lovecraft's favorite neighbors when he lived at 66 College Street in 1933–37 were the members of the Kappa Alpha Tau feline fraternity who sunned themselves atop the backyard shed at 53–55 Waterman Street, whom Lovecraft could observe from the windows of his study in the second-story flat he shared with his aunt Annie E. Gamwell. I leave the subject of Lovecraft's feline friends at his final home to another author. But Lovecraft was also acquainted with some of his non-feline neighbors. My article on Lovecraft's final home, "Can You Direct Me to Ely Court?: Some Notes on 66 College Street," in this volume, covers Alice R. Sheppard (1870–1961) and Mary Spink (1877–1968), who lived in the downstairs flat at 66 College Street during Lovecraft's and his aunt's years of residence. The houses at 53 Waterman, 55 Waterman, and 66 College (1 Ely Court) all belonged to the heirs of merchant Samuel Brenton Mumford (1796–1849) when the 1875 Providence atlas was compiled.[1] The "Garden House" at 66 College Street (removed to 65 Prospect Street in 1959) is dated c. 1825 on its Providence Preservation Society plaque, although Lovecraft himself claimed that he could discern the house in the famous 1809 theatre curtain now at the Nelson W. Aldrich House headquarters of the Rhode Island Historical Society at 110 Benevolent Street.

---

1. By 1918, 53–55 Waterman, 64 College, and 66 College all belonged to C. H. Robinson.

53–55 Waterman in the Nineteenth Century

I do not find either 53 or 55 Waterman Street (the houses across the backyard from 66 College Street) in Providence directories before 1860. (It is possible that the houses, if constructed earlier, bore different street numbers before 1860.) In the 1860, 1862, 1864, and 1866 directories, Mrs. Benjamin D. Earle made her home at 55 Waterman Street. By 1872, Freewill Baptist clergyman Rev. Ammi Ruhamah Bradbury (1810–1899), the son of Samuel Bradbury and Jane Gurney and an 1837 graduate of Bowdoin College, made his home at the same address. Rev. Bradbury still lived there in 1875, by which time his wife Caroline L. J. (Johnson) Bradbury (1814–1890), whom he had married in 1844, was operating a boarding house at the same address. In the 1880 U.S. census, Ida M. Gardner, a 30-year-old MA-born school teacher, was the head of household at 55 Waterman. Her sister Margaret A. Gardner, age 21, a music teacher, also MA-born, and two school teacher boarders were also members of the household. By 1882, John Holden (1811–1887) and his wife Hester (Brown) Holden (1814?–1905), the daughter of James and Lydia G. (Carpenter) Brown, were making their home at 55 Waterman. Holden had been a farmer in Warwick, RI, in the 1870 U.S. census.[2] In the same year (1870), Ida M. Gardner was running a private young people's school at 53 Waterman. Her sister Lillian L. Gardner, also a teacher, boarded at the same address. By 1895, Josiah Westcott (1835–1922), a travelling jewelry salesman, and his wife Hannah Holden (Gorton) Westcott, made their home at 53 Waterman, while the widowed Hester Holden was still the head of household at 55 Waterman. A common entrance for the two houses had been created by the time the 1875 atlas was compiled, perhaps indicating that both houses

---

2. The 1880 Providence directory listed John Holden, farmer, at 1 College Court (the Garden House).

were functioning as boarding houses and shared some facilities. The common entrance is also reflected in the 1889 Sanborn fire map.[3] In 1896, shirt maker A. S. Arnold was co-householder with Hester B. Holden at 55 Waterman. The year 1898 was the last for Hester Holden (by then eighty-four years old) at 55 Waterman, while the Westcotts continued at 53 Waterman through 1901. In 1899, Susanna R. Steere succeeded Mrs. Holden at 55 Waterman. When the 1900 U.S. census was enumerated on 1 June 1900, Francis B. Carleton, a medical doctor, was the renter and head of household at 55 Waterman. He and his wife and their three children had two servants and no boarders in their household.

A view of Waterman Street (postcard). It includes The Arsdale on the south side of the street, three doors down from Prospect Street. Courtesy David Haden and Tentaclii.

---

3. To view the Sanborn fire maps for Providence, go to www.provlib.org/databases/proquest-sanborn-maps-ir/. The vicinity of 53–55 Waterman may be found in plate 47a of volume 2 of the 1889 maps. References for later Sanborn maps include 1900 (v. 2, sheet 105), 1920–21 (v. 2, sheet 15), and 1920–51 (vol. 2, sheet 15).

The Twentieth Century Arrives

By 1903, Ellen A. Donahue [Donohue] had become the householder at 53 Waterman, and Elizabeth B. Dexter at 55 Waterman. Harriet J. Miller succeeded at 55 Waterman in 1907. Ellen Donahue called her boarding house The Paxton in the 1903 Providence directory.

Ellen A. Donohue (1903–22) and Harriet J. Miller (1907–30) had long runs as operators of the boarding houses at 53 and 55 Waterman Street. The 1921 Providence directory listed Miss Ellen A. Donahue as operator of The Paxton at 53 Waterman and Miss Harriet J. Miller as householder at 55 Waterman. Not until the house directory of 1925–26 did Louisa C. Brinkerhoff succeed as operator of the merged rooming houses at 53–55 Waterman, now called The Arsdale. However, Harriet J. Miller returned as operator of The Arsdale in the 1928 and 1929 directories and the 1929–30 house directory. Miss Miller died, age 59, in Rhode Island on 2 February 1930. In the 1910 U.S. census, Miss Miller had nine lodgers and one servant at 55 Waterman, while Miss Donahue had four lodgers and two servants at 53 Waterman. By the time of the Rhode Island state census in 1925, Miss Miller had thirty-one lodgers and one servant at The Arsdale at 53 and 55 Waterman Street. Included among Miss Miller's lodgers in that year were Evelyn Staples (1860–1938) and Marian F. Bonner (1883–1952). Miss Staples remained at The Arsdale through her own death in 1938, while Miss Bonner remained until she removed to lodgings at 156 Meeting Street in June 1936.[4] Lovecraft had a piquant correspondence with Miss

---

4. Miss Bonner's letters from HPL are dated between 22 March 1936 and 7 December 1936. She had moved to 156 Meeting Street by the time HPL wrote on 9 June 1936. His letters to her Meeting Street address were addressed to its former name Gaol Lane, and Miss Bonner wrote of HPL's delight that the post office delivered his letters without a problem (*AAV* 433).

Bonner about the Kappa Alpha Tau fraternity and other subjects, first published in full in *Lovecraft Annual* No. 9 (2015): 3–51.

The Lovecraft Era Nears

John B. and Mary G. Marcett (also spelled Marcette) succeeded Harriet J. Miller as operators of The Arsdale by the time the 1931–32 house directory was compiled. John B. Marcett, the 37-year-old son of Joseph and Zoe [Mary] Marcett, resided in Fairfield, VT, when he married Mary E. Goodroe (1878–1970), the daughter of Israel Goodroe (1853–1928) and Mary Jane Rushford (1855–1945), on 30 June 1902, at St. Patrick's Church in Fairfield, VT. Rev. N. J. LaChance officiated at their wedding. The Marcetts removed to Providence by 1903. John B. Marcett worked as a janitor, and lived at 27 Calais Street and 114 Camp Street in the 1903 and 1908 directories, respectively. He and his wife had children Mildred E. Marcett (1906–1986) and John R. Marcett (b. 1909), both born in Providence. By 1916, John Marcett Sr. was a grocer at 116 Camp Street, still residing at 114 Camp. The Marcetts and their two children still lived at 114 Camp Street when the 1920 U.S. census was enumerated. John worked as a janitor in an office building while his wife Mary operated the retail grocery at 116 Camp. The Marcetts were at the same Camp Street address in the 1925 directory; by then, John was devoting his attentions to the grocery at 116 Camp. In the 1928 directory, John B. and Mary G. Marcett made their home at 178 Bowen Street. By 1930, they resided at 305 Hope and operated a boarding house at 178 Bowen. In the 1930 U.S. census, John B. Marcette, age 64, born VT of VT-born parents, and Mary G. Marcette, age 50, born CT of VT-born parents, were enumerated at their lodging house at 178 Bowen. John Marcett, age 65, died in Providence on 3 July 1931—probably not long after the compilation of the data for the 1931–32 house directory—and was buried in Holy Cross Cemetery in St. Albans VT. In the 1952 and 1953 directories, Mary G. Marcett was still residing at 305 Hope and operating a lodging house at an unspecified location. In 1955–62, she was listed at 155 Medway; the directories no longer listed her lodging house business.

The Lovecraft Era Arrives

The operators of The Arsdale most significant for the period of Lovecraft's residency next door were Leslie Burt Fadden and his wife Florence Loretta Fadden (née Goodroe or Goudreau), who were recorded at 55 Waterman as early as the 1932 directory. Mrs. Fadden was the youngest sister of the preceding manager, Mary E. (Goodroe) Marcett. She was born in St. Albans, VT, on 8 February 1896, the daughter of Israel Goodroe and Mary Jane Rushford. Leslie Burt Fadden had been born in Dunlap, Harrison County, Iowa, on 30 November 1896, the fifth child of Riley W. (1863–?) and Fannie Elizabeth Fadden (1866–?). On 22 September 1914, he married Florence Loretta Goodroe in St. Albans, VT. Leslie worked as a railway conductor, and the couple had children Ruth Eleanor Fadden, born 2 May 1918, and James Forrest Fadden, born 27 January 1920, both in St. Albans, VT. The Faddens continued in St. Albans through the 1930 U.S. census, but came to Providence by 1932 to assume management of The Arsdale. Perhaps the death of John Marcett in 1931 motivated his widow Mary to write her sister Florence concerning the boarding house opportunity at The Arsdale. The Faddens continued as joint operators of The Arsdale until 1938, when they apparently separated. Florence was still managing The Arsdale (with the help of her children) when the 1940 U.S. census was enumerated on 1 April 1940,[5] while Leslie was by then managing a separate rooming house at 3 Greene Street.

---

5. After World War II, Brown University converted The Arsdale to a stu-

Residents of The Arsdale During the Lovecraft Era

Of course, the crucial period for The Arsdale, so far as Lovecraft is concerned, is 1933–37. By searching electronically for "55 Waterman" in Providence city directories on Ancestry.com, I was able to find the following residents in 1934 (where an address is provided, it is the individual's business address; an asterisk indicates an individual not found in 1935 RI state census):

> Bonner, Marian F., assistant, Providence Public Library
> *Crosby, Gretchen R., bookkeeper, 326 Waterman
> Fadden, Leslie B. (Florence L.)
> *Hibbard, Lois H., case worker, 200 Wickenden
> Johnson, Doris D. M., assistant, Providence Public Library, 31 Candace
> Kane, Annise B., librarian, Classical High School
> Leeds, Earl P., clerk, Brown & Sharpe
> Staples, Evelyn, teacher
> *Swartz, Adolphe, jeweler
> *Tinsdale, Edmund J. (Julia V.)
> *Wentworth, Laura E., stenographer, 15 Westminster, room 338

I was able to perform a similar search for 55 Waterman in the 1937 city directory and found the following residents of 55 Waterman (where an address is provided, it is the individual's business address; an asterisk indicates an individual not found in 1935 RI state census):

> Fadden, Leslie B. (Florence L.)
> *Fenner, Eleanor

---

dent dormitory and renamed it Hopkins House. Hopkins House continued in service for a decade or more but was eventually decommissioned and demolished.

*Fiske, Reginald, salesman, 170 Westminster, room 301
*Griffin, Dorothy, teacher
Johnson, Doris E. M., assistant, Providence Public Library, 31 Candace
*Johnson, Muriel S., record librarian, Rhode Island Hospital
Kane, Annise B., teacher, Classical High School
*Mutch, Verona, advertising department, 243 Westminster
Staples, Evelyn, teacher
*Tinsdale, Edmund J.
*Wentworth, Laura E., stenographer
*Wittens, Etta, buyer

Most of these individuals were probably only nodding acquaintances of Lovecraft and his aunt Annie E. P. Gamwell. Mrs. Gamwell took her mid-day meals at The Arsdale, but of course those residents who were working probably did not return to their boarding house for lunch. (It is possible that they were provided "sack lunches" if they had "all meals" contracts.) Lovecraft customarily ate only holiday meals at The Arsdale, most commonly the Thanksgiving feast, since he was often rushed to depart for New Year's visits to New York City at Christmas.[6] (He did not, however, travel at Christmas 1936.) Lovecraft's interactions with the managers and the residents of The Arsdale were probably more substantial during Mrs. Gamwell's illnesses in 1933 (bro-

---

6. However, *contra*, there is the following recollection by HPL's amateur journalist friend Edward H. Cole: "He rarely ventured forth from December to March or April, other than to hurry across to the boarding house where he ate one meal daily (he prepared the others himself)" (*AAV* 25). However, HPL's several discussions of his customary diet in his later years do not, to my knowledge, contain any indication of a daily meal consumed at The Arsdale. On the other hand, he would probably have had a natural inclination to accompany his aunt if she needed any assistance in getting to or from The Arsdale. I am indebted to David E. Schultz for this reference.

ken ankle) and 1936 (mastectomy surgery). She had just moved to 66 College when she broke her ankle in 1933, but by 1936 she was certainly a well-known figure in the dining room of The Arsdale. Lovecraft carried her mid-day meals from The Arsdale to her after she returned home following her injury in 1933.

Lovecraft's best acquaintances at The Arsdale were undoubtedly Marian F. Bonner, for many years the periodicals librarian at the main branch of the Providence Public Library on Empire Street, and Evelyn M. Staples, a retired elementary schoolteacher who spent most of her career at the Charles Street School. Lovecraft's correspondence with Miss Bonner is owned by the John Hay Library; no letters to Miss Staples are known to survive.

A Librarian and Kappa Alpha Tau Associate: Marian Bonner

Marian Frederika Bonner was born in Providence on 6 September 1883 to Robert Bonner (1845–1898) and Marian Barker (1838–1913). Her father, born in Brighton, Sussex, the son of Robert Bonner (1818–1902) and Anne Goldsmith (1819–?), worked as a music teacher in Providence. Her mother, born in Germany of English-born parents, arrived in the United States in 1859 (1900 U.S. census). Marian was the sixth child and fourth daughter of the family, having siblings (all born in Providence) Ethel (1872–1958) (m. Frederic Arthur Wallace), Robert William (1874–1875), Maud Ann (1875–?), Robert (1877–1959) (m. Agnes K. Noyes), Irene D. (1880–1967) (m. France Cornell) and Elinor Agnes (1881–1942). Robert and his wife were living at 60 Williams Street by the time their daughter Marian was born; they had earlier lived at 49 Chestnut (1869), 93 Mathewson (1871) and Angell Court (1873, 1875, 1876). By 1897, Robert and his wife lived at 102 Williams Street, where Mrs. Bonner remained after her husband's death in 1898. Marian's sister Maude was an 1895 graduate of Brown University, while her brother Robert was a special student in 1892–93 and Marian herself in 1902–03. Marian and her sister Irene D. Bonner were enumerated in their widowed mother's household at 102 Williams Street in the 1900 U.S. census. Marian was still in school at the time. Her mother had borne seven children, of whom six were then living. Marian was working for the Providence Public Library[7] by 1905, when she was enumerated at 102 Williams Street with her mother and her sisters, Elinor A., Maude A., and Irene D. The religion of the sisters was stated as Episcopalian. Marian resided with her mother and sisters Maude and Elinor at 102 Williams Street when the 1910 U.S. census was enumerated. After the death of her mother on 5 July 1913, Marian lived as a boarder for the rest of her life. She was boarding with Frederick and Anna Miller at 33 Angell Street when the 1920 U.S. census was enumerated. By 1922, she had taken up residence at The Arsdale, where she still resided when the 1935 Rhode Island census was enumerated (her card is dated 20 January 1936). However, in June 1936 she took up residence with Yolmar and Lillian Bietrum at 156 Meeting Street, where she remained when the 1940 U.S. census was enumerated. She was still at 156 Meeting Street in 1941 and 1942, but was at 95 Benevolent Street in 1943 and 1944. In 1945, 1946, and 1947, she boarded at 167 Evergreen Street. Her affiliation with the Providence Public Library was last listed in 1947, so perhaps she retired around the time of her sixty-fifth birthday in September 1948. In 1952, her final year in the Providence directories, she was boarding at 303 Benefit Street. Marian Bonner died of a cerebral hemorrhage on 13 May 1952 and was buried with her parents in Swan Point Cemetery.

---

7. Between at least 1912 and 1918, Marian compiled an annual "Index to Reference Lists Published in Library Bulletins" for the *Bulletin of Bibliography*, edited by Frederick Winthrop Faxon.

A Teacher and Kappa Alpha Tau Associate: Evelyn Staples

Evelyn M. Staples was born in Barrington, RI, on 1 October 1860, the daughter of paper manufacturer Henry Staples (1828–1901) and his wife Mary Haile Fowler (1831–1878). She was the granddaughter of Providence historian William Read Staples (1798–1868) and his wife Evelina Eaton (1806–1885), and may have been named in honor of her paternal grandmother. Her maternal grandparents were Samuel Metcalf Fowler and Mary (———) Fowler. Evelyn had one sibling, a brother Alfred Bosworth Staples (1863–1892). She was still residing with her widowed father in Barrington when the 1885 RI state census was enumerated. In 1890/91, she was working as a kindergarten teacher in Barrington Center. Evelyn was in Providence by the time the 1900 U.S. census was enumerated, living at 47 Camp Street in the household of Jeannette Towle and her daughters Mary F. Towle (b. 1875) and G. Louise Towle (b. 1883). Daughter Mary F. Towle was working as a kindergarten teacher while G. Louise Towle was still in school. Evelyn remained at 47 Camp in the 1903 and 1904 directories. By 1908, she had removed with the Towles to 118 Lexington Ave. The 1909 directory was the first which listed Evelyn as a teacher at the Charles Street School.[8] Evelyn probably taught at this school for the remainder of her teaching career; the 1931 directory still listed her there. When the 1910 U.S. census was enumerated, Evelyn was still living with the Towles at 118 Lexington Ave. In 1910 both Towle daughters were working as teachers. Evelyn remained with the Towles at 118 Lexington Ave. through at least 1912; by 1914 she had become a boarder at 235 Broadway. By 1916 she was at 563 Public, and then by 1918 at 34 Mawney, where

---

8. A new building for the school was erected in 1917. The 1917 building (480 Charles Street) now houses Esek Hopkins Middle School.

she remained through at least 1920. When the 1920 U.S. census was enumerated, she was a boarder with Nellie Mulligan at 34 Mawney. In 1922, she was boarding at 78 Mawney. By 1924, she was boarding at 53 Waterman, while by 1925 she had begun her long tenancy at The Arsdale (55 Waterman), where she resided until her death on 10 June 1938.[9] Evelyn was buried with her parents and her brother in Princes Hill Burial Ground in Barrington, RI, where she has a handsome marker that can be viewed on Find-A-Grave. Just when she retired from teaching is uncertain. The 1935 RI state census listed no occupation for her, while the 1937 and 1938 directories still listed her as a teacher. Perhaps she continued to work occasionally as a substitute teacher. Like Miss Bonner, Evelyn remained single throughout her life. Her life was not all routine; she traveled to Europe in 1930, returning on the *Lapland,* departing Cherbourg on 23 August 1930 and arriving in New York City on 31 August 1930.

The People of The Arsdale—What They Did and Didn't Mean for Lovecraft

Lovecraft's acquaintances with residents of the neighboring Arsdale were doubtless mostly casual.[10] Probably only Miss Bonner

---

9. She died while visiting relatives in St. Johns, New Brunswick, Canada.

10. HPL and his aunt occupied the second-floor flat at 66 College Street, which can hardly be called a rooming house. His own residences at 169 Clinton Street in Brooklyn in 1925–26 and at 10 Barnes Street in Providence in 1926–33 have not been much studied, despite the availability of enumerations of the two buildings in the 1925 New York census and the 1930 U.S. census, respectively. I do not believe that meal service was offered in either of these two locations, which might more properly be described as apartment or rooming houses, rather than boarding houses. An American boarding house typically provided common areas for residents (in addition to their individual rooms), and optional services such as meals and laundry. I do not know whether meal service was optional or manda-

and Miss Staples could be described as friends, because of their mutual affection for the members of the Kappa Alpha Tau feline fraternity. But young Miss Johnson and Leslie and Florence Fadden probably also had their opinions of their mostly taciturn occasional dining guest. I wish that someone had asked Florence Fadden and Doris Johnson about H. P. Lovecraft before they died in 1982 and 2004, respectively. We must surely always regret that Winfield Townley Scott did not decide to undertake a full biography of H. P. Lovecraft in the 1940s, when The Arsdale still existed, and many of its former residents were still in the midst of their lives. Perhaps Scott concluded that the passage of years was needed before the perspective necessary for a biography could be attained. Biographers L. Sprague de Camp (1975) and S. T. Joshi (1996) had the benefit of the archive of Lovecraft correspondence that has accumulated over the years. While I am not aware that either of the biographers talked to any erstwhile residents of The Arsdale, each of them added his own discoveries to the biographical narrative.

Acknowledgments

I'm grateful to the Rhode Island State Archives and the Reference Department of the Providence Public Library for research assistance. However, I remain solely responsible for all statements, of fact or of opinion, in this paper.

---

tory for the residents of The Arsdale. In any case, cooking in the individual rooms was probably forbidden.

Lovecraftian Places

The Story of 454 Angell Street: The Birthplace of Howard Phillips Lovecraft

In Memory of Whipple V. Phillips

Whipple V. Phillips (1833–1904). Courtesy John Hay Library.

Abbreviations; Notes

PD XXXX means Providence Directory for the year XXXX. PHD XXXX means Providence House Directory for the year XXXX. RI XXXX means RI state census for the year XXXX. US XXXX means US census for the year XXXX. EPD XXXX means East Providence Directory for the year XXXX. USPS abbreviations are used for the states.

194 Angell Street, originally erected c. 1874–75, was renumbered as 454 Angell Street in 1896–97. References to 194 or 454 Angell refer to the same dwelling, demolished in 1961. A modern apartment building stands on the former site of Lovecraft's birthplace on the northwest corner of Angell Street and Elm Grove [Elmgrove] Avenue. The Lovecraft Arts & Sciences Council has placed a marker commemorating Lovecraft's birthplace on the corner.

H. P. Lovecraft and 454 Angell Street

Lovecraft's mother Sarah Susan Phillips apparently eloped to marry Winfield Scott Lovecraft in Boston in 1889. While the couple began their married life in Boston, Sarah Susan returned to her father Whipple V. Phillips's home at 454 Angell Street to give birth to her first and only child on 20 August 1890. Whipple had moved into this spacious home just on the edge of urban development on the East Side of Providence when it was only five or six years old. Here his young grandson was the spend the first thirteen and a half years of his life, until the death of his grandfather on 28 March 1904 resulted in the sale of the property and the removal of Lovecraft and his mother to less spacious (but less expensive) quarters several blocks eastward at 598 Angell Street.

Writing to Rheinhart Kleiner on 16 November 1916, Lovecraft described his birthplace as follows:

In the mid-seventies, my grandfather transferred all his interests to Providence (where his offices had always been) & erected[1] one of the handsomest residences in the city—to me, *the* handsomest—my own beloved birthplace! This spacious house, raised on a high green terrace, looks down upon grounds which are almost a park, with winding walks, arbours, trees, & a delightful fountain. Back of the stable is the orchard, whose fruits have delighted so many of my sad (?) childish hours. The place is sold now, & many of the things I have described in the present tense, ought to be described in the *past* tense. (*RK* 62)

454 (then 194) Angell Street c. 1895. Whipple (seated) and two daughters (standing) on lawn; Robie (seated) on porch. Stable (coach house) can be seen at rear. Courtesy Sean Donnelly.

---

1. As we will see, Whipple V. Phillips purchased the existing home of Samuel Allen at 194 Angell Street in 1880/81. Allen, a successful Providence jewelry manufacturer, had erected the house in 1874/75.

Writing to Edwin Baird on 3 February 1924, he provided further description:

> In 1893, however, his father's health passed into the decline from which it never emerged; so that Lovecraft and his mother returned to Providence, to that materno-grandpaternal roof at 454 Angell St. under which he originally beheld the solar illumination. But what was tragedy for the elder generation was nothing of the sort to the younger. The future dictator of literature was intensely attached to his grandfather, whose travels in Europe and taste for Italian art made him a varied & piquant converser, and to the whole place with its trees and terraces, fountains and stables, walks and gardens—and best of all, its proximity to the dreaming fields and mystic groves of antique New-England (now solid blocks of homes and apartment-houses) which the young sage's vibrant imagination peopled with every conceivable sort of unreal presence. Within the house was a vast array of books—the fusion of two hereditary libraries—and to this the rising aesthete turned when, at four, the ars legendi became his. (*WH* 36)

He provided yet a third perspective in his letter to Maurice W. Moe dated 5 April 1931: "This[2] moved the family to Providence, where a happy financial recovery took place; so that I was born into a very comfortable home in the best part of the city—you saw the house on its terrace in 1923, though both it and the locality are not what they were in 1890" (*JFM* 297).

He described the end of his idyllic childhood days in his letter to Rheinhart Kleiner dated 16 November 1916:

> But my progress received its severest blow in the spring of 1904. On March 28th of that year my beloved grandfather passed away as the result of an apoplectic stroke, & I was deprived of my closest companion. I was never afterward the same . . . My mother & I

---

2. HPL refers to a financial collapse in 1870. While Whipple Phillips had business interests in Providence as early as 1868, he did not in fact remove his family to the city until 1874.

were forced to vacate the beautiful estate at 454 Angell Street, & to enter the less spacious abode at 598, three squares eastward. The combined loss of grandfather & birthplace made me the most miserable of mortals . . . My home had been my ideal of Paradise & my source of inspiration—but it was to be profaned & altered by other hands. Life from that day has held for me but one ambition—to regain the old place & re-establish its glory—a thing I fear I can never accomplish. For twelve years I have felt like an exile. (*RK* 73)

Lovecraft wrote of the loss of his birthplace as the worst event of his life in a letter to Elizabeth Toldridge, 24 January 1933:

> The worst experience I ever had was losing my birthplace, & I dread the thought of the day when still worse circumstances may force me out of my present comfortable quarters—where I have all my old things around me. But even if I had to seek a cheaper habitat,[3] I'd never give up accustomed furniture & accessories if I could help it. I'd rather live in a tumble-down stable[4] with my lifelong-known possessions than in a luxurious hotel with unfamiliar things. (*ET* 231)

He wrote of the sense of foreboding before and after the loss of his grandfather:

> But actual decline did set in when I was about ten years old;[5] so that I saw a steady dropping of servants, horses, and other adjuncts

---

3. He and his younger aunt Annie Gamwell did combine their households in the second-floor flat at 66 College Street on 15 May 1933. It was probably the most commodious living space HPL had enjoyed since 454 Angell Street, and many household items long in storage were restored to their everyday environment.

4. Was he thinking of the former stable (coach house) at 454 Angell Street, which had been demolished in August 1931?

5. HPL wrote to Edwin Baird on 3 February 1924: "But this whole history is one of slow impoverishment and decay. HPL was born to a household of four servants and three horses—and he has seen them all go . . . all of these, and the old home as well, for the death of his grandfather with a

of domestick management. Even before my grandfather's death a sense of peril and falling-off was strong within me, so that I felt a kinship to Poe's gloomy heroes with their broken fortunes. And of course the frightful crash itself—in 1904, when the death of my grandfather broke up all his recuperative plans and forced the sale of the old house—gave me a tremendous and positive melancholy. All the air rotted with decay, and the moon itself was putrescent. I had been vastly attached to my grandfather and to my birthplace, and when both—to say nothing of my beloved black cat Nigger-Man—were swept away in the course of a few months, I was about ready to cash in myself. (*MWM* 301)

Reduced to lesser quarters, the Phillips family put many treasured pieces of Victorian furniture from 454 Angell Street into storage. Having had to surrender 454 Angell Street itself to strangers, Lovecraft cautioned his aunt Lillian D. Clark on 8 August 1925 that he would hang onto his surviving relics from his former residence at all costs:

so in order to avoid the madness which leads to violence & suicide I must cling to the few shreds of old days & old ways which are left to me. Therefore no one need expect me to discard the ponderous furniture & paintings & clocks & books which help to keep 454 always in my dreams.[6] When they go, I shall go, for they are all that

---

burdened estate forced a removal to a small flat three blocks east on the same street . . . the flat where this machine is now clicking, but which will probably go in turn during the coming spring, when finances will decree a final disintegration landing me in all probability in New York" (*SL* 1.298). Of course, HPL's marriage to Sonia Greene on 3 March 1924 was already being planned as he wrote to Baird.

6. Writing to Mrs. Clark on 20 May 1925, he described secluding himself on "one of our 454 dining-room chairs" in his alcove for an evening of reading (*LFF* 289). Sonia Davis recalled: "Yet HPL took pride in telling me that he was born on the mattress on which we both slept. This, I believe, he told no one but me" (R. Alain Everts, "Howard Phillips Lovecraft and Sex," *Nyctalops* 2, No. 2 [July 1974]: 19). Writing in "A

make it possible for me to open my eyes in the morning to look forward to another day of consciousness without screaming in sheer desperation & pounding the walls in a frenzied clamour to be waked up out of the nightmare of "reality" to my own room in Providence. (*LFF* 339)

He wrote to J. Vernon Shea on 4 February 1934:

The one time that I seriously thought of suicide was in & after 1904, when my grandfather died in the midst of business tangles (he was president of a land & irrigation corporation exploiting the Snake River in Idaho, & the total destruction of the dam on which everything depended had caused a frightful situation) & left us all relatively poor. I was (being predominantly geographical-minded) tremendously attached to the old home at 454 Angell (now hous-

---

Consanguineous Union: Incest Imagery in Lovecraft," T. R. Livesey comments: "Presumably, this mattress was Susan's from 454 Angell Street, unused after moving from that place or after her death, since the Eddys claim to have gotten HPL's own bed when he moved to New York. If anything inappropriate did happen between HPL and his mother, the significance that his mattress might have had to him boggles the imagination. He might have had pride in the mattress, but he kept it a secret. Even if it was nothing more than the mattress he was born on, it is still bizarre that he would focus on this thought while he and his wife slept on it" (untitled submission, Esoteric Order of Dagon Amateur Press Association mailing 135 (Lammas 2006): [i–ii], 1–36, 77–79; in *Redux: A Journal of Reflection* No. 1, mailing 136 (Hallowmass 2006): 37–76; see 60–61. HPL's aunts did assist the newlywed couple by shipping various household goods in the spring of 1924. In his letter to Mrs. Clark dated 30 March 1924, HPL mentioned not only "all blankets and bedding, especially the ancestrally-woven blankets" as among needed goods, but added that "the double bed mattress here is 74 by 53 inches in size, and we would appreciate anything in the mattress line which may conform to these dimensions" (*LFF* 128). So perhaps Mrs. Clark did ship Susie Lovecraft's old mattress. I am grateful to David E. Schultz for these references from HPL's letters to Mrs. Clark.

ing 12 physicians' offices[7]—I walk by it still as often as I can) with its grounds & fountain, & stable, but this now had to go ... indeed, there had been drastic economies for 5 years before that. My mother & I moved into a 5-room-&-attic flat two squares farther east (598 Angell St., where I dwelt till 1924), & for the first time I knew what a congested, servantless home—with another family in the same house[8]—was. (*JVS* 221)

Striking a similar chord, Lovecraft wrote to Helen V. Sully on 28 October 1934: "I was altogether disorganised when I lost my original home in 1904, but I have at least managed to hang on to the books, furniture, pictures & other objects most vital to me. When *these* have to go, it will be about time for the old man to follow them into nothingness!" (*WBT* 393).

Despite his general dislike for all things Victorian, he could relish the mementos of his birthplace that he retained. For example, he even recalled with pleasure the hallway and parlor wallpaper from his birthplace:

> As to a decorative scheme for your future room—well, tastes differ, but I never liked any other colour combination so well as *black-and-gold*. To my naïve and undeveloped aesthetic sense that represents about the apex of dignified beauty—perhaps because that was the scheme in the front hall of my birthplace, 454 Angell Street ... Ebony and gold is the aesthetic mixture—although old gold and rose is a great scheme, as the front parlor of my birthplace proved. There was an almost Oriental richness in that room, as in the palace of a caliph—I used to read the *Arabian Nights* there with an especial zest. (*SL* 2.165)

Lovecraft's commonplace book [entry 159] may even reflect a memory retained from his grandmother Robie Place Phillips's

---

7. I do not find as many as eleven physician tenants until PD 1945, but there may have been physician tenants not recorded in the Providence directories available to me online.

8. 598–600 Angell Street had first- and second-story flats.

wake in 1896: "Certain kind of deep-toned stately music of the style of the 1870's or 1880's recalls certain visions of that period—gas-litten parlours of the dead, moonlight on old floors, decaying business streets with gas lamps &c.—under terrible circumstances" (*CE* 5.229). This note is remarkable in its melding of aural and visual images. Had Lovecraft added smell and taste and touch, he would have covered the universe of human senses. Doubtless, 454 Angell had its own characteristic smells which he would have recalled from his boyhood.

Whipple Phillips had traveled to Italy in connection with his visit to the Paris Exhibition of 1878 to promote a fringing machine invention, and acquired statuary and art that adorned his Providence home. Lovecraft's attachment to the relics of his birthplace even extended to his grandfather's cufflinks: "He always wore a pair of mosaics in his cuffs for buttons—one a view of the Coliseum (so *tiny* yet so *faithful*); the other of the Forum. I wear them now—for I still adhere to the old-style round cuff that most have discarded in favour of the modern 'link'" (*RK* 64).

Of course not all Lovecraft's recollections of 454 Angell Street were of the interior. He recalled the miraculously warm Christmas Day of 1903, when he used his bicycle to visit Mr. and Mrs. Franklin C. Clark at 38 Barnes Street: "Yesterday, for example, was the mildest and most genial Christmas I can recall since 1903, when I wore a summer weight coat (and short trousers!) as I rode my bicycle from home (454 Angell Street) over to see my aunt, (Mrs. Clark) who then lived not far from where I am—and she is—now [10 Barnes Street]. Good old days!" (*JFM* 171).

Lovecraft and his aunts mourned every change that diminished their erstwhile residence in their eyes. Along these lines, he wrote to Mrs. Clark on 15 September 1925: "Here's hoping for an early fortune, which I shall spend on buying 454 & the barn, tearing down Angell Court & putting back the stone wall, & rebuilding my 'Engine House'" (*LFF* 394). When Lovecraft was a boy, the three lots on the north side of the street immediately west of 454 Angell Street were still undeveloped,[9] and Whipple V. Phillips had the coachman (perhaps with the help of the gardener) build a playhouse and miniature railroad for his grandson. Then in 1895, when he was five, the coachman, carriages, and horses were disposed of, and Lovecraft was left in possession of the erstwhile coach house:

> Then came changes—one day there was not any coachman to help me, whereat I mourned; but later on I had compensation—the horses and carriages were sold too, so that I had a gorgeous, glorious, titanic, and unbelievable new playhouse—the whole great stable[10] with its immense carriage room, its neat-looking "office", and its vast upstairs, with the colossal (almost scareful) expanse of the grain loft, and the little three-room apartment where the coachman and his wife had lived. All this magnificence was my very own, to do with as I liked! (*Misc.* 107)

The carriage room became the main terminal for Lovecraft's miniature railroad, while he and his friends added "a pastoral countryside" to provide an appropriate setting for the railroad. Despite his increasing age, he and his friends similarly transformed another vacant lot once he and his mother removed to 598 Angell Street (see *Mics.* 108).

---

9. The three lots were converted into Angell Court some time between the 1918 Providence atlas map and the 1921 Sanborn fire map.
10. The stable can be seen at the rear of the house in the c. 1895 photograph on p. 139. The stable still appears in the 1921 Sanborn fire map and the 1921–52 Sanborn fire map update. However, HPL's letter to August Derleth dated 2 September 1931 recounted the demolition of the stable in August 1931.

Although Lovecraft did not live to witness the demolition of 454 Angell Street, he did witness a lesser loss in 1931:

> I hate to see the old things go. Just now my greatest loss has been the stable of my birthplace; for years in decay, though the house on its high terrace has been rehabilitated as a doctors' building. The old barn went down a month ago to make way for a modern dwelling, and it seemed as though half of my linkage with youth went with it—for it was my exclusive playhouse after the financial decline wiped out our horses & carriages [c. 1895]. My younger aunt [Annie Gamwell] felt desolated, too, for she had seen it built—it being newer than the house. Last month she recovered from the shattered walls the baking-powder tin with "historical data"—tintype, newspaper sheet, and "to whom it may concern" letter—which she had put in it in 1881, for the benefit of future archaeologists. How melancholy—and how illustrative of the emptiness of human designs—that she should have to reclaim herself that which was intended for a remote posterity. (*ES* 372)

The third floor of 454 Angell Street probably comprised mostly servants' quarters and store rooms. Here were probably housed the ancient the long-s'd books that the young Lovecraft discovered. The colossal grain loft of the erstwhile stable was not the only part of his home that frightened the young Lovecraft:

> No—we[11] are never scared of the dark *now*, though we used to be prior to 1895 or '96. Our grandfather cured us of this tendency by daring us (when our years numbered approximately five) to walk through certain chains of dark rooms in the fairly capacious old home at 454 Angell. Little by little our hardihood increased—and by the time we graduated from the fully-inhabited 2nd floor to the merely servant-and-store-and-guest-room-occupied 3d floor, we were reasonably hard-boiled so far as the Amorphous Entities of Shadow were concerned. (*LFF* 1032)

---

11. HPL used the royal "we" to interject a feeling of antiquarianism into his correspondence with Miss Bonner.

Lovecraft recalled especially the bucolic setting of his birthplace, which was located at the very edge of the then urban development on Providence's East Side. He wrote to Frank Belknap Long on 27 February 1931:

> My house, tho' an urban one on a paved street, had spacious grounds & stood next to an open field with a stone wall (now urbanized into a modern little court [Angell Court], as you saw when we drove past) where great elms grew & my grandfather had corn & potatoes planted & a *cow* pastured under the gardener's care. Here, when I was five, they built me a playhouse—to which I added others in later years. I never knew what it was to play on a city street; for from the age of three my mother always took me walking in the fields & ravines, & along the high wooded riverbank . . . I knew the old New England country as well as if I had been a farmer's boy . . . (*SL* 3.317)

Similarly, he wrote to August Derleth on 2 September 1931:

> I have never been able to live without the ancient woods and fields. My birthplace, though an urban house on a solidly built-up street, was just on the edge of the settled district—with a rural vacant lot next door, and the whole stretch of unchanged farming countryside (now all built up in streets) only a block away. (*ES* 371)

He wrote to E. Hoffmann Price on 15 February 1933:

> The house where I was born & grew up (about a mile southeast of 10 Barnes) was near the edge of the built-up streets when I was very small, & it was only a stone's throw to the rolling, stone-walled meadows, trim white farmhouses, rambling barns & byres, gnarled old orchards, dim twilight woods, & ravine-pierced river-bluffs of primitive colonial New-England. (*EHP* 59)

Perhaps most importantly, 454 Angell Street remained a strong component of Lovecraft's dreams. Writing to J. Vernon Shea on 4 February 1934, Lovecraft described a strange, time-shifting dream in which he lived at 598 Angell Street, 66 College

Street, and 454 Angell Street—all seemingly at once. Of the importance of the past for his imaginative life, he wrote to R. H. Barlow on 8 August 1933:

> It takes no effort at all—especially when I am out in certain woods and fields which have not changed a bit since my boyhood—for me to imagine that all the years since 1902 or 1903 are a dream . . . that I am still 12 years old, and that when I go home it will be through the quieter, more village-like streets of those days—with horses and wagons, and little varicoloured street cars with open platforms, and with my old home at 454 Angell St. still waiting at the end of the vista—with my mother, grandfather, black cat and other departed companions alive and unchanged. (*OFF* 73)

Perhaps most poignantly, he wrote near the end of his life to Willis Conover on 10 January 1937: "My own dreams usually go back very far in time, and it takes a long while for any new experience or scene or acquaintance to get worked into them. At least ¾ of them are laid at my birthplace, where I haven't lived since 1904, and involve those who were living in those days" (*RB* 413).

Lovecraft wrote of the importance of his dream life in the past to Helen V. Sully on 15 August 1935:

> It might be said that I am just about two inches from the suicide level—among that vast majority for whom existence is the *barest shade* preferable to non-existence. But of course that bare shade makes a vast amount of difference. What keeps me alive is the ability to look back to the past & imagine I am still in 1902 or 1903. Of all my dreams, about 0.8 are of that period—with myself in short trousers & at the old home, with my mother, grandfather, black cat Nigger-Man &c. still alive. Thus the world of the early 1900's still exists for me in about a third of the hours of my lonely life. As long as I can retain the books & pictures & furniture & accessories of those days, as I still do, I have something to live for. When I no longer can, I shall move to that lot in Swan Point Cemetery which is reserved for me. (*WBT* 429–30)

Of course, not every dream that came to Lovecraft as a youth was pleasurable. In one of his very last letters, to Harry O. Fischer dating to late February 1937, he recorded:

> In infancy I was afraid of the dark, which I peopled with all sorts of things; but my grandfather cured me of that by daring me to walk through certain dark parts of the house when I was 3 or 4 years old. After that, dark places held a certain fascination for me. But it is in *dreams* that I have known the real clutch of stark, hideous, maddening, paralysing *fear*. My infant nightmares were classics, & in them there is not an abyss of agonizing cosmic horror that I have not explored. I don't have such dreams now—but the memory of them will never leave me. At the ages of 3, 4, 5, 6, 7, & 8 I have been whirled through formless abysses of infinite night and adumbrated horrors as black & as seethingly sinister as any of our friend Fafhrd's "splatter-stencil" triumphs. That's why I appreciate such triumphs so keenly. *I have seen these things!* Many a time I have awaked in shrieks of panic, & have fought desperately to keep from sinking back into sleep & its unutterable horrors. At the age of six my dreams became peopled with a race of lean, faceless, rubbery, winged things to which I applied the home-made name of *night-gaunts*. Night after night they would appear in exactly the same form—& the terror they brought was beyond any verbal description.[12] (*CLM* 323)

454 Angell Street remained in physical existence from 1874/75 until 1961, when it was demolished. (Lovecraft had envisioned that he would probably live to about 1960, "in view of the average death-ages of near kinsfolk" (see Lovecraft to J. Vernon Shea, 4 February 1934, *JVS* 221). While we may justifi-

---

12. Susie Lovecraft kept her son in long hair and dresses until the age of six. That she might have taken her son to bed to comfort him with hugs and kisses when he suffered such nightmares is certainly within the realm of belief. When she was hospitalized at Butler Hospital in 1919, her doctors remarked a "psycho-sexual contact" with her son (see Winfield Townley Scott, "His Own Most Fantastic Creation" [1944], in Peter Cannon, ed., *Lovecraft Remembered* [Sauk City, WI: Arkham House, 1998], 16).

ably mourn the works of genius of which Lovecraft's premature death deprived us, we may be thankful that he did not live to witness to demolition the house at 454 Angell Street. Given its importance for Lovecraft's boyhood and his subsequent imaginative life, it is worthwhile to trace the history of 454 Angell Street—from its first ownership by jewelry manufacturer Samuel Allen (1874/75–1880/81) to its ownership by Lovecraft's grandfather Whipple V. Phillips (1880/81–1904) to its gradual transformation in 1914 and later to a "warren" of doctors' offices, primarily under the direction of Dr. Emery Moulton Porter.

454 Angell Street Before Whipple V. Phillips

Whipple V. Phillips began his life in Foster, RI, and apart from a year spent with his uncle James Phillips in Delavan, IL, in 1852–53, remained in Foster through at least 1857. He probably taught in the local schools in 1853–55 and then conducted the Tyler Store in Moosup Valley in 1855–57. By 1859, he had moved his residence to Greene, in the town of Coventry, RI. His first two children, Lillie and Susie, had been born in Foster in 1856 and 1857, but his three youngest children, Emeline, Edwin, and Annie, were born in Greene in 1859, 1864, and 1866, respectively. Whipple first appears in Providence directories as a dealer in coal, wood, and kindlings in 1868, but he did not move his family to Providence until 1874. He was first listed as a householder at 53 Vernon Street in PD 1875; then at 75 Courtland Street in PD 1876; and then at 276 Broadway in PD 1877, PD 1878, PD 1879, and PD 1880. He had various business interests during the period 1868–80, including a sewing machine, a fringing machine, a 99-cent store, and a carburetor. He first appeared at 194 Angell Street in PD 1881 and remained resident there until his death in March 1904.

As Donovan K. Loucks has observed, many Lovecraftians have the misimpression that Whipple V. Phillips erected the home at 454 Angell, on the northwest corner of Angell Street and Elm Grove Avenue. However, this is false. Witness the following section of Plate K from the 1875 Providence atlas:

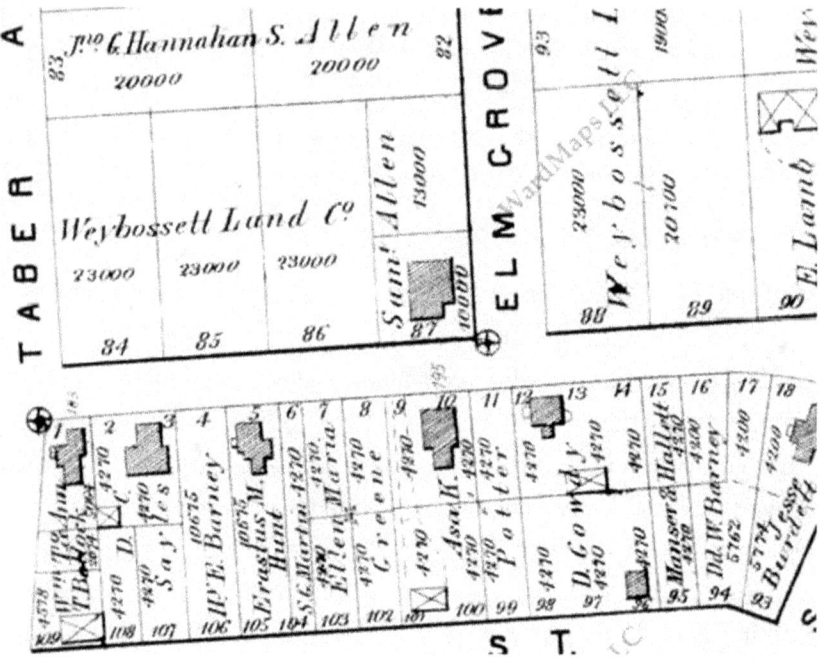

One can see that the south side of Angell Street between Taber Avenue and Wayland Avenue was already built up in 1875. But Sam'l Allen owns the house on the northwest corner of Angell Street and Elm Grove Avenue and two lots to the north on Elm Grove Avenue.[13] On the north side of Angell Street, the

---

13. Note that the barn or coach house did not yet exist in 1875. Whipple Phillips erected it after he purchased his home at 194 Angell Street in 1880/81. I believe that Whipple must have purchased not only Samuel Allen's houselot but his undeveloped lot immediately to the north on the west side of Elm Grove Avenue. I believe that it was on this northward lot that Whipple built his barn/coach house and laid out his fountain and gar-

Weybosset Land Company owns three lots to the west of Sam'l Allen's property and one lot to the east of Sam'l Allen's property across Elm Grove Avenue.

Who was this Samuel Allen? He was born in Barrington, RI, on 2 March 1811, the son of Capt. Sylvester Allen (1778–1832) and his wife Nancy Luther (1789–?), who married on 15 February 1807 in Barrington, RI. Samuel Allen was listed as a jeweler at 7 North Court, residing on Field Street, as early as PD 1832.[14] PD 1835 and PD 1836 listed Samuel Allen as a jeweler on Richmond Street (rear). PD 1838 listed him as a jeweler doing business on President Street, residing on Hope Street; PD 1841, as a jeweler doing business on President Street, residing on Arnold Street. PD 1850 listed him as a manufacturing jeweler at 43 Canal; PD 1860, as a manufacturing jeweler at 43 Canal, with house at 36 Arnold.

Samuel Allen married before 1838 Esther Walker Armington (1813–1880), the daughter of Benjamin Armington (1772–1831) and Sally Paine (1776–1845). They raised a large family of which we first get a glimpse in US 1850's enumeration of this household in Providence Ward 3 (all members born RI except for Esther W. Allen): Samuel Allen, age 39, jeweler; Esther W.

---

dens as well. According to HPL, the stone wall was on the west side of his grandfather's property where Angell Court was later built between 1918 and 1921. It is possible that Whipple asked the permission of the Weybosset Land Company for the play railway and village erected for his grandson. These could have been taken down at short notice when and if the land was sold for house-building. My belief is that the play railway and village extended west of Whipple's home to the three lots eventually developed as Angell Court in 1918–21. There is certainly much about the interior and exterior layout of Whipple's property that is probably lost to us.

14. A mariner, Sylvanus Allen, was also listed as residing on Field Street in PD 1832. Could this have been Samuel Allen's father Captain Sylvester Allen? There was no Samuel Allen listed in PD 1830.

Allen, age 36, born MA; Juliette A. Allen, age 11, at school; Sylvester Allen, age 9, at school; Willard Allen, age 7, at school; Sarah A. Allen, age 5, at school; Henry W. Allen, age 3; Esther A. Allen, age 6 months. There were also three Irish-born servants in their household, so Samuel Allen was apparently prospering.

USD 1860 enumerated Samuel Allen's household in Providence Ward 3: Samuel Allen, age 49, master jeweler, $2000 real property, $500 personal property, born RI; Esther W. Allen, age 47, born MA; Juliett A. Allen, age 21, school teacher, born RI; Sylvester Allen, age 19, clerk, born RI; Willard J. Allen, age 17, jeweler, born RI; Sarah A. Allen, age 14, born RI; Henry W. Allen, age 12, born RI; Esther A. Allen, age 10, born RI; Stella C. Allen, age 8, born RI; Eunice F. Allen, age 4, born RI; Lucy Barry, age 21, servant, born RI. PD 1861 listed Samuel Allen, manufacturing jeweler, at 43 Canal with house at 36 Arnold and Sylvester Allen, post office clerk, as a boarder at 36 Arnold. PD 1864 listed Sylvester Allen, post office clerk, with house at 133 Williams, and Willard J. Allen, jeweler, Friendship corner Dorrance, boarding at 133 Williams.

In RI 1875, Samuel Allen and his growing family were enumerated in their home at 194 Angell Street in Providence Ward 2. US 1880 enumerated Samuel Allen's family at 194 Angell Street in Providence. Sometime in 1880–81, Samuel Allen sold 194 Angell Street to Whipple V. Phillips. Perhaps the loss of his wife on 3 December 1880 was a motivating factor for the sale. Samuel lived on for almost fifteen more years. PD 1882 listed Sylvester Allen (Samuel Allen & Co.), 38 Friendship, boarding at 17 S. Angell, and Samuel Allen & Co. (Sylvester Allen), manufacturing jewelers, 38 Friendship, house 17 S. Angell. PD 1885 listed Samuel Allen & Co. (Sylvester Allen), manufacturing jewelers, at 38 Friendship with house at 245 Waterman and Sylvester Allen (Samuel Allen & Co.), with business at 38 Friendship and house at 245 Waterman. The *Jewelers' Circular and Horological Review* (1 November 1893, 37) reported: "Samuel Allen, one of the oldest manufacturing jewelers of this city [Providence] and for many years at 34 Potter St., has been forced to retire from active business on account of ill health." Samuel Allen died of a ruptured aortic aneurysm at his home at 44 East Manning Street in Providence on 13 July 1895, aged 84 years 4 months and 11 days. He was buried with his wife in Swan Point Cemetery in Providence.

I have not fully established just when Samuel Allen acquired or built the house at 194 Angell. We know that he was head of household there when RI 1875 and US 1880 were enumerated. PD 1871 listed Samuel Allen & Co. (Willard J. & Sylvester Allen), jewelers, at 96 Pine, house 160 Williams and Sylvester Allen and Willard J. Allen (both of S. Allen & Co. at 96 Pine) as boarders at 160 Williams. I conclude that 160 Williams was Samuel Allen's address in 1871. PD 1874 listed Sylvester Allen (S. Allen & Co.), 96 Pine, house 113 Williams. Then PD 1875 and PD 1876 had the listings: Samuel Allen & Co. (Sylvester Allen), manufacturing jewelers, 96 Pine, house Elm Grove Ave., cor. Angell; Sylvester Allen (S. Allen & Co.), 96 Pine, house 113 Williams. I conclude that Samuel Allen was at 194 Angell in 1875; his son Sylvester, at 113 Williams. PD 1878 and PD 1879 had the listings: Samuel Allen & Co. (Sylvester Allen), manufacturing jewelers, 96 Pine, house Elm Grove Ave. cor. Angell; Sylvester Allen (S. Allen & Co.), 96 Pine, house 171 Angell. I conclude that Samuel Allen remained at 194 Angell while Sylvester Allen had removed from 113 Williams to 171 Angell.

We may regret that Lovecraft is not known to have had the opportunity to speak with any of the children of Samuel Allen. They probably would have shared many common memories of the home at 454 Angell Street.

454 Angell Street as the Home of Whipple V. Phillips (1880/81–1904)

Howard Phillips Lovecraft was born at 454 Angell Street on 20 August 1890. While part of his early years were spent in Dorchester and Auburndale, MA, he was back in Providence for good by the time his father was hospitalized at Butler Hospital in April 1893. He had many poignant memories of his birthplace. He and his aunts Lillie and Annie mourned every change to the premises, especially the demolition of the erstwhile stable in 1931.[15] While he walked by his birthplace as often as he could, he had no occasion to enter the premises. I suspect he might have enjoyed talking to Dr. Emery M. Porter, who was connected with the property for forty-three years—opening his medical office there in 1914, residing there in 1915, becoming the property owner no later than 1937, and continuing to maintain his office through his death in 1957.

---

15. There are a number of puzzles pertaining to the coach house/barn. The 1900 Sanborn map shows only one structure to the north of the house, marked with an "X"—it is adjacent to the west property line. The 1918 atlas map shows one darkly shaded structure north of the house and then the house of F. E. Maynard (with its driveway) farther north on Elm Grove Avenue. The 1921 Sanborn maps appears to show two structures to the north of the house on the property—one of them heavily shaded, the other marked with an "X." I assume that the shaded structure was the barn or coach house. The 1937 atlas still shows the shaded structure to the north of the house, with another property owned by M. L. Cavanaugh (with its own outbuilding) to the immediate north on Elm Grove. (Of course, compilation of information for the 1937 atlas could have lagged the 1931 demolition of the barn or coach house on the 454 Angell Street property.) Curiously, the 1921–52 Sanborn fire map revision still shows the shaded outbuilding to the north of the house at 454 Angell Street. It appears to straddle the property line between 454 Angell Street and the next house to the north on the west side of Elm Grove Avenue.

The Providence directories for the years of Whipple's residence at 454 Angell do reveal to us the names of two of his employees: PD 1884 and PD 1885 list Dennis A. Mathewson (1855–1938), coachman, at 194 Angell. PD 1887 lists William H. Wilson (1854–1901), coachman, at 194 Angell. At the time of Lovecraft's birth, the staff at 194 Angell probably included at least four persons: a coachman, a gardener, a cook and a maid.[16] As Whipple's fortunes diminished, the staff was gradually cut back until only a single servant, 23-year-old Irish-born Maggie Corcoran,[17] remained by the time US 1900 was enumerated:

[census record image]

Delilah (Robinson) Townsend (ca. 1868–1944)

A special case is Delilah (Robinson/Robertson) Townsend, who in later years served as a personal assistant to Lovecraft's aunt Lillie and may have also provided laundry service for Lovecraft when she lived at 6 Olney Street (a dilapidated dwelling which

---

16. Perhaps the maid also served as waitress for meals. A staff of six, with a dedicated cook's assistant or scullery maid, would certainly have been fuller. Some of the women's work of the household—like laundry—was heavy work. Robie Phillips and her daughters doubtless helped with some tasks.

17. Maggie claimed emigration year 1895 in US 1900. It is possible that she was the Maggie Corcoran, age 19, female, single, servant, resident of County Waterford, able to read and write, who arrived in Boston on 26 April 1896, having sailed on the *S.S. Bothnia* from Queenstown on 17 April 1896. She stated that her passage had been paid by her brother. Her final destination was Boston, where her aunt Miss K. O'Brien lived at 15 School Lane (Box 5). The manifest originally stated that she had arrived with $5, but this was struck out and "none" substituted. I have not succeeded in finding vital records for Maggie subsequent to US 1900.

served as inspiration for Joseph Curwen's house in *The Case of Charles Dexter Ward*. Delilah Townsend may have been waitress, cook's assistant or maid at 194/454 Angell as early as the 1890s, although she was not a resident staff member by the time US 1900 was enumerated. (See further the essay "The Site of Joseph Curwen's Home . . ." in this volume.)

454 Angell Street After Whipple V. Phillips

Sarah Susan Lovecraft and her son relocated to 598 Angell Street soon after the death of Whipple V. Phillips. However, selling the property apparently took some time. We find the widow Fannie M. Lines listed as householder in PD 1906, followed by Frank E. Maynard in PD 1908, John D. E. Jones in PD 1909–12, and Frederick W. Jones in PD 1911–12. Physician and surgeon Emery M. Porter first had offices at 454 Angell Street in 1914 and remained through his death in 1957. In 1918–20, householder Lily J. H. Barton, widow of William, evidently made efforts to obtain boarders. She had at least four in 1918: Preserved W. Arnold, Christiana Rankin, George F. Bliven, and his wife Olive S. Bliven. In addition, Arthur C. Miller was general manager of Mount Hymettus Apiaries at 454 Angell in PD 1918. The 1918 Providence atlas showed H. Brudley as owner of 454 Angell Street. His efforts to build tenancy in 1918–20 do not appear to have been very successful. Dr. Emery M. Porter had opened medical offices in the building in 1914, but he was not joined by another physician until 1920. By 1937 (and probably significantly earlier), Dr. Emery M. Porter had taken ownership of 454 Angell.

Dr. Emery Moulton Porter (1884–1957)

Emery Moulton Porter was born in Providence on 10 September 1884, the son of surgeon George Whipple Porter (1847–1910) and Emogene Louise Hoyt (1853–1912). His father had been trained at Women's Hospital in New York City and founded the department of gynecological surgery at Rhode Island Hospital in 1877. George Whipple Porter was the first of three generations of Porter surgeons to practice at Rhode Island Hospital. His son Emery Moulton Porter served as chief of surgery at Rhode Island Hospital, and his grandson Arnold Porter also practiced surgery at the hospital.[18]

Emery Moulton Porter attended Brown University, where he was a member of the Class of 1906. On 29 June 1907, in RI, Porter married Mary Emerson Bradley (1884–1963), the daughter of Charles Bradley (1845–1898) and Jane W. Bailey (1849–1927). Dr. Porter's medical offices at 454 Angell were first listed in PD 1914. However, RI 1915 captured Dr. Porter and his family actually living at 454 Angell:

By 1915, the family had grown to include son George W. Porter (b. 18 July 1910), son Arnold Porter (b. 24 December 1914), and daughter Nancy Porter (b. 17 February 1916). There were two servants in the household, one of them a black woman from the West Indies. By the time he registered for the draft on 12 September 1918, Dr. Porter had moved to 12 Keene Street in Providence; his medical office was still at 454 Angell Street. PD 1919 listed Emery Moulton Porter as a member of the University Club. He became a well-known surgeon, rising to become chief of surgery at Rhode Island Hospital.

---

18. See Robert W. Hopkins, M.D., Robert Bowen, M.D. and Warren W. Francis, M.D., "History of Surgery in Rhode Island," *JAMA Surgery* (April 2001).

Changes were afoot in the Porter family by the 1930s. In PD 1934, daughter Nancy Porter was listed as a resident of 454 Angell Street. In PD 1936 and PD 1937, son Arnold Porter was listed as a student residing at 454 Angell Street. Emery and Mary (Bradley) Porter had divorced by 1935, when RI 1935 enumerated Mary Porter as a divorced woman residing at 110 Waterman Street. I do not know exactly when Dr. Porter took ownership of 454 Angell Street, but the 1937 Providence atlas showed him as owner.[19] By 1 April 1940, Dr. Porter had taken Alice Stanton Bennett, the former wife of Lester Ralston Thomas, as his second wife.

Starting with Alexander M. Burgess [Sr.] in 1920, Dr. Porter brought more and more physicians into his practice at 454 Angell Street. There were four physicians by PD 1922; six, by PD 1928, eight, by PD 1942, ten, by PD 1944; and only reached a peak with eleven physicians in PD 1945. Dr. Alexander M. Burgess Jr. joined the practice in 1942. Dr. Porter's own son Arnold Porter joined the practice in 1949. Some of the great early recruits like Dr. Alexander M. Burgess Sr., Clinton S. Wescott, and Herman A. Lawson began to retire or die by the early 1950s. Practice totals dropped to eight in 1950 and to six in 1952. Finally, Dr. Emery M. Porter himself died on 4 November 1957, leaving only Alexander M. Burgess Jr., Arnold Porter and John B. Lawlor in the practice.

Beginning in 1941, Emery M. Porter had begun to take tenants in the available living space at 454 Angell Street. He had John Reighard Lynch and his wife Gertrude in 1941; Isaac Butts Merriman, Jr. and his wife Ellen, in 1942–47; his own stepson Lester

---

19. PHD 1933–34 and PHD 1935–36 listed him as householder at 454 Angell. None of the other physicians and surgeons practicing there was listed as householder.

Ralston Thomas Jr. and his wife Ruth, in 1949–51;[20] Walker Mason Jr. and his wife Constance, in 1952; and finally Marsden Perry Earle and his wife Elizabeth, in 1953. (Their daughter Denise Earle also resided at 454 Angell and served as secretary to Dr. Porter in 1953.) Finally, Dr. Emery M. Porter died on 4 November 1957 in Providence. He was buried at Swan Point Cemetery in Providence, where his second wife Alice Stanton Bennett Thomas Porter (1895–1981) eventually joined him. His two early-deceased children Emery M. Porter, Jr. (1908–1909) and Jane Bennett Porter (1911–1912) also rest with him there.

The writing was probably on the wall for 454 Angell Street by the time Dr. Emery Porter died in 1957. What spelled the end of 454 Angell as a "warren" of physicians' offices? Increasing reliance on the automobile for transportation was probably a significant factor. Parking was undoubtedly at a premium in the congested Wayland Square area.[21] The number of patients willing and able to travel to 454 Angell using trolleys and buses and their own two feet probably decreased. In addition, maintenance costs for the aging structure first built in 1874/75 were probably increasing. Perhaps the householders of 1941–53 were dissatisfied with living conditions; I did not find record of householders or other residents after 1953. Dr. Arnold Porter probably did not share the same sentiments toward 454 Angell Street felt by father, who practiced there for forty-three years from 1914 until his death in 1957 and had taken ownership of the property no

---

20. It is possible that we will see the last appearance of 454 Angell Street in the US census when US 1950 is released in 2022. This census should capture the residence of Lester Ralston Thomas Jr. and his wife Ruth there in 1950.

21. The former stable north of 454 Angell was demolished in 1931. However, the space made available may have been used primarily by the physicians and surgeons or the residents for their own parking.

later than 1937 and probably years earlier.

Renovating 454 Angell Street either as a medical office building or as a private residence would probably have been prohibitively expensive. The cost of installing an elevator to allow greater usage of the second and third floors would surely have been excessive. So within three years of the death of Emery Porter, the decision to abandon 454 Angell Street was taken. PD 1960 is the last edition to list the three-member medical practice (Alexander M. Burgess Jr., Arnold Porter, John B. Lawlor). The house was demolished in 1961.

Robert and Mary (Black) Martin—
Service Staff at 454 Angell After Whipple V. Phillips

PD 1922, 1924, 1925, 1928 and 1930 all reported Robert Martin, gardener, as householder at 454 Angell. PD 1925, 1928 and 1930 reported his wife Mrs. Mary B. Martin as a resident. PHD 1931–32 and PHD 1933–34 listed Robert Martin, gardener, at 454 Angell; PHD 1935–36 no longer listed him at 454 Angell. When he applied for a U.S. passport on 18 November 1924, Robert Martin stated that he had been born in County Cavan, Ireland on 4 January 1878, the son of Robert Martin, deceased, and that he had sailed from Liverpool for the United States in April 1901. He stated that he had become a naturalized U.S. citizen on 27 June 1908, and that he had married Mary Black (born 24 June 1880 in Scotland) on 6 July 1910. He and his wife intended to sail on the *Columbia* from New York on 13 December 1924, to visit relatives in Ireland and to do sightseeing in England and Scotland. They intended to be absent for four months or less. Dr. Emery M. Porter of Lincoln, RI, served as witness for Robert Martin and stated that he had known him for ten years (i.e., since he had first opened offices at 454 Angell in

1914). The photograph that Mr. and Mrs. Martin took for their passport application is preserved with the application.

Robert Martin was first enumerated at 241 Blackstone Street in Providence Ward 5 in US 1910. He was 32, single, born in Ireland of Irish-born parents, an emigrant of 1901 and a naturalized U.S. citizen. He was a boarder in the home of his cousin Thomas J. McCullagh. Both he and Thomas were rubber workers. But Robert Martin was soon to find more congenial work. Some time after marrying Mary Black in Rhode Island on 6 July 1910, he began to work on his own account as a gardener. PD 1912 listed him as a gardener with house at 261 Benefit; PD 1914, as a gardener with house at 355 Williams. He probably already had Dr. Emery M. Porter of 454 Angell as one of his clients by this time. In RI 1915, Martin was enumerated at 355 Williams and described himself as a private family gardener. When he registered for the draft on 12 September 1918, Martin was living at 357 Williams.[22] He called himself a jobbing gardener with thirty or forty employers (i.e., customers). In US 1920, Martin and his wife were enumerated at 357 Williams in Providence. He was working as a gardener and claimed emigration in 1905 and naturalization in 1908. His wife, born in Scotland or Irish-born parents, claimed emigration in 1898 and naturalization in 1908. RI 1925 enumerated Robert and Mary Martin at 454 Angell. In US 1930, Martin and his wife were enumerated at 454 Angell. He described himself as a private family gardener and stated his emigration year as 1899. His wife called herself a private family caretaker, stated her emigration year as 1900, her birthplace as Scotland of Scottish-born father and Northern Ireland-born mother.

---

22. PD 1918 and PD 1920 also listed Martin as a gardener with house at 357 Williams.

I doubt that Robert Martin worked fulltime on the grounds of 454 Angell for Dr. Emery M. Porter. I suspect he retained other gardening clients. Lovecraft's account of the demolition of the former coach house (stable) in August 1931 leads me to believe that the Martins may have resided on the third floor of the main house with kitchen privileges. Perhaps Mrs. Martin provided "inside" services like cooking and cleaning. In RI 1935, Robert and Mary were enumerated at 48 Ide Avenue in East Providence. Robert continued to work as a private family gardener. His wife stated her birthplace as Northern Ireland rather than Scotland. EPD 1944, 1946, 1951, 1953 and 1957 continued to list Robert Martin (wife Mary B.) as a landscape gardener with house at 48 Ide Avenue. I have not found death or burial records that I can positively identify with Robert and Mary (Black) Martin. I do not know who was responsible for cleaning and maintenance at 454 Angell after Robert's final appearance as gardener at 454 Angell in PHD 1933–34. It is possible that Robert Martin continued to perform outside maintenance subsequent to their departure as householders.

Closing Reflections

If it were not for the fact that Howard Phillips Lovecraft spent the first fourteen years of his life at 454 Angell Street in 1890–1904 and left many poignant accounts of his residence there, the most notable figures associated with the residence would surely be (1) Samuel Allen (1811–1895) (resident in 1875–80), (2) Whipple V. Phillips (1833–1904) (resident in 1881–1904), and (3) Emery M. Porter (1884–1957) (office in 1914–57, resident in 1915, owner from at least 1937 onward). In many ways, Whipple V. Phillips was a father figure for his grandson. After Whipple died in 1904, Dr. Franklin C. Clark (1847–1915),[23]

---

23. I wonder whether Dr. Clark knew Dr. Emery M. Porter. Of course,

who married Whipple's eldest daughter Lillie in 1902, served to a lesser degree in that role. Edward F. Gamwell (1869–1936), who married Whipple's youngest daughter Annie in 1897, was a journalist but played a lesser role model than Dr. Clark, especially after he and Annie separated. Whipple's own son Edwin E. Phillips (1864–1918), who dealt in investments, mortgages, and property management (with a fling into refrigeration in 1910–15), is hardly mentioned in Lovecraft's letters.

Lovecraft and his aunts Lillie and Annie kept close track of changes at 454 Angell Street after the death of Whipple V. Phillips in 1904. They mourned every change which in their eyes diminished the value (at least the sentimental value) of their erstwhile home. I have to admit that Emery M. Porter's spare features suggest to me those of Lovecraft. If they had ever had the occasion to meet on the sidewalk outside 454 Angell Street, I wonder whether the busy Dr. Porter might not have found enough of interest in Lovecraft to make an appointment to show him over 454 Angell Street in its post–Whipple Phillips incarnation. One can envision Lovecraft's saying ordinary things like "this was the parlor," "this was my bedroom," "these were servants' quarters." I think we can be certain that Lovecraft would have told at least some of his correspondents about the occasion if such a tour had ever occurred.

I do not know whether any post–Whipple Phillips era photographs of 454 Angell Street survive. We shall probably have to be content with the c. 1895 photograph that passed from Phillips family friend Nelson Rogers to editor Sean Donnelly and adorned the cover of the paper edition *The Case of Charles Dexter Ward* (University of Tampa Press, 2010). The constraints of

---

they were of different generations. Dr. Clark died the year after Dr. Porter opened his office at 454 Angell Street.

spacetime will forever prohibit a discussion of 454 Angell Street with the simultaneous participation of Samuel Allen, Whipple V. Phillips, Emery M. Porter, and Howard Phillips Lovecraft. If it could happen in some kind of multiverse scenario, I suspect there would be many interesting things to be said. After all, home remains home, and for all four of these men I believe it can truthfully be said that 454 Angell Street was home.

Perhaps even now Delilah Townsend is consulting with Robie Phillips over the evening's meal. Or Maggie Corcoran is consulting with Susie Lovecraft over the bedroom arrangements for a visitor. Or Dr. Emery Porter is making his stepson Lester R. Thomas and his wife feel welcome in the home where he has his offices. Or consulting with Robert Martin over some detail of the grounds keeping or with his wife Mary (Black) Martin over some detail of the housekeeping. The photograph of 454 Angell Street taken c. 1895 leaves us with questions we cannot definitely answer—e.g., is one of Whipple's daughters holding Lovecraft's famous black cat in her arms? For that matter, which of Whipple's and Robie's daughters are included, and why is Lovecraft himself missing? Is one of Whipple Phillips prized Italian statuary pieces visible in a ground floor window? There are many things concerning 454 Angell Street and its occupants that we will probably never know. But the bare facts which remain can fuel our imaginations. Perhaps that is all that we can ask for.

Acknowledgments

I am grateful to Donovan K. Loucks for first suggesting the subject of this article and to David Haden for his stimulating discussions of 454 Angell Street. All opinions and any errors in this article are my sole responsibility.

I thank S. T. Joshi for his superb work *An Index to the Selected Letters of H. P. Lovecraft* (West Warwick RI: Necronomicon

Press, second edition, 1991), which facilitated the quotations from Lovecraft which appear in this article.

I depended upon the on-line Providence city directories (PD) available on Ancestry.com. These are far from complete and woefully so for the 1890s. I mourn the Providence House Directories (PHD) formerly available online at the Providence City Archives. Donovan K. Loucks kindly provided me with electronic copies of PHD 1896, 1897, 1898, 1915, 1931–32, 1933–34, and 1935–36.

Monument to Samuel Allen, his wife Esther and their daughters Stella, Sarah and Juliet at Swan Point Cemetery, Providence. Courtesy: RI Historical Cemeteries Commission.

Note: Paris Fletcher Allen (b. 14 November 1854, d. 6 January 1855) was a son of Samuel and Esther (Armington) Allen who died in infancy. He received his middle name in honor of Elijah Timothy Fletcher (1824–1877), the husband of his aunt Eunice B. Allen (1826–1855).

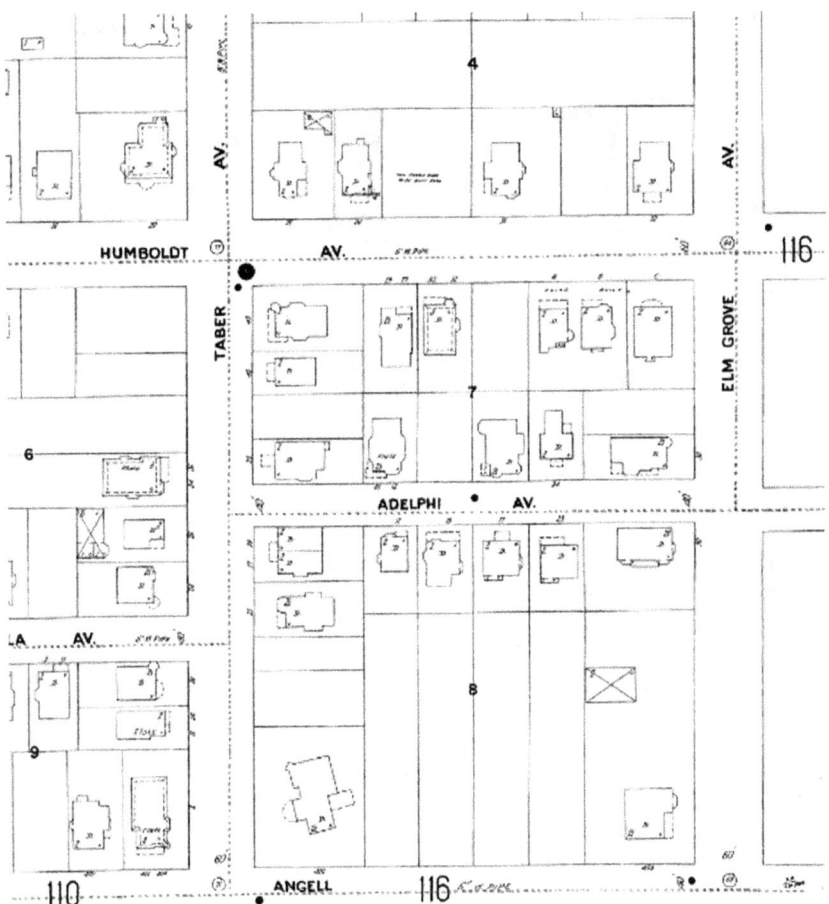

*Sanborn Map 1900 v 2 plate 115: locality of 454 Angell Street.
Courtesy: Providence Public Library.*

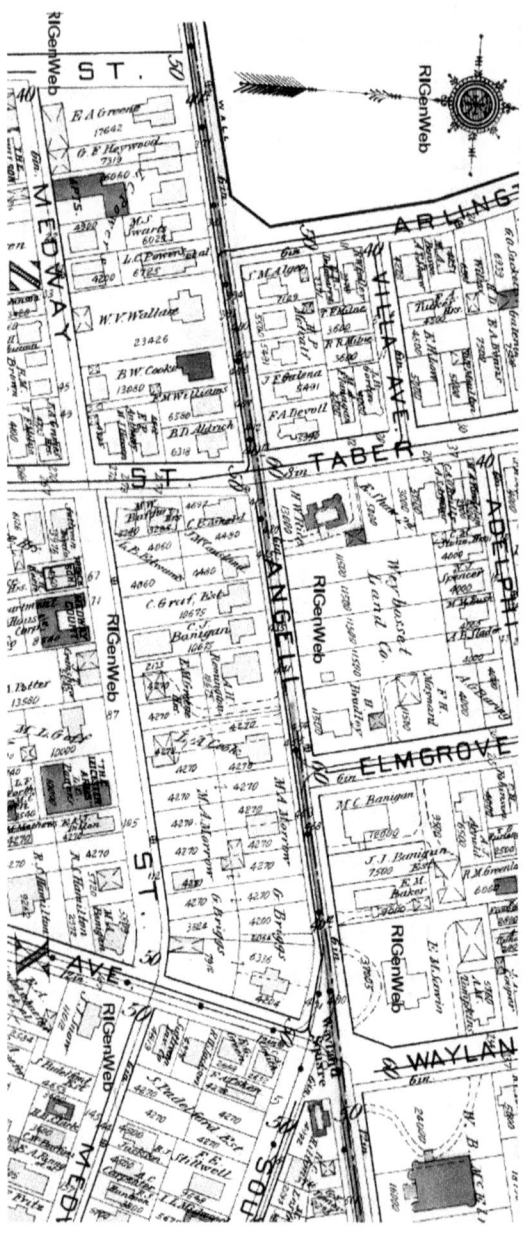

Providence 1918 atlas, plate 20: locality of 454 Angell. Note H. Brudley as owner. Four lots to immediate west still undeveloped. Courtesy: RI Gen Web.

The Story of 454 Angell Street 171

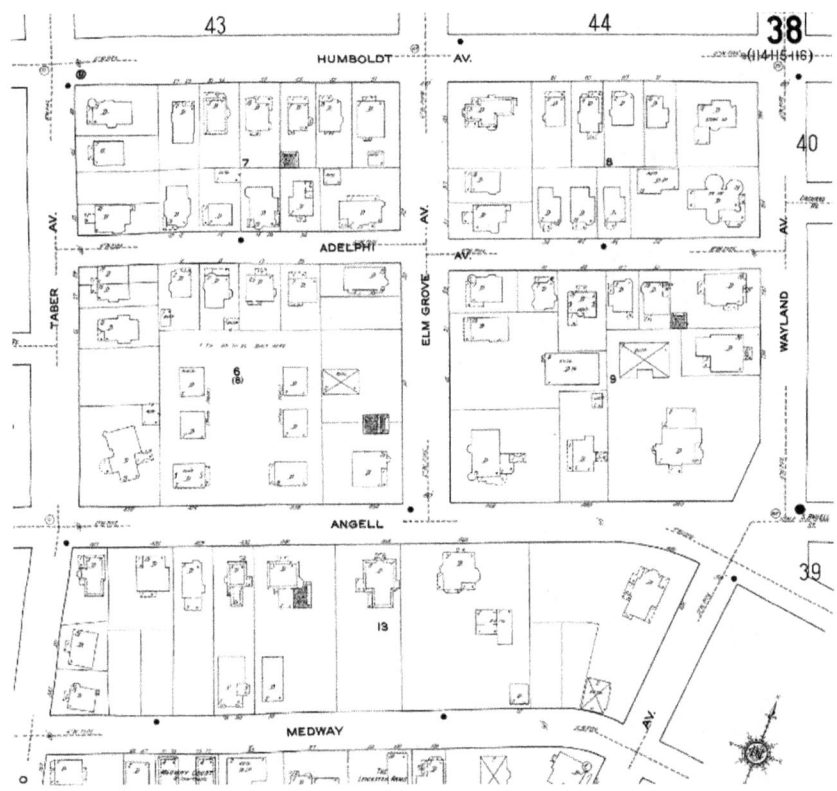

*Sanborn Map 1921, v 2 sheet 38: locality of 454 Angell.
Note development of Angell Court homes immediately west.
Courtesy: Providence Public Library.*

Providence 1937 atlas, plate 20: vicinity of 454 Angell. Note Angell Court to the immediate west. Courtesy: www.historicmapworks.com

Dr. Emery Moulton Porter (1884–1957) owned 454 Angell Street in 1937 and practiced medicine there from 1914 to 1957. Courtesy: Find-A-Grave (Priscilla Porter).

Marker for Dr. Emery M. Porter and his second wife at Swan Point Cemetery, Providence. Courtesy: Find-A-Grave.

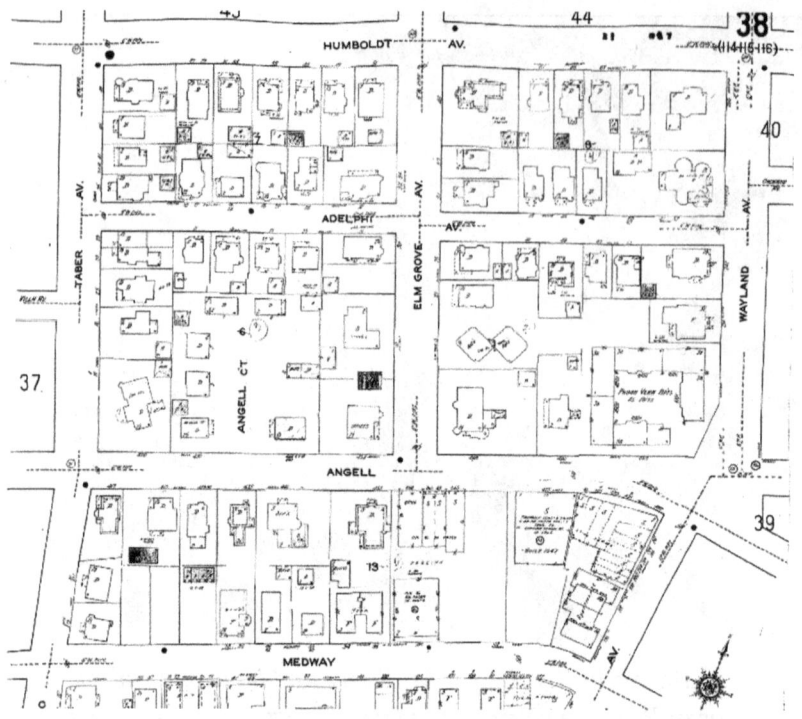

*Sanborn map – 1921–52, v. 2, plate 38. Vicinity of 454 Angell.
Courtesy: Providence Public Library.*

*Modern apartment building at northwest corner of Angell Street and
Elm Grove Avenue. Note Lovecraft birthplace marker on corner.
Courtesy: Google Maps.*

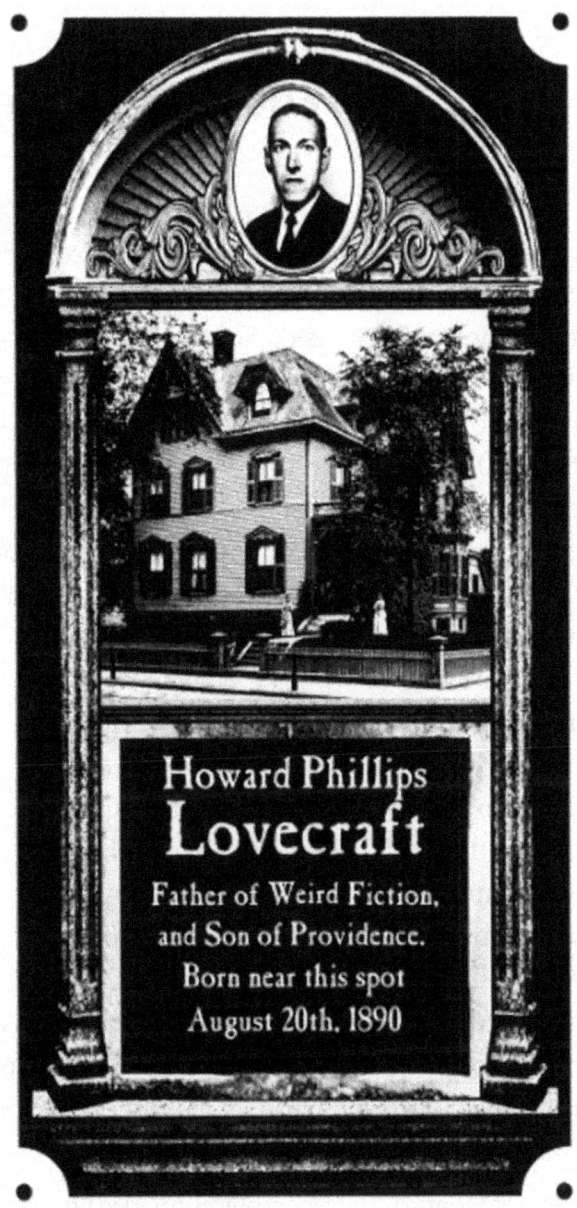

Lovecraft birthplace marker placed by Lovecraft Arts & Sciences Council.

The People of 598–600 Angell Street

For Douglas A. Anderson

Of the three Lovecraft homes remaining in Providence—598 Angell Street (1904–24), 10 Barnes Street (1926–33), and 66 College Street [now 65 Prospect Street] (1933–37)—I suspect that 598 Angell is the least-visited. Of course, it is in close proximity to the site of Lovecraft's first Providence home—454 Angell Street (1890–1904)—but that site is now occupied by a modern apartment building with only a marker on the corner of Angell and Elmgrove to remind the visitor of Lovecraft's birthplace. There is little in the trendy Wayland Square area to attract the Lovecraftian visitor—unless he or she wishes to linger over lunch at a sidewalk café or to make bold to explore some of the adjoining residential streets.

Certainly, 598 Angell consumes much less space in Lovecraft's letters than his 454 Angell birthplace. Of the former, W. Paul Cook wrote: "I shall never forget his outburst as he walked past the old estate of his grandfather in Providence. He lived with but one ambition—to repatriate the old property before he died and restore it as it was in his grandfather's day" (*AAV* 34). While he admitted that 598 Angell was hardly a slum, he missed spaciousness of 454 Angell and its grounds and the amenities of the erstwhile service staff. He wrote to J. Vernon Shea on 4 February 1934:

> I was (being predominantly geographical-minded) tremendously attached to the old home at 454 Angell St. (now housing 12 physicians' offices—I walk by it still as often as I can) with its grounds & fountain, & stable, but this now had to go . . . indeed, there had been drastic economies for 5 years before that. My mother & I

moved into a 5-room-&-attic flat two squares farther east (598 Angell St., where I dwelt till 1924), & for the first time I knew what a congested, servantless home—with another family in the same house—was. There was a vacant lot next door (although even that was later built up—during my adulthood), which I promptly exploited as a landscape garden & adorned with a village of piano-box houses, but even that failed to assuage my nostalgia. (*JVS* 221)

Writing to Edwin Baird on 3 February 1924, Lovecraft stated that his grandfather's "burdened estate forced a removal to a small flat three blocks east on the same street" (*WH* 37).

Most of the few recollections of 598 Angell Street that we possess come from visitors rather than the occupant himself. (Lovecraft apparently met his first Providence amateur visitor, W. B. Stoddard, at the Crown Hotel, rather than 598 Angell, in 1914.) W. Paul Cook recalled being nearly turned away at the door of 598 Angell by Lovecraft's mother and his aunt Mrs. Clark, who insisted that the sleeping Lovecraft could not be disturbed, until Lovecraft himself appeared in his dressing gown and slippers (*AAV* 37). On the other hand, the debonair Rheinhart Kleiner was graciously welcomed by Lovecraft's mother and ushered into her son's quarters:

> I noticed that at every hour or so his mother appeared in the doorway with a glass of milk, and Lovecraft forthwith drank it. Something was said about a cup of tea for me, but by that time I had become aware of the heat of the room and thought it might be a good idea to suggest that we take a short walk. I digress sufficiently to say that the room in which I sat was fairly small and lined on three sides with books, mostly old ones. On the wall near his desk were small pictures of Robert E. Lee, Jefferson Davis, and one or two others. An almanac hung against the wall directly over his desk; it was a *Farmer's Almanac* with which he had been familiar for many years. (*AAV* 100)

Recalling his own and Mrs. Gamwell's love of 454 Angell Street, Sonia Davis nevertheless recalled the affection which he felt for 598 Angell: "After some years H. P. became accustomed to the small, five-room house in Angell Street. THAT was home until he married; and in time he learned to love it. As he reached full manhood it was with even a more deepened affection that he came to love it and call '598' his 'Blessed Home'" (*AAV* 120–21).

While about eighty percent of his dreams centered on his boyhood home at 454 Angell, Lovecraft recalled for Clark Ashton Smith a somewhat darker dream set at 598 Angell (29 November 1933:

> Only last night I had another dream—of going back to 598 Angell Street after infinite years. The neighbourhood was deserted and grass-grown, & the houses were half-falling to pieces. The key on my ring fitted the mouldering door of 598, & I stepped in amidst the dust of centuries. Everything was as it was around 1910—pictures, furniture, books, &c., all in a state of extreme decay. Even objects which have been with me constantly in all later homes were there in their old positions, sharing in the general dissolution & dust-burial. I felt an extreme terror—& when *footsteps* sounded draggingly from the direction of my room I turned & fled in panic. I would not admit to myself what it was I feared to confront . . . but my fear also had the effect of making me shut my eyes as I raced past the mouldy, nitre-encrusted *mirror* in the hall. Out into the street I ran—& I noted that none of the ruins were of buildings newer than about 1910. I had covered about half a block—of continuous ruins, with nothing but ruins ahead—when I awaked shivering. At the last moment my great fear seemed to be of passing my birthplace & early home—the beloved 454 Angell St.—toward which I was headed. (*DS* 486)

A psychologist might attempt to make much of this dream of 598 Angell Street fallen into ruin. Lovecraft also suffered nightmares—especially of the dreaded "night-gaunts"—as a boy at

454 Angell Street. In this dream, his fear seems to have been based on the dislocation in time—even though he professed elsewhere that escaping from the bounds of time was a primary aesthetic theme in his work.

S. T. Joshi writes that "Lovecraft and his mother occupied only the western side of the smallish house" (*IAP* 96). Taking a look at 598–600 Angell Street (see below), I'm driven to wonder whether the separate living quarters for two families were in fact on the first and second stories. If the building was divided into western and eastern halves, then only the western half would enjoy the first- and second-story "bays" facing Angell Street. A vertical division, on the other hand, would enable similar if not identical floor plans for each of the two flats. Both flats might have enjoyed basement and attic access via a rear staircase. If in fact 598 Angell was the first-story flat, then the front entrance of 600 Angell probably allowed access to a stairway leading to the second-story flat. Of course, this is only my idea. Any former resident of 598–600 Angell could probably dispose of the matter in an instant. Lovecraft's description of the quarters shared with his mother at 598 Angell as a "flat" may add just a bit of evidence to the supposition that they occupied the first story of the house rather than the western half. It is possible that the reverse was true and that 598 Angell was the upstairs flat and 600 Angell the downstairs flat. However, if this was the case, wouldn't Lovecraft have dreamed of ascending the stairs after admitting himself to 598 Angell in his dream of 28–29 November 1933?

For many years, the duplex (double house) at 598–600 Angell Street presented a tired appearance. But the owners have recently added new shingles and some plantings. I for one think that H. P. Lovecraft would be pleased to see the recent improvements.

Here's an aerial view of the immediate neighborhood (credit Google Maps):

I have mostly constructed the occupancy history of 598–600 Angell from electronic city directories as maintained by Ancestry.com. However, it must be noted that these are far from complete and especially lacking in the 1890s. Through the kindness of Donovan K. Loucks I had access to Providence House Directories for 1896, 1897, 1898, 1915, 1931–32, 1933–34, and 1935–36; I mourn the full set of the house directories which used to be maintained online by the Providence City Archives.

598–600 Angell appears to be the second house on the north side of Angell Street east of Butler Avenue. Actually, I believe it is the first house on the north side of Angell Street east of Butler Avenue with an Angell Street address. The house to its immediate west has its address on Butler Avenue. It is not easy for me to determine when this house was first erected—certainly, by 1896, when occupants were listed in the first Providence House Directory. The house did not exist when the 1875 Providence atlas was compiled:

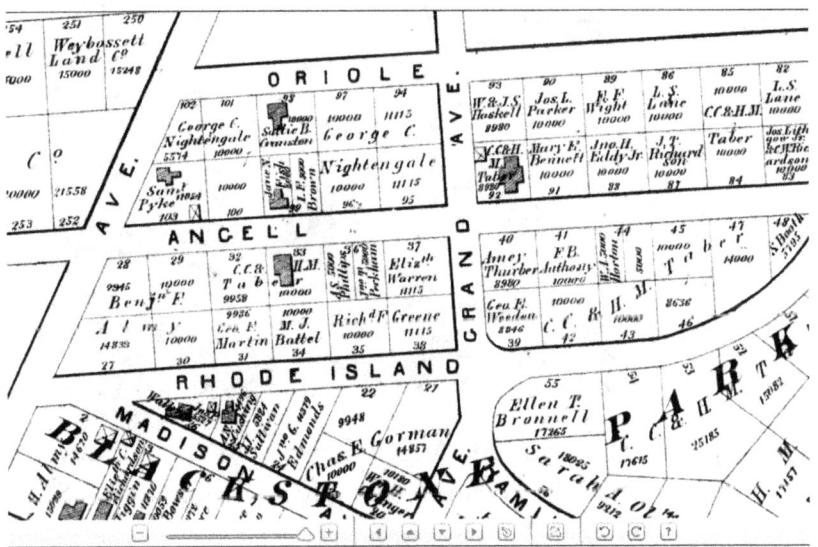

Butler Avenue is on the left side of this detail from Plate K of the 1875 Providence atlas. (I do not think the structure with an

"X" mark on the property of Samuel Pyke at the corner of Butler Ave. and Angell St.—while at the approximate location of 598–600 Angell—actually represents that structure.)

Had it been erected before 1896, 598–600 Angell would of course have borne a different number on Angell Street. In 1896, Lovecraft's birthplace was renumbered from 194 Angell Street to 454 Angell Street. If 598–600 Angell existed before 1896 and underwent a comparable numbering change, it would probably have been originally numbered 338–340 Angell Street.

Alas, the Sanborn maps of 1889 and 1900 do not appear to cover the vicinity of 598–600 Angell. The 1918 Providence atlas displays the locality:

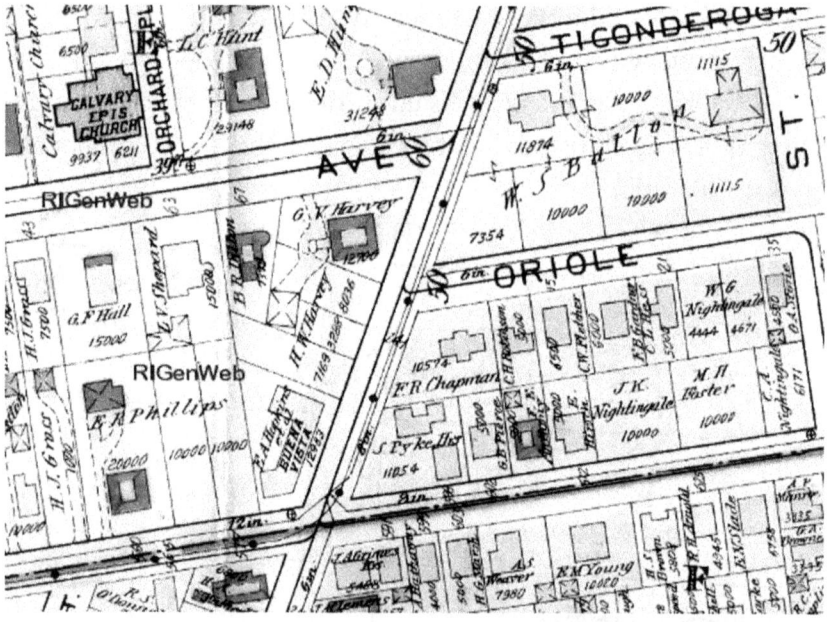

In this detail from plate 20, Angell Street runs slightly upward from left to right at the bottom. The only street it crosses is Butler Avenue. 598–600 Angell is the first building on the north side of Angell east of Butler Avenue, part of the property owned by the S. Pyke Est[ate].

The situation in the 1921 Sanborn fire map is similar:

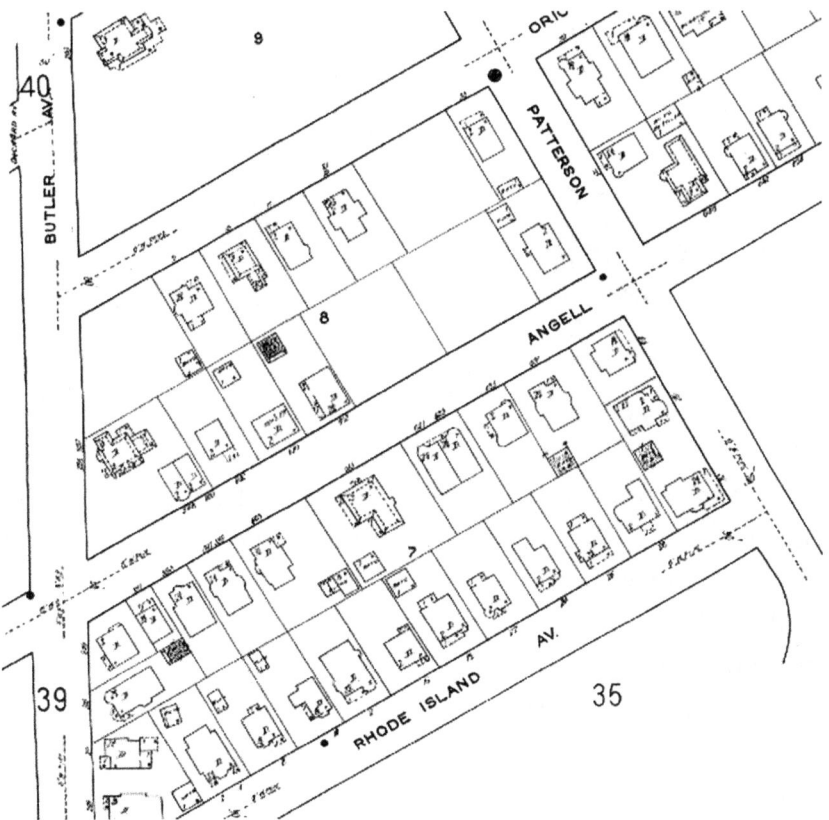

In this detail from plate 41 of the 1921 Sanborn fire map, 598–600 Angell is the double house on the north side of Angell Street just east of Butler Avenue.

By 1937, the property was owned by George C. Calef[1] (Providence 1937 atlas, plate 20):

---

1. Calef and his wife Dorothy resided at 598 Angell Street in 1933–38 and at 600 Angell Street in 1940–42.

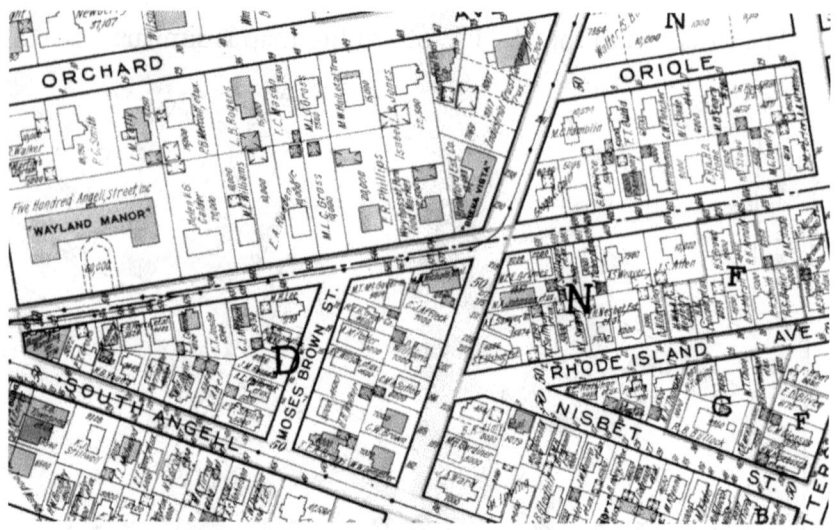

Here Angell Street can be identified by Wayland Manor at 500 Angell Street. The intersecting street to the east of Wayland Manor is Butler Avenue. The 1921–52 revision of the 1921 Sanborn fire map does not really reflect any material changes to the immediate surroundings of 598–600 Angell Street.

The most interesting period of the history of 598–600 Angell Street for the Lovecraft scholar is the period of his residency from 1904 to 1924. When Lovecraft and his mother arrived at 598 Angell in 1904, their neighbors at 600 Angell were the widow Jennie T. Metcalf (1854–1939) and her sons Henry Knight Metcalf (1879–1964) and Houghton Metcalf (1881–1955). The Metcalfs remained at 600 Angell at least through 1911. The next neighbors that I discovered for Lovecraft and his mother at 600 Angell were draftsman George Manning Leonard (1877–1932), his wife Emily Hastings (Lyman) Leonard (1878–1944), and his sister-in-law, librarian Bertha H. Lyman (1873–1944). In the 1915 RI state census they had a seven-year-old daughter Frances B. Leonard. The Leonards remained at 600 Angell through at least 1928—after Lovecraft's departure in

1924. Here are the Lovecrafts and the Leonards next to each other in the schedule for the 1915 RI state census:

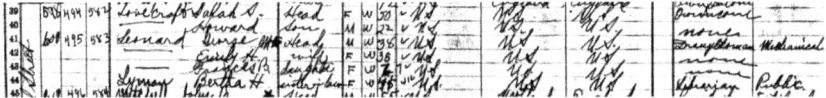

The same families were enumerated at 598–600 Angell in US 1920:

(Note that the census taker recorded the surnames of the members of the Leonard family as Manning—from head of household George M. Leonard's middle name. Also note that Susie Lovecraft's sister Annie P. Gamwell, a public school teacher, was also a member of the household at 598 Angell.)

Occupants of 598–600 Angell Street came and went in the years after Lovecraft departed. One interesting resident was Frederic James Farnell, M.D., who kept his offices at 598 Angell Street in 1928–31. Lovecraft had had his chemistry laboratory in the basement of 598 Angell, and the story is told that Dr. Farnell (who had conducted a psychiatric examination of Susie Lovecraft at Butler Hospital in 1919) found Lovecraft's name carved on a wooden beam or post in the basement. Lovecraft had only been gone for four years when Dr. Farnell opened his office at 598 Angell Street.[2]

---

2. For more on Dr. Farnell, see my work *Frederic James Farnell (1885–1968)—Susie Lovecraft's Psychiatrist* (Glenview, IL: Moshassuck Press, 2020).

Older view of 598–600 Angell. Credit: Chris Perridas blog.

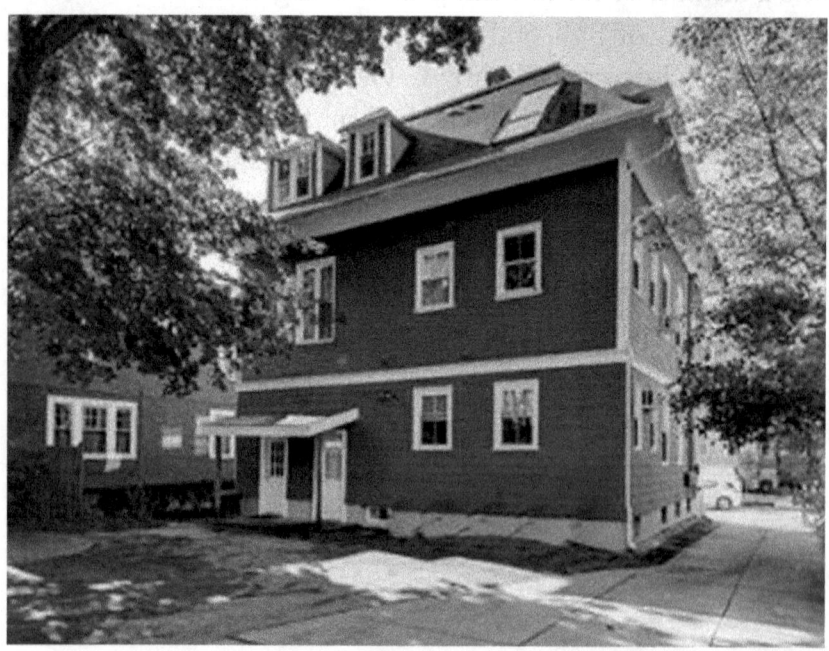

Rear view of 598–600 Angell. Credit: Redfin.

The Site of Joseph Curwen's Home in *The Case of Charles Dexter Ward*

with Jason C. Eckhardt

For S. T. Joshi

> The authors wish to express their thanks to Donovan K Loucks, David E. Schultz, and the Rhode Island State Archives for their assistance. However, the authors remain solely responsible for all opinions and errors contained in their text.

Catherine R. Williams on the old North Side of Providence, Rhode Island (from her work *Annals of the Aristocracy*):

> In the course of a few years, the settlement continued to extend, and the aristocracy of those days, progressed upwards, not downward. From the top of Constitution Hill almost to the North Burial Ground, you might see their spacious and commodious dwellings; while the poor and hard-working class were constrained, for the most part, to retreat further down town.
>
> Of all the grandeur that once distinguished this neighborhood, but little now remains. Some of the old houses remain; and being composed of durable materials, very unlike the present style of building, they have survived generations-and their sturdy oak timbers, in many instances, borne up six or seven families at a time. (41–42)

*Portrait of Catherine Read Williams (1787–1872)
Painted ca. 1835 by Susanna Paine (1792–1862)
Mrs. Williams and her grandson Lewis Cass De Wolf
lived in "Olney Court" in 1862–63.
Source: Wikimedia Commons
Original: Rhode Island Historical Society (RHi X3 4475)
Gift of Henry J. Steere et al. (1885) (Goodyear 269)*

Introduction: The Curwen House in Lovecraft's Novel

H. P. Lovecraft has skillfully woven the tapestry of his narrative in *The Case of Charles Dexter Ward* (1927) around the history and geography of his native Providence and the surrounding area.

There can be no doubt whatsoever about the identification of the residence of his protagonist Charles Dexter Ward with the Thomas Lloyd Halsey House at 140 Prospect Street:[1]

> His home was a great Georgian mansion atop the well-nigh precipitous hill that rises just east of the river; and from the rear windows of its rambling wings he could look dizzily out over all the clustered spires, domes, roofs, and skyscraper summits of the lower town to the purple hills of the countryside beyond. Here he was born, and from the lovely classic porch of the double-bayed brick facade his nurse had first wheeled him in his carriage; past the little white farmhouse of two hundred years before that the town had long ago overtaken, and on toward the stately colleges along the shady, sumptuous street, whose old square brick mansions and smaller wooden houses with narrow, heavy-columned Doric porches dreamed solid and exclusive amidst their generous yards and gardens. (*CF* 2.221–22)

---

1. The Rhode Island volume in the American Guide Series has this to say of the Halsey Mansion: "100. The *Halsey Mansion (private),* 140 Prospect St., was built in 1801 by Thomas Lloyd Halsey, 'away out on his farm.' He was a famous *bon vivant* in Colonial days, and there is a legend that he kept live terrapins in his cellar. For many years during which the mansion was empty, Negroes in the vicinity were convinced that a piano-playing ghost haunted the property. They would not enter the house under any circumstances, and at night always gave it a wide berth. It is also said that a blood-stain on the floor has defied many years of scrubbing" (*Rhode Island: A Guide to the Smallest State* 290). M. Eileen McNamara and S. T. Joshi describe the members of the Mauran family who later resided in this mansion in their article "Who Was the Real Charles Dexter Ward?"

Lovecraft is perhaps even more specific about the Providence home of Ward's ancestor Joseph Curwen, whom he states to have left Salem for Providence in March 1692 (*CF* 2.225). Lovecraft writes of Curwen and his Providence home:

> He had fled from Salem to Providence—that universal haven of the odd, the free, and the dissenting—at the beginning of the great witchcraft panic, being in fear of accusation because of his solitary ways and queer chemical or alchemical experiments. He was a colourless-looking man of about thirty, and was soon found qualified to become a freeman of Providence; thereafter buying a home lot just north of Gregory's Dexter's at about the foot of Olney Street. His house was built on Stampers' Hill west of the Town Street, in what later became Olney Court; and in 1761 he replaced this with a larger one, on the same site, which is still standing. (*CF* 2.227)

When Ward discovers a letter from Curwen to Simon Orne of Salem, he finds that it contains specific directions to Ward's house in Providence: "My House opp. Mr. Epenetus Olney's Tavern off ye Towne Street, 1st on ye N. side of Olney's Court. Distance from Boston Stone abt. XLIV Miles" (*CF* 2.270). In fact, this letter enables Ward to identify Curwen's still-standing second home:

> The discovery was doubly striking because it indicated as the newer Curwen house built in 1761 on the site of the old, a dilapidated building still standing in Olney Court and well known to Ward in his antiquarian rambles over Stampers' Hill. The place was indeed only a few squares from his own home on the great hill's higher ground, and was now the abode of a negro family much esteemed for occasional washing, housecleaning, and furnace-tending services. (*CF* 2.270–71)

Of the house, wherein upon second examination Ward discovers the hidden portrait of his ancestor, Lovecraft writes:

> Young Ward came home in a state of pleasant excitement; and spent the following Saturday in a long and exhaustive study of the

house in Olney Court. The place, now crumbling with age, had never been a mansion; but was a modest two-and-a-half story wooden town house of the familiar Providence colonial type, with plain peaked roof, large central chimney, and artistically carved doorway with rayed fanlight, triangular pediment, and trim Doric pilasters. It had suffered but little alteration externally, and Ward felt he was gazing on something very close to the sinister matters of his quest. (*CF* 2.71)

Curwen, who seemed never to age, had always fit poorly into Providence's close-knit society. In the same year he erected his new home on his property on Olney Court, he had contributed generously to the rebuilding of the Colony House after its destruction by fire (*CF* 2.234). Lovecraft remarks: "About this time, also, he built the plain but excellent new house whose doorway is still such a triumph of carving" (*CF* 2.234).

Curwen maintained at least nominal church membership (*CF* 2.235). After exerting considerable pressure on her father, Curwen married Eliza Tillinghast at the Baptist Church on 7 March 1763 (*CF* 2.237). Curwen and his new bride compromised their Congregational and Baptist backgrounds by joining King's Church (Episcopal), where their only daughter Ann was baptized 7 May 1765 (*CF* 2.239). Lovecraft writes that Curwen's marriage somewhat improved his acceptance by Providence society; in any case, he removed his alchemical and other secret dealings to a farmhouse in Pawtuxet so that "the new house in Olney Court was now free from disturbing manifestations" (*CF* 2.238). Curwen's nefarious dealings were finally brought to an end by a party of one hundred Providence men, led by some of the town's leading citizens, on the night of 12–13 April 1771. By common consent, the name of Joseph Curwen was soon obliterated from the memory of Providence. The inscription was chiseled off his tombstone (*CF* 2.263) and his monogram effaced from the brass knocker of his home in Olney Court (*CF* 2.272). His widow resumed her maiden name of Tillinghast, sold the house in Olney Court, and removed with her daughter to her father's home on Power Street, where she lived until her death in 1817 (*CF* 2.264). It remained for Curwen's descendant Charles Dexter Ward, with his discoveries in 1919–20, to revive his ancestor's memory, with disastrous consequences, after so many years of oblivion.

The Stampers Hill locale which Lovecraft describes is very much an historical reality, and it is not to be wondered that students of Lovecraft's fiction have pondered the exact location of Joseph Curwen's house in Olney Court.

Lovecraft's Knowledge of the Stampers Hill Neighborhood

Whether Lovecraft's own juvenile explorations of his native city extended to the Stampers Hill neighborhood may be questioned. As an infant, he was probably not taken farther down College Hill than Congdon Street (Prospect Terrace) by his mother or his nurse, as mirrored in his narrative of Charles Dexter Ward's infancy (*CF* 2.222). He remarks that Charles Dexter Ward's own solitary explorations as a youth extended as far as the Judge Durfee house at 49 Benefit Street, where the neighborhood was "getting to be a slum" (*CF* 2.222). By the 1920s, sometimes accompanied by his friends, Lovecraft was undertaking explorations into some slum districts of his native city. On 27 December 1923, a visiting James F. Morton joined Lovecraft and Clifford M. Eddy to explore first of all the First Baptist Meeting House and nearby sights adjoining Benefit Street However, then they:

> finally struck north in quest of the oldest brick house in Providence, (1750) which I had never seen, and which lies in a region that my foot had never trod. And such a region! Antient . . . unbelievably ancient cottages and sheds and houses, some of them urban, and some of them farmhouses overtaken in 1740 or 1745 by the growing town. Networks of dusty unpav'd byways darting narrowly and

nervously hither and thither off the main streets, and leading down
from the crest of old Constitution Hill to the brow of the vertigi-
nous slope that frowns over the river.... the antient Moshassuck,
at the falls where Goodman Smith's mill and the foot-bridge were
put up in 1642. There were all the symbols of the antient town—
Olney's Lane, with the gambrel-roof'd tavern where the Boston
coach us'd to leave every Thursday with passengers and His Majes-
ty's mail—and the first brick house itself, freshly painted and admi-
rably presev'd, tho' in the worst sort of mongrel slums. Then we
turn'd into the maze of colonial alleys toward the river, and suddenly saw a sight of incredible picturesqueness. From one of these lanes
an abrupt declivity fell, descending at a steepness almost prohibitive
to human feet, and provided with an iron hand-rail. Intersecting at
intervals several hidden Georgian lanes on the hillside, it reach'd a
group of early stone mill buildings—1815 or 1820—and slid be-
twixt two of them whose second stories were connected above it
with a passage like the Bridge of Sighs,[2] finally crossing the river by
a wooden bridge and coming out near Randall-Square, a hideous
polyglot slum district. (*MWM* 508–9)

The Providence weather must have been favorable on Thursday, 27 December 1923, for Lovecraft to have undertaken such an extended wintertime exploration with his friends. We can say with near certainty that on this occasion Lovecraft, Morton, and Eddy explored the Stampers Hill neighborhood around the foot of Olney Street, descending Stampers Hill at some point to the American Screw complex (mostly destroyed by fire in July 1971)

---

2. The original Bridge of Sighs (1602) crossed one of the canals and con-
nected the prison with the interrogation rooms of the Doge's palace in
Venice, Italy. Cambridge, Chester and Oxford, England and New York
City all had structures with the same name-those in Chester, England and
New York City serving a similar purpose. The former Bridge of Sighs in
lower Manhattan connected the Tombs Prison with the Criminal Courts
Building. Given the connections of Morton and Loveman with New York
City, HPL's intended reference may have been the Manhattan structure.

and finally ending in Randall Square. (At this point, Eddy had to leave the party, but Lovecraft and Morton and one of Lovecraft's aunts—probably Annie—continued to explore more of College Hill and then other slum districts adjoining downtown Providence.) So, by the time he returned to Providence to write *The Case of Charles Dexter Ward* in January and February of 1927,[3] Lovecraft had some personal acquaintance with the Stampers Hill neighborhood where he placed Joseph Curwen's home.

The History of the Stampers Hill Neighborhood

Stampers Street, which ran along the crest of the onetime Stampers Hill from 4S6 North Main to 7 Hewes Street, was obliterated when North Main Street was widened in 1931.[4] Bark Street, which ran along the foot of the hill from 55 Mill Street to 23 Stevens Street, through the area once known as Stampers Bottoms, also no longer exists. The tavern of Epenetus Olney was located on the northeast corner of Olney Street and North Main Street (see Maps 1 and 2).[5]

---

3. The surviving manuscript of *The Case of Charles Dexter Ward* indicates that HPL completed his work on 1 March 1927 (*IAP* 664).

4. North Main Street had been widened to a width of 99 feet between Sexton Street and Cemetery Street in 1882 (Cady 160). The widening of North Main was continued from the North Benefit Ground south to Randall Street in 1922 (Cady 238). Cady continues: "By a subsequent project, in 1931, the North Main Street widening was continued southerly to Benefit Street, involving the condemnation of land on the western side of the highway and the absorption of Stampers Street (page 24). This provided a maximum width of about 150 feet with two 40-foot roadways and landscaped center islands, identified as Captain J. Carleton Davis Boulevard" (238).

5. Epenetus Olney was born 14 February 1632/33 in Hertford, England and died in Providence on 3 June 1698. He married Mary Whipple. His tavern at the northeast corner of Town Street and Olney Lane was continued oy his son James Olney (b. 9 November 1670, Providence; d. 6 Oc-

The name Stampers goes back more than three and a half centuries in the history of Providence. Stampers Hill was a bluff overlooking the east side of the Moshassuck River. Stampers Bottoms was the lowland area on the east side of the Moshassuck River, below the bluff. In the Stampers Bottoms area, at the falls of the Moshassuck River, John Smith erected the first mill in Providence about the year 1646. One venerable tradition regarding the naming of Stampers Hill was provided by William Staples in his *Annals of the Town of Providence:*

> At a town meeting in January [1655/56], permission was given to such as pleased to erect a fort on "Stampers' hill." It has been handed down by tradition, that soon after the establishment of Providence, a body of Indians approached the town in a hostile manner. Some of the townsmen by running and stamping on this hill, induced them to believe that there was a large number of men stationed there to oppose them, upon which they relinquished their design and retired. From this circumstance the hill was always called Stampers' hill, or more generally, Stampers. Stampers street passes along the brow of this Hill. (117)

Citing Judge Staples's work, Samuel Greene Arnold repeated this tradition for the naming of Stampers Hill in his *History of the State of Rhode Island* (1.258). However, in a note Arnold expressed a different opinion:

> The earliest mill grant in R.I. was made in 1646 to John Smith to establish a grist-mill. He was to pay the cost of "the stampers" that had been imported from England by the colonists, amounting to about £100. These wooden stampers were used to pulverize corn. The mill was located just above Mill Bridge, in Providence. The street leading up the hill from the mill was called Stampers street, probably from these works rather than from the tradition cited in note 3, p. 258, vol. i. In excavating for the Blackstone Canal, many

---

tober 1744, Providence; m. Hallelujah Brown) and his grandson Joseph Olney (d. 1777).

years ago, some of the old timbers forming the bottom of the dam were discovered. This was no doubt the first hydraulic work in this State, if not in New England. (2.121)

In his work *The History of the State of Rhode Island and Providence Plantations* (3.893), Thomas W. Bicknell stated his opinion that the name Stampers took its origin from John Smith's mill, which used wooden stampers (rather than gears) to crush grain. In her sketch of "Stampers Street" in *Streets of the City,* Florence Simister repeats the traditional story told by Judge Staples but adds:

> Historians tell another tale. If it wasn't the stamping of the white men to scare off the Indians, then perhaps it was this. Once; there was a grist mill on this site and the owner imported from England what were known as "stampers," wooden tools for pulverizing corn. It was from these that the street took its name. Choose whichever story you prefer . . . (21)

The record apparently does not disclose whether a fort was erected on Stamper's Hill after permission was granted in 1655/56. On 30 March 1676, the Indians burned nearly all of Providence except for William Field's garrison house (Cady 12). Included among the structures burned were the mill and the miller's house. The then miller, John Smith, Jr., saved the town records from burning by throwing them into the mill pond. Simister recounts the developments after the burning of the town:

> Roger Williams wrote, "I pray the town will give me leave . . . to put some defence on the hill between the mill and the highway for the like safety of the women and children in that part of town." Between the mill and the highway would have been Stampers Street. A King's Garrison was formed, too, and the Garrison House was near Stampers Street, at the foot of Constitution Hill. (21)

The name "Stampers" appears in the Providence town records as early as "28 of the 5th m. 51" (28 July 1651), when the Council ordered "that James Leonard shall have 25 acres of

Land according to our late Order, as his home Lot neere the Stampers" (*The Early Records of the Town of Providence* 2.58). Then on 28 January 1655/56, the Quarter Court, sitting with Thomas Olney Sr. as moderator, ordered "that libertie is giuen to so many as please to erect a fortification upon the Stompers hill or about theire owne houses. Tho: Olnie Junr hath so much of the Stampers boottom as could be spared from a highway for his home share & 80 akers at Wainskock" (*Early Records* 2.91–92). The Town Meeting held March 23, 1665/66 with Thomas Olney Sr. as moderator confirmed grants of land to Thomas Olney, Jr., including "also one percell of Land lieing and being in the place Commonly called Stampers Bottom, the which land being laid out for a howse Lott or home share, Jt lieing in Two Pcells by reason of a high way" (*Early Records* 3.75).

It is probably not unreasonable that Lovecraft's fictional Joseph Curwen would have purchased his home lot on Stampers Hill about March 1692; Carly's map of the 1636–1650 home-lots (10) shows that a lot immediately north of the original grant to Gregory Dexter would have been about at the present location of Olney Street By the beginning of the eighteenth century, Stampers Hill was a well-settled neighborhood within the town of Providence. As early as 3 February 1717/18, the town proprietors accepted a plat drawn by Andrew Harris of the home lots on Stampers Hill—a plat reproduced between pp. 36–37 of James Pierce Root's *Steere Genealogy: A Record of the Descendants of John Steere* (1890). In this wonderful plat, reproduced herein as Map 2, one may note a 20-foot-wide way between the Towne St. (now North Main) and Stampers Street, at the foot of Olney Street. (By way of contrast, the Towne Street is a 45-foot-wide highway.) On either side of this small way, on the east side of Stampers Street, are the home lots of Arthur Goodwin to the north and Edward Smith to the south. Two narrow lanes, each

20 feet wide, descend the bluff from Stampers Street to Stampers Bottoms, where another highway of 20 feet (which became Bark Street) has been laid out. It is interesting to note that the home of Epenetus Olney[6] is the second from northernmost on the west side of Stampers Street. Note that in 1717/18 an Olney owned the land on the east bank of the Mohassuck River in Stampers Bottoms at the foot of Stampers Hill.

We find account of the Quakers' constructing their first Providence meeting house on Stampers Hill in Edward Field's *State of Rhode Island and Providence Plantations at the End of the Century: A History:*

> In 1718 Providence Monthly Meeting was set off from Greenwich and in 1724 or 1725 a meeting-house was built, through tJie influence of members of the Arnold family, mentioned above, on Stamper's Hill, in the northern part of the town. This was removed in 1745 to the corner of Meeting and North Main streets and replaced in 1844–5, by the present house of worship. (2.112)

Rhode Island: A Guide to the Smallest State records:

> The Old Friends Meeting-House *(not* open), 77–79 Hope St., is a severely plain structure recalling the austerity of the early Quakers, Built in 1723, it was originally located on Stampers Hill near the foot of Olney Street. In 1784 it was moved to the corner of North Main and Meeting Sts., the site of the present Friends Meeting-House. When the latter structure was erected in 1844–45, the old building was moved to the location it now occupies. (289)

As early as 27 January 1695/96, the Town Meeting had granted to petitioners a 40-foot-square lot for a schoolhouse on Stampers Hill:

---

6. Epenetus Olney Jr. (b. 18 January 1675 Providence, d. 17 September 1740 Providence; m. Mary Williams), son of the original tavern-keeper Epenetus Olney.

Towne Meeting Jan. 27, 1695–6. Where as, there hath hen a Request made unto ye Town by Jon Dexter, William Hopkins, Epenetus Olney, Willm Turpin, Joseph Whipple, John Smith, Philip Tillinghast and Joseph Smith, that the Town would accommodate them with a Small spot of Land to set a School House' upon in some place in this Town about ye Highway called Dexter Lane or about ye Stampers hill, the Town have Considered of the matter and Do by these presents freely Grant unto ye aforesaid persons . . . a Spot of Land of Forty foot, square . . . about the place where it may be most convenient. (Field 2.253)

Field comments that there is no evidence that a schoolhouse was built at this time.[7] A schoolhouse, known as Whipple Hall, was finally erected at the north end of Benefit Street, on land donated by Captain John Whipple, in 1768 (Field 2.256–57). According to Cady (43, 62, 103), Whipple Hall was replaced by the Benefit Street School, a 70 × 40 two-story brick building at the corner of Benefit and Halsey Streets, in 1840. Enlarged in 1893, the Benefit Street School was still in use in 1950.

Plate VI of Henry R. Chace's *Maps of Providence, R.I.: 1650–1765–1770* (1914) provides a wonderful view of the Stampers Hill neighborhood in 1770. An enlargement of a portion of this plate appears as Map 2 in this essay. Here we note the Olney Tavern on the north side of Olney's Lane, east of the Town Street. Joseph Olney and George Taylor occupy land on the north and south side of Olney's Lane at the juncture with the Town Street. The twenty-foot way between Stampers Street and the Town Street has M. Hearn on the north side and Samuel

---

7. In his work *The Providence Plantations for 250 Years*, Welcome Arnold Greene asserts that William Turpin and associates erected a schoolhouse on Stamper's Street "about the year 1687" (261). Chace, *Maps of Providence, R.I.* (Plate VI) also shows a schoolhouse between Stampers Street and North Main Street, immediately north of the residence of M. Hearn, in the year 1770 (see Map 3).

Currie on the south side. Immediately north of Hearn is a School House. E. Burr is immediately north of the School House. Simeon Thayer already resided at the southern end of Stampers Street, just north of the juncture of the Town Street (later North Main) and Back Street (later Benefit Street). After Epenetus Olney's grandson Joseph Olney ceased operation of the Olney Tavern, Thayer founded here the Montgomery Inn, named in honor of Revolutionary War General Richard Montgomery (1738–1775), whose head was depicted on the tavern's outside sign and whose portrait was found inside.

Plate VI of Henry R. Chace's work *Owners and Occupants of the Lots, Houses and Shops in the Town of Providence, Rhode Island in 1798* (1914) (Chace-b) gives us a look at the Stampers Hill neighborhood toward the end of the eighteenth century. Now we find L. Burr on the north side of the way between Stampers Street and Olney Lane. I. Angell is immediately north of him, where the School House was formerly. The Stampers Bottoms land is called Dr. Sterling's Meadow, now in the possession of Thomas Jackson. Olneys cluster-aplenty about the foot of Olney's Lane at the Town Street.

By 1831, the intersection of North Main and Olney Streets had become a predominantly Negro neighborhood known as "Hardscrabble" or "Addison Hollow." The Negro population of Providence had grown from 980 in 1820 to 1200–1400 in 1830. Houses of entertainment—providing food, drink, and sex—clustered in the area. When one of a group of seamen was shot and killed in the neighborhood, his fellow sailors rioted in Hardscrabble on 21–24 September 1831.[8] Three residents were wounded and two houses burned on 21 September. On the fol-

---

8. An earlier riot resulting in the destruction of eleven houses had occurred in the area on 18 October 1824.

lowing day, a mob of 700–800 men destroyed six houses in the neighborhood. Another riot occurred in the Snow Town neighborhood, whose exact location has been the subject of debate. On 23 September 1831, a mob of one thousand men crossed the Smith Street Bridge to Snow Town.[9] The militia fired and killed four men.

Simister (p. 21) calls Stampers Street "a narrow, dark street." By the time of the 1911 Providence House Directory, the length of the street, running from 456 North Main to 7 Hewes, was definitely a working class neighborhood. The even street numbers were on the west side of Stampers Street, the odd numbers on the east side. The short stretch of Olney Street between Stampers Street and North Main Street originated at 28 Stampers Street. Stevens Street crossed at numbers 46–47, Hewes Street at numbers 76–77.

In the 1920 U.S. census, the racial mix on the stretch of Stampers Street from numbers 6 to 28 (inclusive) was 10 white, 15 black/mulatto. Occupations included bleacher-dye works (2), domestic-private family (2), spinner-cotton mill, freight handler-freight yard, laundress-private family, laborer-buildings, weaver-cotton factory, painter-houses, shoe dealer-shoe store, and clerk-shoe store. In the 1930 U.S. census, the same stretch of Stampers Street had 11 white and 21 negro residents. Occupations included expressing-furniture moving (2), domestic-private family (2), janitor-office building (2), helper-baker shop, butler-private family, servant-private family, porter-shoe store, pharmacist-drug store, cook-hotel, cook-private family, tailor, upholstering, machine operator-file shop, and carpenter. While clearly a working class neighborhood for the entirety of its existence, Stampers Street

---

9. Rhode Island historians have debated the exact location of Snow Town. One authority places it where the Rhode Island State House lawn is today.

had a variety of residents: the *Providence Journal* reported in 1908 that an 1818 fire in Stampers Street had been "caused by explosion of fireworks a Chinaman was making" (see Tsai).

Was 6 Olney Street the Joseph Curwen House?

S. T. Joshi had this to say in 2001 about the Joseph Curwen house in note ten of his annotations for *The Case of Charles Dexter Ward* in the Penguin edition of Lovecraft:

> Olney Court was an extension of Olney Street on the west side of North Main Street. The area was called Stampers' (formerly Stompers') Hill. HPL appears to have had a specific house in mind for Joseph Curwen's 1761 residence, but the entire area has now been razed to make way for new development. Olney Court is no longer in existence. (Lovecraft, *Thing on the Doorstep* 390–91)

A discussion of whether a specific residence informed Lovecraft's depiction of the Joseph Curwen House took place in the Internet discussion group alt.horror.cthulhu in 2000–03. In a post, Karl Kluge placed the Curwen House west of the Moshassuck River, but Donovan K. Loucks maintained that the house was east of the river and placed it near the intersection of Stevens and Hewes Streets. However, the most notable post in this discussion was made by Karl Kluge on 22 May 2003. He had access to the 1921 Sanborn Fire Map of Providence through a proprietary database, and identified the Curwen house as 6 Olney Street, on the then-section of Olney Street west of North Main (see Map 6). In 1921, this residence stood around the corner from a broom factory at 502–504 North Main Street. Based on his examination of the Sanborn Fire Map, Harms asserted that the southwest corner of the residence at 6 Olney Street had stood 42 feet west of the intersection of North Main and Olney Street. The short section of Olney Street west of North Main and Stampers Street were both obliterated when

North Main was widened to form Captain J. Carleton Davis Memorial Boulevard in 1931.

The authors believe that Kluge was the first to identify correctly the residence that was probably the principal inspiration for Lovecraft's description of the new residence erected by Joseph Curwen in 1761. As early as the 3 February 1717/18 plat of the Stampers Hill neighborhood, there had been a 20-foot-wide highway extending west from the Towne Street (now North Main) at the foot of Olney's Lane (now Olney Street). This highway extended a short distance from the Town Street to what later became Stampers Street. In February 1717/18, Arthur Goodwin resided on the north side of this short highway, and Edward Smith on the south side. Plate VI of Chace's 1770 map shows M. Hearn on the north side of this, short stretch of highway, and Samuel Currie on the south side. There is a schoolhouse immediately north of Hearn. Plate VI of Chace 1798 map (*Owners and Occupants*) shows L. Burr on the north side of the short stretch of highway, and the south side vacant (no resident named). Providence Directories beginning with the first in 1824 and extending at least through 1867 indicate that Olney Street[10] begins at North Main. It is certainly perfectly reasonable that the appellation "Olney Court" might have been used for the short highway extending between Stampers Street and North Main Street, opposite the foot of Olney Street. Starting with the 1868 directory, Olney Street is listed as running from "Stampers to Neck road." The usage of "Olney Court" for the short stretch of highway linking Stampers Street and North Main probably died out from this time forward.

---

10. In the 1824 directory, Olney Street is still called by its original name, Olney's Lane.

The addresses on the north side of Olney Street between Stampers Street and North Main Street were number 2 and number 6. Since Curwen specifically identifies his residence as "1st on Ye N. Side" in his letter to Orne, it seems that Kluge is correct in his assertion that number 6 Olney Street, which stood on the northwest corner of Olney Street and North Main, was the probable inspiration for Curwen's new house erected in 1761.

G. M. Hopkins's *Plat Book of the City of Providence, Rhode Island* (1918) provides a detailed layout of the properties on the north side of this short stretch of Olney Street. The images may be found on scan 4 of plate 22 of the online edition of this work. S. W. Greene owns a tract on the north side of this short stretch of Olney Street (extending from Stampers Street on the west to North Main Street on the east), which includes the residences at number 2 and number 6 (the putative Joseph Curwen House). Greene's property (which bears identification number 4620 on the plat map) extends north to include two structures on North Main, the southernmost of which apparently included a side-building or shed. Perhaps this was the broom factory at 502–504 North Main Street noted by Kluge in the 1921 Sanborn Fire Map. All four buildings in S. W. Greene's tract 4620 are shown in light brown in the 1918 plat book, which the authors presume indicates wooden structures. How far forward or backward from 1918 property records can trace the property at 6 Olney Street remains to be demonstrated.

Donovan K Loucks (communication to Faig, 8 July 2011) found that the City of Providence acquired the property in 1931 for the widening of *North* Main Street, presumably by eminent domain. The exact date of demolition of the dwelling at 6 Olney Street has not been determined. Since the property is listed as "vacant" in the 1931–32 Providence House Directory and the address is no longer listen in the 1933–34 Providence House Directory, Mr. Loucks assigns 1933 as the probable demolition year for the dwelling at 6 Olney Street.[11] We can be certain that if the dwelling at Olney Street was erected as early as 1761, we are not going to be able to find any building permits or plans. However, we know that the Stampers Hill neighborhood was laid out for residences as early as February 1717/18, and that many eighteenth-century structures did survive into the early twentieth century. The authors believe it is very probable that Lovecraft, Eddy, and Morton saw an old frame house at 6 Olney Street when they explored the Stampers Hill and adjoining neighborhoods on 27 December 1923.[12]

Delilah Townsend—An Additional Link Between
H. P. Lovecraft and 6 Olney Street

Co-author Jason C. Eckhardt and Donovan K. Loucks (proprietor of the hplovecraft.com website) independently discovered that Mrs. Delilah Townsend was the occupant of the dwelling at 6 Olney Street in the 1927–28 Providence House Directory.

---

11. Cady (238) states that the widening of North Main from Randall Street to Benefit Street to create Captain J. Carleton Davis Boulevard occurred in 1931. It is possible that the data for the 1931–1932 Providence House Directory, which listed the dwellings at 2 and 6 Olney Street as "vacant," was compiled in advance. The authors believe that the search for newspaper accounts of the widening of North Main Street to create Captain J. Carleton Davis Memorial Boulevard is a worthy project.

12. In an email to Faig, S. T. Joshi, and David E. Schultz dated 27 October 2012, Donovan K. Loucks (proprietor of the hplovecraft.com electronic archive) announced that he had discovered a surviving photograph of 6 Olney Street owned by the Colonial Dames of Rhode Island. It is amazing how faithfully this actual house was described in HPL's narrative in *CDW*. The authors congratulate Mr. Loucks on this amazing discovery and express the hope that he will publish the jpg of this apparent 1920s photograph of 6 Olney Street electronically.

During the period 1926–32, Mrs. Townsend, a black woman, provided housekeeping, laundry, and attendance services for Lovecraft's aunt Lillian D. Clark (1856–1932) at 10 Barnes Street. Mrs. Townsend also worked for Mrs. Clark at prior addresses including 115 Waterman Street and 598 Angell Street. Her ex-husband William Townsend may have helped Lovecraft and his aunt with some heavier work, including possibly Lovecraft's removal from 10 Barnes Street to 66 College Street in May 1933. The following passage from Lovecraft's novel thus provides additional identification of the dwelling at 6 Olney Street as the inspiration for Joseph Curwen's abode (emphasis added by the authors):

> The discovery was doubly striking because it indicated as the newer Curwen house built in 1761 on the site of the old, a dilapidated building still standing in Olney Court and well known to Ward in his antiquarian rambles over Stampers' Hill. The place was indeed only a few squares from his own home on the great hill's higher ground, and was now the abode of *a negro family much esteemed for occasional washing, housecleaning, and furnace-tending services.* (CF 2.270–71)

Numerous letters from Lovecraft to his aunt Mrs. Clark refer to their housekeeper "Delilah" but it is only Lovecraft's letter to Mrs. Clark dated 1 August 1924 which provides her surname: "On this occasion I met for the first time the Michigan amateur Clyde G. Townsend (no relative of Delilah's, but a fine Nordic specimen with yellow hair and blue eyes!)" (*LFF* 139). In his letter to Mrs. Clark dated 22–23 December 1925, Lovecraft appears to suggest that Delilah Townsend may have been employed by the Phillips family as early as the first decade of the twentieth century:

> Yes indeed—I certainly wish that you could be a Wendell heir, so that you might be here for the Christmas dinner; or that *I* could be; so that 454 Angell St. might be the home of both, & the dinner prepared by Norah or Delia (sober, I trust) or Svea or Jennie or

Bridget under your own direction, & served by honest Delilah in proper uniform & apron! (*LFF* 515)

In his correspondence with Mrs. Clark, Lovecraft's references to Delilah Townsend range from openly appreciative to the blatantly racist. He wrote of Delilah's "effective aid in the locomotive process" when Mrs. Clark was afflicted with arthritis. As Mrs. Clark was then in the process of removing from 598 Angell Street to 115 Waterman Street, Lovecraft advised her: "Don't work too hard at your moving—remember that Delilah is on hand to do all the heavy lifting" (*LFF* 451). When Mrs. Clark suffered another spell of illness, Lovecraft wrote to his friend Frank B. Long: "For some time in the evening the faithful old negress Delilah comes in to supply my place as I go home to collect my mail and eat my dinner" (*SL* 2.219). On the other hand, he could write to his aunt Mrs. Clark of her faithful helper Delilah Townsend: "She certainly is a valuable nigger, & ought to bring a good $900 or $1000 in any fair market north of Savannah" (*LFF* 476).

Recounting his reading of Gertrude Selwyn Kimball's *Providence in Colonial Times* (Houghton Mifflin, 1912) at the New York Public Library to his aunt, he mentioned casually the alleged haunting of the Halsey mansion:

> In the last chapter of the Kimball book I learnt of the spectre which haunts the Halsey Mansion in Prospect St. It is a *thing* which plays the piano during the sinister small hours . . . . & there is a bloodstain on the floor which cannot be washt out. Niggers from the neighbouring darktown will not pass the place after dark—or at least, would not at one time. Ask Delilah about it. (*LFF* 414)

Today of course we can take a more enlightened view of Delilah Townsend. The 1900 U.S. census of Providence found her and her family residing at 46 Thayer Street on the East Side on 1 June 1900:

> Townsend, William, head, negro, male; born May 1872, age 28, married for 6 years, born New Bedford MA of NY-born father and MA-born mother, occupation: day laborer, can read & write, speaks English, rents;
> Townsend, Delilah, wife, negro, female, born December 1872, age 28, married for 6 years, mother of 2 children (1 living), born VA of VA-born parents, can read & write, speaks English;
> Townsend, William, son, negro, male, born March 1896, age 4, single, born RI of RI-born father [*sic*] and VA-born mother, at school.

There is no notation that Delilah Townsend might then have been a domestic employee of Whipple V. Phillips at 454 Angell Street. William J. Townsend was the son of Robert and Sarah (Turgerson) Townsend of New Bedford, MA. The 1880 U.S. census recorded Robert Townsend as Massachusetts-born of Massachusetts-born parents and his wife Sarah as Virginia-born of Virginia-born parents; Robert was employed as a sailor. There were three children in their household in that year: Robert H., age 12, Martha M., age 10; and William J., age 7. It is possible that William Townsend was in Providence as early as 1892 and 1893, when the city directory recorded a William Townsend as a coachman a 476 Broad Street, residing at the same address.

The earlier history of William's wife Delilah is less certain, but the authors believe she can be identified in the following household in the 1870 U.S. census of Pine Top, Middlesex County, Virginia:

> Robinson, George[13] age 25, male, negro, farmer, born VA, cannot read or write;
> Robinson, Amanda, age 22, female, negro, keeping house, born VA, cannot read or write;

---

13. Most records indicate that the name of Amanda Robinson's husband was Henry Robinson. Perhaps her husband George as enumerated in the 1870 U.S. census was also known as Henry, or perhaps Henry Robinson was: a second husband of Amanda Robinson.

Robinson, Lelia F., age 2, female, negro, at home, born VA;
Robinson, Mary A., age 4 months, female, negro, at home, born VA.

Amanda Robinson was apparently widowed or separated from her husband when her household was enumerated in the same place in the 1880 U.S. census:

Robinson, Amanda, black, female, age 28, born VA, keeping house;
Robinson, Lelia F., black, female, age 12, daughter, born VA, at home;
Robinson, Mary E., black, female, age 10, daughter, born VA, at home;
Robinson, Annie B., black, female, age 8, daughter, born VA;
Robinson, George W., black, male, age 5, son, born VA.

By the time of the 1905 RI Census, Delilah Townsend, age 36, was already divorced from William J. Townsend and was the head of household at 46 Thayer Street. She claimed thirty years' residence in RI and was unable to read or to write. Her occupation was private family laundress and her religious affiliation Baptist. The other three persons in Delilah's household in at 46 Thayer Street in 1905 were her mother Mandy Robinson (widow, age 60, born VA), her sister Mary Robinson (single, age 35, born August 1870 VA, private family cook), and her son William J. Townsend [Jr.]. In the 1915 RI Census, Mandy Robinson, black female, age 68, was the head of a four-person household in Providence Ward 2. The other three household members were daughter Mary Robinson, black female, age 43, private family cook; daughter Lila Townsend, black female, age 39, housekeeper-general work; and grandson William Townsend, black male, age 19, laborer-general work. In the 1918 Providence Directory, Delilah Townsend was listed as a widow at 91 Bates Street.

6 Olney Street, Courtesy Donovan K. Loucks.

Doorway detail, 6 Olney Street. Courtesy Donovan K. Loucks.

William J. Townsend had remarried in 1911. On 8 May 1911, in New Bedford, MA, he married Mary E. Brooks, the daughter of Joseph Brooks and Lucy Homan. In the 1914 Providence Directory, William J. Townsend, a clerk at 169 South Water Street, resided at 42 Wickenden Street. Tragically, Delilah's and William's son William Joseph Townsend [Jr.], then residing at 91 Bates Street, died on 21 July 1915, aged only 19 years 4 months 20 days.[14] His cause of death was recorded as angina pectoris. He had been working as a chauffeur at the time of his death. He was buried in Grace Church Cemetery.

The Providence Directories show Delilah Townsend at 6 Olney Street as early as 1918. We next encounter Delilah Townsend with her sister and her mother at 7 Olney Street (southeast corner of Olney and North Main) in the 1920 U.S. census on 7 January 1920:

> Townsend, Lila, rents, female, negro, age 45, widow, cannot read or write, born VA of VA-born parents, occupation: laundress-private family;
> Robinson, Mary, sister, female, negro, age 54, single, cannot read or write, born VA of VA-born parents, no occupation;
> Robinson, Amanda, mother, female, negro, age 72, widow, cannot read or write, born VA of VA-born parents, no occupation.

However, Delilah Townsend and sometimes her mother Amanda Robinson [Robertson] and her sister Mary Robinson [Robertson] were recorded at 6 Olney Street in Providence directories for the years 1918–28. The 1929 Providence directory recorded Mrs. Delilah Townsend and Clara L. Rodrigues as domestics in the home of Mrs. Ruth M. Ridley at 489 North Main Street. In

---

14. The inferred date of birth for William Joseph Townsend, Jr. (1 March 1896) agrees with his month and year of birth as stated in the 1900 U.S. census.

the 1930 U.S. census, Delilah and her family were recorded nearby at 474 North Main Street on 17 April 1930:

> Townsend, Delilah, head, rents ($22/month), female, negro, age 50, divorced, cannot read or write, born VA of VA-born parents, occupation: none;
> Robinson, Mary, sister, female, negro, age 54, single, cannot read or write, born VA of VA-born parents, occupation: cook-private family;
> Robinson, Amanda, mother, female, negro, age 80, widowed, cannot read or write, born VA of VA-born parents, occupation: none;
> Johnson, Sarah, lodger, female, negro, age 52, widowed, cannot read or write, born VA of VA-born parents, occupation: laundress-private family.

The 1942 and 1944 Providence directories listed Delilah Townsend's home as 45 East Transit Street. Delilah Townsend herself followed her sister and her mother in death on 21 November 1944, aged 74 according to her death certificate. Her last residence had been 45 East Transit Street in Providence, but she spent the last eleven days of her life in the State Infirmary in Cranston, RI. She was listed as the widow of William Townsend and the daughter of Henry and Amanda Robinson. Her birthplace was given incorrectly as North Carolina. Like her mother, sister, and son, Delilah Townsend was buried in Grace Church Cemetery.

Of Delilah's erstwhile husband William Townsend, we can find a few records. In the 1915 RI Census, 43-year-old William Townsend and his wife 37-year-old Mary Townsend were recorded at 42 Wickenden Street. William was working as a fish cleaner at a fish market and his wife Mary as a private family cook. In the 1925 RI Census, William Townsend, male, black, age 52, born MA, was recorded alone at 42 Wickenden Street. William Townsend married Sarah J. Johnson in Providence on 26 October 1930. In the 1935 RI Census, William Townsend, born 6 May 1872 MA, residing at 185 North Main Street, was recorded on 12 May 1936. His occupation was given as fishery laborer but he had been unemployed for twelve months in 1935. Also recorded in his household at 185 North Main Street was Sarah Townsend, born 22 October 1889 VA, unemployed. William Townsend last appeared in the 1937 Providence Directory. He was then living at 185 North Main Street, with no occupation listed. It is possible that he returned to his Massachusetts birthplace to spend his final years. However, the California Death Index lists a William John Townsend, born 30 May 1872 MA, who died in Stanislaus County CA on 2 December 1949. Delilah's ex-husband William Joseph Townsend died in Providence on 6 August 1966 at the age of ninety-four.

We know that Lovecraft explored the Stampers Hill neighborhood with James F. Morton and Clifford M. Eddy on 27 December 1923. It seems likely that he renewed his acquaintance with the neighborhood after his return to Providence in April 1926, since it would have been only a short walk down the hill from his home at 10 Barnes Street. During most of the period of Lovecraft's residency at 10 Barnes Street (1926–33), Delilah (Robinson) Townsend was still performing housekeeping and attendance duties for his aunt Lillian D. Clark (1856–1932). During this entire period, Delilah Townsend lived in the immediate neighborhood of 6 Olney Street It is possible that Lovecraft paid occasional visits to the neighborhood to drop off laundry parcels or conduct other business.

Closing Reflections

Names from the past flicker through the present. Olney's Tavern, Friends' Meeting House, Whipple School, Montgomery Inn, 6 Olney Street, Levi Burr, Samuel Currie, Catherine Read Williams, Stephen Mathewson Greene, Sarah Williams (Olney) Greene, Amanda Robinson, Delilah Townsend. Whether it was the stampers used to crush grain in John Smith's mill, or the colonists' stamping to frighten off the Indians, that provided the Stampers neighborhood with a name, we shall probably never know for certain. We can recapture Lovecraft's experience of the Stampers neighborhood in his letter to Samuel Loveman of 5 January 1924. But *The Case of Charles Dexter Ward* provides us with an imagined past woven by a genius of rare talent. Much as we might wish to assemble from the fragmented records of the past, the exact context for the author's imaginings, we are likely to achieve at best only partial answers to our questions. Armed with correct information and a time machine, one might hope to experience the precise inspiration for Joseph Curwen's 1761 Olney Court house. But as Charles Dexter Ward discovered, the past can be a dangerous place for residents of the present. A time machine operating from the center median of North Main Street at Olney Street could well deliver its operator into the midst of the Hardscrabble riots of 1824 and 1831. Certainly, Lovecraft's fictional Joseph Curwen would have been a dangerous person to encounter. In the end, both the real past and the imagined past collapse into the unknown, the imaginary domain in which H. P. Lovecraft excelled. We believe that the erstwhile residence at 6 Olney Street formed a small part of the rich tableau that informed the creation of Lovecraft's *The Case of Charles Dexter Ward*. Despite the denigrating racist comments of which he was capable, Lovecraft seems to have appreciated the faithful service of Delilah (Robinson) Townsend to his aunt Lillian D. Clark. That Mrs. Townsend resided at 6 Olney Street in 1927–28, when Lovecraft was busy with the composition of *The Case of Charles Dexter Ward*, and that he saw fit to make glancing reference to her and her family in his description of the Curwen house at 6 Olney Street ("Olney Court" in his novel), is yet another rich aspect of the Providence background for his composition. Delilah Townsend could doubtless have told H. P. Lovecraft much about the traditions of the black neighborhood at the foot of Olney Street, which had been the scene of violence one hundred years prior to their time. Her actual inhabiter's knowledge of this neighborhood probably helped to inform the rich tapestry of *The Case of Charles Dexter Ward*.

Bibliography

althorror.cthulhu. See posts on "Olney's Court" by Karl Kluge (7 April 2000; 12 June 2002; 22 May 2003); Donovan K. Loucks (1 April 2000; 8 April 8 2000). Viewed 5 February 2011.

Arnold, Samuel Greene. *History of the State of Rhode Island and Providence Plantations*. New York: D. Appleton, 1859–60. 2 vols.

Bicknell, Thomas Williams. *The History of the State of Rhode Island and Providence Plantations*. New York: American Historical Society, 1920. 3 vols.

Cady, John Hutchins. *The Civic and Architectural Development of Providence*. Providence, RI: The Book Shop, 1957.

Chace, Henry R. *Maps of Providence, RL: 1650–1765–1770*. Providence, RI: Henry R. Chace, 1914. Reprinted together with *Owners and Occupants* by Higginson Books (Salem, MA).

———. *Owners and Occupants of the Lots, Houses and Shops in the Town of Providence, Rhode Island in 1798*. Providence, RI: Henry R. Chace, 1914. Reprinted together with *Maps of Providence* by Higginson Books (Salem MA).

City Plan Commission. *College Hill: A Demonstration Study of Historic Renewal Area*. Providence, RI: City Plan Commission, 1967.

Early Records of the Town of Providence. Providence, RI: Snow & Farnham, 1892–1915. 21 vols.

Field, Edward. *State of Rhode Island and Providence Plantations at the End of the Century: A History*. Boston & Syracuse, NY: Mason Publishing Company, 1902. 3 vols.

Goodyear, Frank H., Jr. *American Paintings in the Rhode Island Historical Society*. Providence, RI: Rhode Island Historical Society, 1974.

Greene, Welcome Arnold. *The Providence Plantations for 250 Years*. Providence, RI: J. A. & R. A. Reid, 1886.

Hopkins, Charles Wyman. *The Home Lots of the Early Settlers of the Providence Plantations*. Providence, RI: [Privately published], 1886.

Hopkins, G. M. *City Atlas of Providence*. Philadelphia: O. M. Hopkins, 1875. 3 vols. On-line at www.historicmapworks.com.

———. *Plat Book of the City of Providence*. Philadelphia: G. M. Hopkins, 1918. Online at www.rootsweb.ancestry.com/-rigenweb/1918prov/.

Loucks, Donovan K. "The Search for Joseph Curwen's Town Home." *Lovecraft Annual* No. 9 (2015): 98–104.

Lovecraft, H. P. *The Thing on the Doorstep and Other Weird Stories*. Edited by S. T. Joshi. New York: Penguin, 2001.

McNamara, M. Eileen, and S. T. Joshi. "Who Was the Real Charles Dexter Ward?" *Lovecraft Studies* Nos. 19/20 (Fall 1989): 40–41, 48.

Paine, Susanna. *Roses and Thorns; or, Recollections of an Artist*. Providence, RI: B. T. Albro, 1854.

Rhode Island: A Guide to the Smallest State. Boston: Houghton Mifflin, 1937. A volume in the American Guide Series.

Rider, Sidney S. *Bibliographical Memoirs of Three Rhode Island Authors*. Rhode Island Historical Tracts No. 11. Providence, RI: Sidney S. Rider, 1880.

Root, James Pierce. *Steere Genealogy: A Record of the Descendants of John Steere*. Cambridge, MA: Riverside Press, 1890. Contains 3 February 1717/18 plat of home lots between pp. 36–37.

Simister, Florence. *Streets of the City: An Anecdotal History of Providence*. Providence, RI: Mowbray Co., 1968.

Staples, William. *Annals of the Town of Providence*. Providence, RI: Rhode Island Historical Society, 1843.

Tsai, Luke. "Providence's Black Chinese: A. Love Story." dl.lib.brown.edu/pdfs/ 117269371193125.pdf. Viewed 5 February 2011.

Updike, Wilkins. *Memoirs of the Rhode-Island Bar*. Boston: Thomas H. Webb & Co., 1842.

Williams, Catherine R. *Annals of the Aristocracy*. Providence, RI: B. T. Albro, 1845.

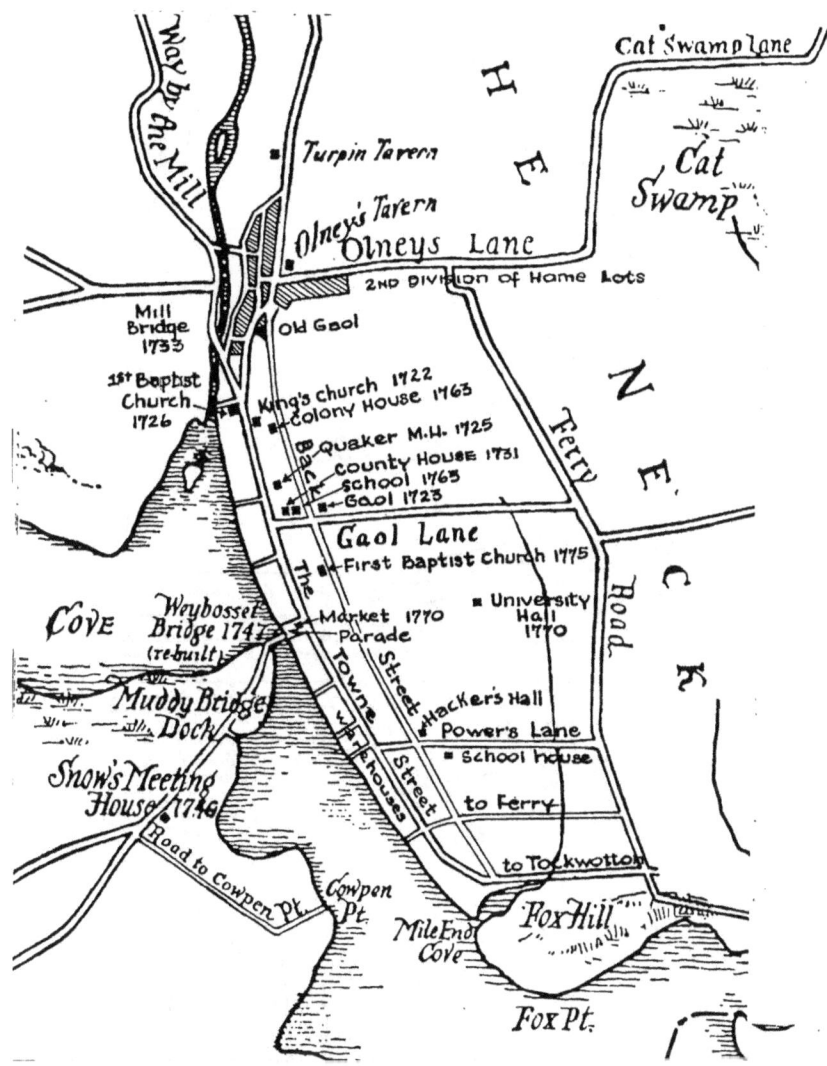

Map 1. *East Side Map showing Olney Tavern*
(City Plan Commission, p. 24)

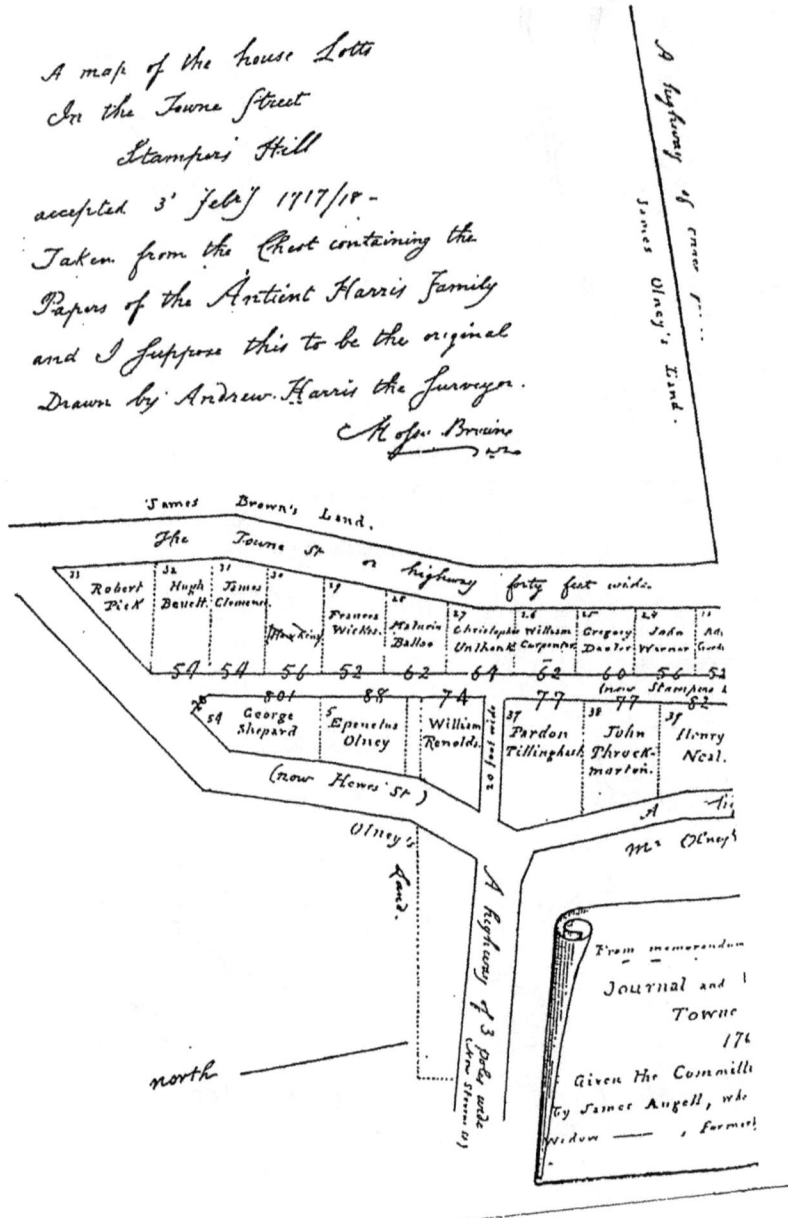

Map 2 (left). 3 February 1717/18 Plat of Home Lots
(Root, between pp. 36–37)

The Site of Joseph Curwen's Home

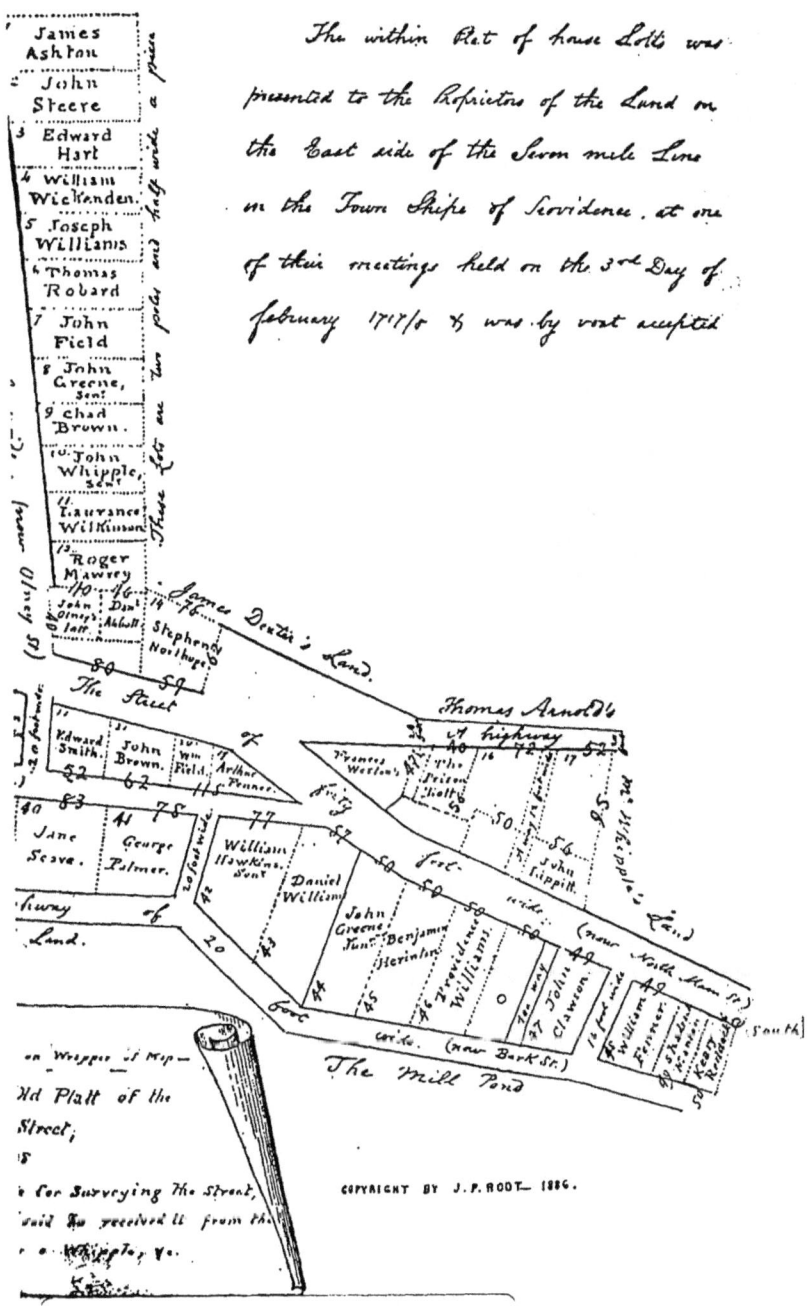

Map 2 (right)

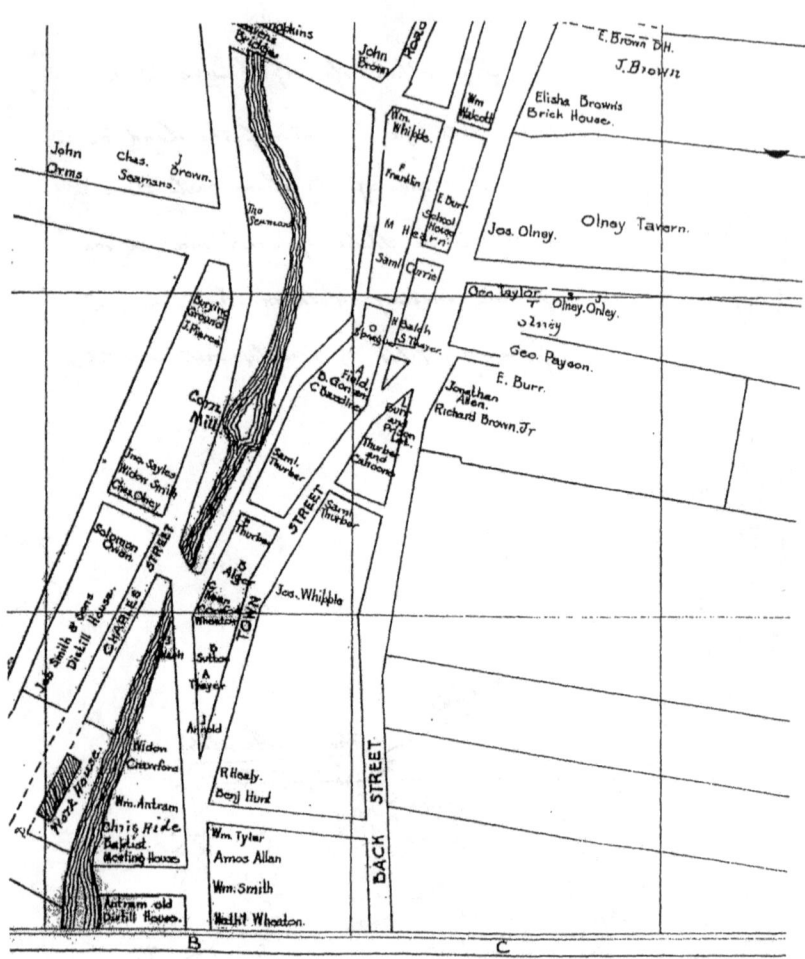

Map 3. Stampers Street Neighborhood 1770 (Chace-a, Plate VI)

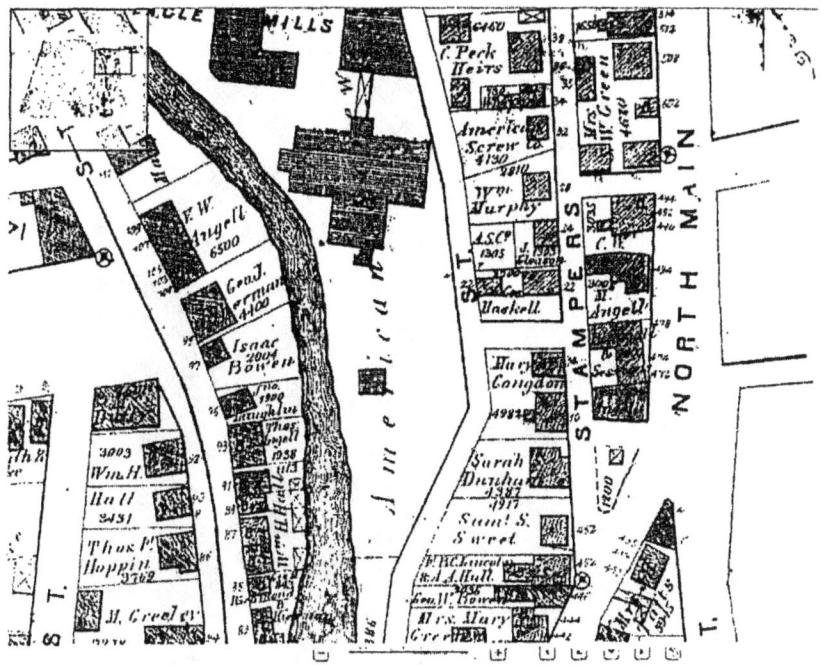

Map 4. Vicinity of 6 Olney Street, 1875 City Atlas of Providence (www.historicmapworks.com)

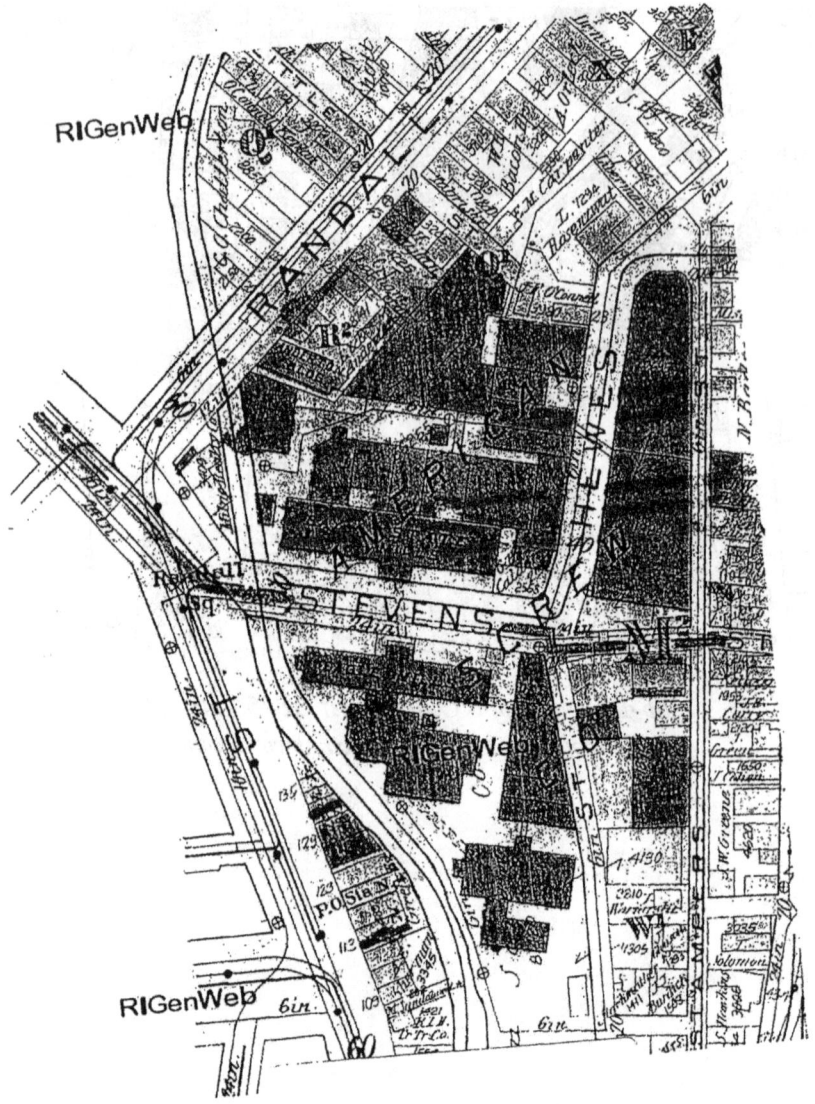

Map 5. Vicinity of 6 Olney Street, 1918 Providence Plat Book (r.i. genweb)

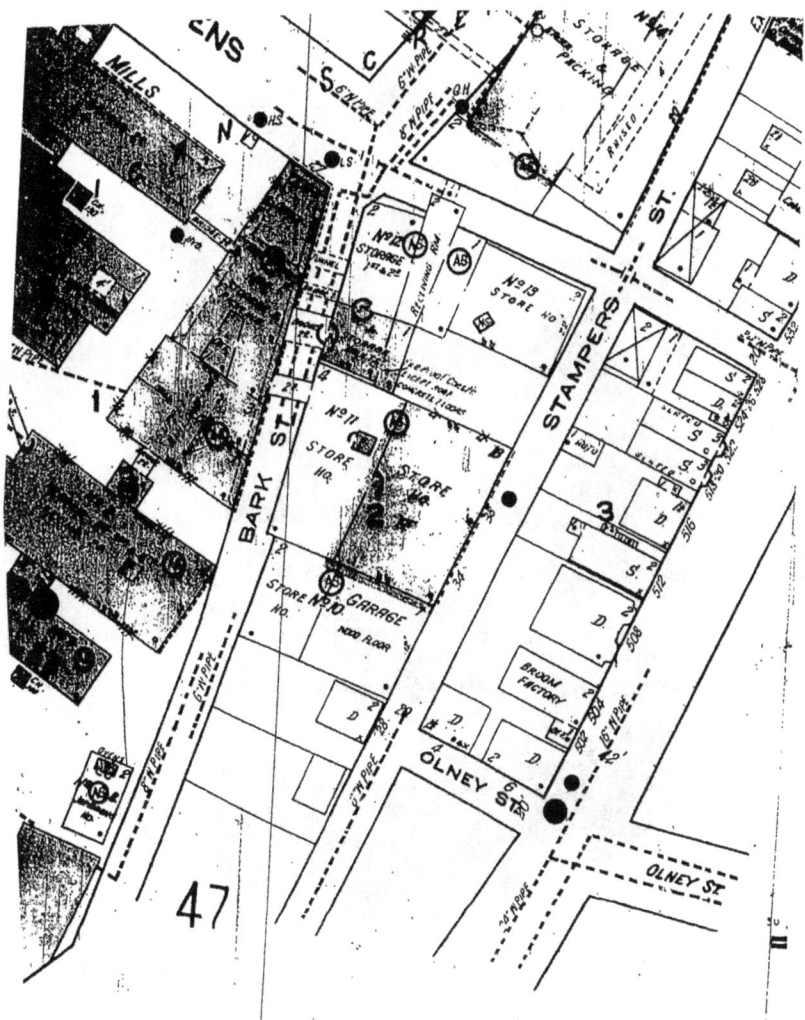

Map 6. *Vicinity of 6 Olney Street, 1921 Sanborn Fire Map*

*Undated drawing of the Olney Tavern and the Liberty Tree.
Courtesy of the Rhode Island Historical Society.*

The Site of Joseph Curwen's Home

Nineteenth-century photograph of the Sabin Tavern from Mary C. Crawford's Little Pilgrimages Among Old New England Inns. *Photo by James Allen.*

Can You Direct Me to Ely Court? Some Notes on 66 College Street

In Memory of Alice Rachel Sheppard (1870–1961)
and Mary Spink (1877–1968)

H. P. Lovecraft had only a cramped single room with alcove when he lived at 10 Barnes Street from 1926 to 1933. His elder aunt Lillian D. (Phillips) Clark (1856–1932) had a room on the floor above, and Lovecraft usually spent an hour every evening with his aunt. After she died in 1932, Lovecraft and his younger aunt Annie E. (Phillips) Gamwell (1866–1941), then residing on Slater Avenue, decided to seek common quarters. As luck would have it, they found a wonderful flat on the second floor of 66 College Street, tucked just behind Brown University's John Hay Library.

Lovecraft claimed that his new home was of colonial origin and cited several architectural features to support his contention. The rear wing, down three steps from the main part of the building, had wide colonial floorboards. Lovecraft's aunt had her quarters in this wing. His own study looked out from the southwest windows of the main part of the structure. The photographs that Robert H. Barlow took of Lovecraft's study when he came to Providence to organize his mentor's papers in 1937, first reproduced in *Marginalia* (Arkham House, 1944), speak to the sensibilities that guided Lovecraft when he furnished his study. Many family heirlooms, in storage since the dissolution of the 454 Angell Street household following the death of Whipple V. Phillips in 1904, were able once more to be displayed. Lovecraft purchased new bookcases the better to accommodate his growing collection. Beginning in 1933, he and his aunt even had a decorated Christmas tree during the holiday season. In a word, Lovecraft and his aunt were delighted to find themselves in a genuinely old building perched atop the "antient hill" overlooking downtown Providence.

The author's final years at 66 College brought challenges as well as blessings. Only a few weeks after taking up residence there on 15 May 1933, Mrs. Gamwell slipped on the stairs and broke her ankle. After being hospitalized, she recovered in a nursing home. But once she returned to 66 College, many support tasks devolved upon her nephew. Then in the spring of 1936, Mrs. Gamwell was hospitalized once more, this time for removal of a cancerous right breast. Once again, she spent a period of nursing home recovery and then returned to 66 College Street, where her nephew was once again pressed into service to provide necessary help. In the end, it was Lovecraft himself who fell ill, dying of cancer of the small intestine on 15 March 1937. His aunt survived him by nearly four years, dying on 29 January 1941.

The house at 66 College Street was removed to 65 Prospect Street in 1959 and continues to be one of the "must-sees" for Lovecraftian visitors to Providence. The Providence Preservation Society (PPS) plaque for the house does not agree with Lovecraft's contention that the house was of colonial origin: it dates the house to c. 1825 and names the first owner as Samuel B. Mumford. Lovecraft claimed that he could discern the "Garden House" on the famous 1809 Providence theatre curtain now owned by the Rhode Island Historical Society and kept at its Aldrich House headquarters at 110 Benevolent Street. Samuel Brenton Mumford, the first owner of the house according to PPS, was born in Providence on 12 September 1796, the son of Joseph Mumford and Mary Carr. He became a prosperous commission merchant, with offices at 19 South Main in 1826, 7 South Water in 1844, and 9 South Water in 1847. He married

Louisa G. Dexter, the daughter of Benjamin G. Dexter, in Providence on 9 February 1818. Perhaps he and his new bride moved into the so-called Garden House, set back a considerable distance from College Street, soon after their wedding. The 1826 Providence directory stated his home address as Angell Street.

Samuel Brenton Mumford died on 27 February 1849. He was survived by his widow Louisa for more than a quarter-century. The widow Louisa D. Mumford was listed at 25 Waterman Street in the 1853 Providence directory. When she applied for a passport to travel to Cuba in 1864, she stated her date of birth as 2 January 1801; perhaps she was shaving a few years, since her age at death was recorded as seventy-eight when she died on 12 February 1876. She had been listed at 45 College Street in the 1871–73 Providence directories. Then, in 1875–76, she was listed at 151 Benefit St. Samuel Brenton Mumford and his wife Louisa (Dexter) Mumford are buried in the North Burial Ground in Providence. The heirs of S. B. Mumford still owned the Garden House and the lot on which it stood when the 1875 Providence atlas was published. Perhaps they only disposed of the property after Mumford's widow died in 1876.

The 1899 Providence *House Directory and Family Address Book* provides a hint to us concerning 66 College Street: the addresses on the north side of College St. immediately west of Prospect St. are listed as follows (see end of paper for directory abbreviations):

64	Sheldon, F. J., Mr. & Mrs., h.	
	Sheldon, Frank A., ins. agt., b.	
68	Pegram, John C., Jr., physician, h.	
70	Bowen, Cordelia J., widow, h.	
	Bowen, E. G., Miss, teacher, h.	
	Bowen, Frank, hardware, etc., b.	

Note there is no house listed at 66 College Street. The mystery is solved by a separate listing for College Court:

1   Cushing, Kate P., tchr., rms.
Cushing, Rebecca R., Mrs., tchr., r.
Dart, Willard C., publisher, rms.
Peck, Robert H., draughtsman, h.
Whipple, Inez, Miss, rms.

The directory indicates that College Court runs [northward] from College in Ward 1. In the 1875 Providence atlas,[1] a walkway separates the President's House[2] of Brown University from the residence of W. H. and C. J. Bowen on the north side of College Street. To the north of these two residences, on Waterman Street, are the homes of S. K. Parsons (abutting the Bowen residence on College Street) and of J. W. C. Ely, abutting the President's House. To the west of the W. H. and C. J. Bowen residence, is property owned by the "Heirs of S. B. Mumford," stretching all the way north to Waterman St. The Garden House, set back a considerable distance from the north side of College Street, occupies this property. The two joined buildings on Waterman St. that eventually became The Paxton (and then The Arsdale), also owned by the Mumford heirs, abut the Garden House property to the north. The Bowen residence was re-

---

1. Plate N on Historic Mapworks. See www.historicmapworks.com/Map/US/32343/Plate+N/Providence+1875+Vol+1+Wards+1+-+2+-+3++East+Providence/Rhode+Island/
2. According to Martha Mitchell's *Encyclopedia Brunoniana*, Brown University's second President's House was dedicated on the corner of Prospect and College Streets In 1840. It was last occupied by Brown's president in 1898. Brown's third President's House was dedicated at 180 Hope Street in 1901. It was replaced by the current President's House (originally built in 1922) at 55 Power Street in 1947.

moved as part of the construction of the John Hay Library in 1910. The President's House was moved further down College St. and was demolished as part of an expansion of the Rhode Island School of Design in 1936.

In the 1918 Providence atlas,[3] a wall separates the John Hay Library from the setback Garden House and the residence of C. H. Robertson to the west on the north side of College Street. The residences of R. Ely and S. K. Parsons abut the John Hay Library to the north on Waterman St. Behind the Garden House and the Robertson residence on Waterman Street is The Paxton, a boarding house later known as The Arsdale.[4]

College Court pops up from time to time in the Providence directories after the Mumford era. In 1847, Frank Thompson ran an eatery and oyster saloon at South College Court and at the Mansion House.[5] In 1865, Anthony Dougherty, partner in the firm of Haywood & Dougherty at 9 Market Square, resided in College Court By 1880, 1 College Court had clearly been cut up into apartments:

---

3. Map 19 scan 4 on Rootsweb. See www.rootsweb.ancestry.com/~rigenweb/maps/1918prov/1918Providence19-2a.jpg

4. HPL's friends Marian Bonner (1883–1952) and Evelyn M. Staples (1860–1938) resided at The Arsdale (55 Waterman Street) in the mid-1930s. They owned several of the cats who loved to sun themselves on the shed behind the Garden House. Helen V. Sully stayed at The Arsdale when she visited in 1933, and Robert H. Barlow stayed there when he visited for over a month in 1936. HPL and his aunt customarily took their holiday meals at The Arsdale.

5. I am not sure that "South College Court" corresponded to "College Court." Edgar Allan Poe had stayed at the Mansion House (formerly the Golden Ball Inn) on Benefit Street when he was courting Sarah Helen Whitman (1803–1878) in 1848. By the twentieth century, the Mansion House had become a cheap rooming house and was demolished in 1941.

> Bowers, Mrs. Lloyd, bds.
> Fish, Sarah, Miss, h.
> Holden, John, farmer, h.
> Jenckes, Thomas, bds.
> Manton, Mary, Mrs., bds.

The 1884 directory listed the residence of Mrs. Leon Chappotin at 1 College Court; and the 1887 directory listed the residence of Mrs. Sarah Rodman at the same address. The five residents of 1 College Court in 1899 were already listed above.

My belief is that the reassignment of 1 College Court as 66 College Street dates to about 1905. In 1906, we find three residents listed at 66 College Street:

> Peck, Robert H., draughtsman, City Engineer's Office, h.
> Price, Albert G., foreman, 157 Orange, 3rd floor, h.
> Roxbury, Harriet E., teacher, State Normal School, h.

The residences that formerly stood at numbers 68 and 70 College Street were eventually removed or demolished for the construction of the John Hay Library, which was dedicated on 11 November 1910.

However, College Court was not the only name for the lane leading back to the Garden House before the number 66 College was assigned in 1905. The 1901 directory contained the following listings for "1 Ely Ct.":

> Crahan, Morris, prop. Crahan Engraving Co., 193 Westminster, h. 1 Ely Court & at Edgewood
> Dart, Willard C. (Dart & Bigelow[6]), 35 Westminster, rm. 3, rms. 1 Ely Ct.

---

6. Dart & Bigelow were translators and correspondents, fluent in English, French, German, and Spanish.

The 1913 and 1923 Providence directories listed Ely Court running from 64 College in Ward 1. The 1917 street directory listed the following addresses on the north side of College Street approaching Prospect Street:

64	Forbes, Anna R. H., Mrs.
	Hayes, Frederick, lawyer, b.
	Ely Ct. begins
000	cor Prospect, John Hay Library

Then, in the 1948 directory, there is an apparent final reference to Ely Court: the listing of streets indicates that Ely Court runs "from College northerly [in] Ward 1."

When H. P. Lovecraft corresponded with Marian Bonner as third assistant secretary on behalf of the Kappa Alpha Tau feline fraternity in 1936, he gave the fraternity's address, as #1, Ely's Court. Whether Ely Court or Ely's Court was ever an official postal address or a public way remains to be determined.[7] It seems that College Court was the more common usage for the lane back to the Garden House during the period 1850–99. The name Ely Court clearly seems to lead back to the Ely family who resided on the southwest corner of Waterman and Prospect (36 Prospect Street) both in 1875 and in 1918.

James Winchell Coleman Ely was born in Vermont in October 1820,[8] the son of Rev. Richard M. Ely (1795–1861) and his

---

7. In 2015, a private walkway (probably Brown University property) ran between the John Hay Library and the List Art Building from College Street to Waterman Street. There is a seating area on lawn of the List Art Building on the Waterman St. side. Several stairways allow the walkway to ascend from College Street to Waterman Street. I am not sure that it is fair to say that this walkway replicates the path of the former Ely Court. However, it is doubtless as good a proxy as we are likely to have for now.

8. The 1900 U.S. census recorded that James W. C. Ely was born in October

wife Lora. He had a younger brother, Francis W. Ely, born eight years later in Springfield, Vermont, who married Sarah E. Hill on 4 April 1859, in Cavendish, Windsor County, Vermont. James Ely became a physician, while his younger brother Francis Ely became an engineer. James Ely married Susan Backus, the daughter of Thomas and Almira (———) Backus, born in Connecticut in September 1824. By 1850, we find the following household in Providence:

> Joseph Cady, age 76, born CT
> Susan Cady, age 73, born VT
> James W. C. Ely, age 29, physician, born VT
> Susan B. Ely, age 25, born CT
> Joseph C. Ely, age 1, born RI
> Mary A. McLane, age 19, born Ireland
> Ann Tierney, age 25, born Ireland

By 1860, James W. C. Ely had his own household in Providence:

> James W. C. Ely, age 39, born VT
> Susan B. Ely, age 35, born CT
> Joseph C. Ely, age 11, born RI
> Edward F. Ely, age 2, born RI
> Joseph Cady, age 89, born CT
> Ann Tierney, age 32, born Ireland

By 1870 the household consisted of:

> James W. C. Ely, age 49, born VT, physician
> Susan B. Ely, age 45, born CT, housekeeper
> Joseph C. Ely, age 21, born RI, student
> Edward F. Ely, age 12, born RI, at school
> Ann Tierney, age 50, born Ireland, servant

1821, but his Swan Point Cemetery record gives his year of birth as 1820.

Joseph Cady Ely (b. 24 March 1849, Providence, R.I.; d. 21 June 1897, Providence, R.I.) and Edward Francis Ely (b. 12 February 1858, Providence, R.I.; d. 1920, Providence, R.I.) were the sons of James W. C. and Susan (Backus) Ely. Joseph C. Ely was an attorney and married Alice Peck (b. November 1854, Massachusetts; d. 14 December 1924, Providence, R.I.). Edward F. Ely was a partner in the firm of Hoppin & Ely, architects and remained single. The 1880 census enumerated James W. C. Ely, his wife Susan, their son Edward F., and two servants at 36 Prospect St.[9] The 1900 census enumerated James W. C. Ely, Susan (Backus) Ely, and their son Edward F. Ely and two servants at 36 Prospect St. The same census recorded Alice P. Ely, widow of James C. Ely, and her daughter Ruth Ely (b. 3 May 1881, Providence, R.I.; d. June 1973) at 94 Waterman Street. In 1903, James W. C. Ely and his son Edward F. Ely still resided at 36 Prospect Street; James still kept his doctor's office at 61 Waterman, and the firm of Hoppin & Ely, architects, was located at 32 Westminster Street. In the same year, Alice (Peck) Ely, widow of Joseph C. Ely, was residing at 94 Waterman Street.

James W. C. Ely and his wife Susan (Backus) Ely were both long-lived. James died in Providence on 6 May 1906, age eighty-five, and his widow Susan followed him in death on 23 December 1909, also age eighty-five. In 1910 and 1915, their son Edward F. Ely lived at 36 Prospect Street with two servants. In 1920, Alice Ely, widow of Joseph C. Ely, and her daughter Ruth Ely lived at 94 Waterman Street with two servants. Ruth Ely obtained a passport for European travel on 11 December 1923—a photograph accompanied her passport application. Ruth Ely remained single and was still living at 94 Waterman Street (with

---

9. 36 Prospect Street, on the southwest corner of Waterman and Prospect Streets, is still standing in 2015.

two servants) in 1940.[10] The whole extended Ely family—James W. C. Ely (1820–1906), Susan (Backus) Ely (1824–1909), Edward Francis Ely (1858–1920), Joseph C. Ely (1849–1897), Alice (Peck) Ely (1854–1924), and Ruth Ely (1881–1973)—are buried in Swan Point Cemetery in Providence.

The Ely family left such an imprint on the immediate neighborhood that Ely Court (once known as College Court) appeared in Providence directories as late 1948, twelve years after Lovecraft corresponded with Marian Bonner. From 1905 until its removal to 65 Prospect Street in 1959, the Garden House bore 66 College Street as its postal address. I will pass by most of the tenants from 1905 until 1941: we already know two of them, Annie E. (Phillips) Gamwell in 1933–41 and H. P. Lovecraft in 1933–37. They occupied the second-floor flat. The 1928–42 tenant of the first-floor flat, Alice Rachel Sheppard, deserves to be better known to Lovecraftians than she is. Alice Rachel Sheppard was born in Phoenix, Warwick, R.I., on 10 September 1870 to Rev. Theodore William Sheppard (b. 2 December 1833, New Jersey; d. 16 December 1892, R.I.) and his wife Jane (Porter) Sheppard (b. 9 August 1833, Rochester, N.Y.; d. 9 March 1915, Providence, R.I.).[11] Her father was the son of Nathan Sheppard and Rachel Cook,[12] who married in Cumberland County, New Jersey, on 7 April 1814. In 1850, Theodore Sheppard, age fifteen, was apparently apprenticed to

---

10. 94 Waterman Street, on the north side of Waterman Street between Brown Street and Thayer Street, is still standing in 2015.

11. The death certificate of Alice Rachel Sheppard's brother William Carey Sheppard gives the names of his parents as Theodore W. Sheppard and Jane P. Richardson. I follow the Find-A-Grave record from Greenwood Cemetery in Coventry, R.I., in giving her mother's maiden name as Jane Porter.

12. Perhaps the Rachel Sheppard who died in Bowentown, N.J., of dropsy on 28 July 1849.

James A. Welden as a tailor in Bridgeton, Cumberland County, New Jersey.[13] The 1880 census recorded the following family in Warwick, R.I.: Theodore W. Sheppard, age forty-six, born New Jersey of New Jersey–born parents, clergyman; Jane P. Sheppard, age forty-six, wife, born New York of New Hampshire–born father and New York–born mother; William C. Sheppard, age thirteen, son, born New Hampshire of New Jersey–born father and New York–born mother; and Alice R. Sheppard, daughter, age nine, born Rhode Island of New Jersey–born father and New York–born mother. Rev. Theodore W. Sheppard served as pastor of the Mt. Vernon Christian Society in Foster, R.I., from 1889 until his death in 1892.[14] His son Rev. William Carey Sheppard (b. 1866 New Hampshire; d. 14 January 1909, Plaistow, Rockingham, N.H.) was also a clergyman.[15]

---

13. This fact leads me to believe that he probably did not belong to the following Fairfield, Cumberland County, N.J., family (all born N.J.) in 1850: Nathan Sheppard, age 53, farmer; Sarah Sheppard, age 54; William Sheppard, age 19, farmer; Cornelia Sheppard, age 17; Benjamin Sheppard, age 15; and Joseph Sheppard, age 10. This Nathan Sheppard (b. 26 July 1796, N.J.; d. 9 March 1855, Fairfield Township, Cumberland County, N.J.) married Sarah B. Rose (b. 7 March 1794; d. 3 July 1879) on 19 March 1817 in Cumberland County, N.J. They are buried in Old Stone Church Cemetery, Fairfield, Cumberland County, N.J. Alternative dates of b. 12 December 1797, N.J., d. 11 January 1881, Cumberland, N.J. are also found for Sarah B. (Rose) Sheppard. Her son William Rose Sheppard (b. 22 September 1831, Cedarville, Cumberland County, N.J.; d. 12 March 1879, Cape May, N.J.) became a physician.

14. The new church was dedicated on 29 August 1889. Rev. Theodore W. Sheppard preached the dedication sermon, and Rev. George W. Kennedy (1824–1900) offered the dedication prayer. Thereafter, Rev. Sheppard preached three Sundays per month at Mt. Vernon Christian Society until his death in 1892.

15. William Carey Sheppard married Annie Nye Peaslee (1866–1952), the daughter of Ruben Peaslee (1810–1875) and Harriet —— (1823–1893)

66 College ca. 1920 showing the doorway in back annex section and The Arsdale (with fire escape) across the backyard. Courtesy Providence Public Library, John Hutchins Cady Scrapbook No. 119.

Alice Rachel Sheppard had a distinguished career as a language teacher. She graduated from Boston University with an A.B. degree in 1892. She was a member of Kappa Kappa Gamma sorority, and was president of the Gamma Delta chapter, as well as vice president of her class, in her senior year in 1891–92. She was also assistant editor of the student magazines *Beacon* and *Hub* and a member of the Philological Society. She specialized in the German language and pursued her studies in Göttingen in 1899. She returned to Providence, where she obtained her A.M. degree from Brown University in 1900.[16] She was living with her

---

on 28 December 1889, in Haverhill, Mass. They had children William Theodore Sheppard (1891–1907), Katherine Sheppard (1897–1984), Edson Peaslee Sheppard Sr. (1900–1978), and Harriel Rachel Sheppard (1909–1925). William Carey Sheppard, his wife, his son William Theodore Sheppard, and his daughters Katherine and Harriet Rachel Sheppard are buried with his sister Alice Rachel Sheppard and their parents in Greenwood Cemetery, Coventry, R.I.

16. *Liber Brunensis* for 1899 listed her as a master of arts candidate in fine arts and German.

widowed mother Jane (Porter) Sheppard at 38 Congdon Street and teaching at Classical High School in 1901. She studied in Berlin in 1902–03 and returned to become head of the German Department at Classical High School in Providence. She went on to serve as director of the New England Modern Language Association in 1912–15 and as president of the Rhode Island chapter of the Association of Collegiate Alumnae in 1914–16.[17]

In 1908–09, Miss Sheppard took her seventy-four-year-old widowed mother Jane (Porter) Sheppard along with her while she taught a term at Fontainebleau in France. She continued to live at 38 Congdon Street after the death of her mother in 1915, and still lived there as late as 1924. Then, in 1928, she took up residence at 66 College Street, where she remained through 1942. In the 1930s, she took annual trips to Europe, returning to New York City from Bremen on the *Europa* on 7 September 1932; from Bremen on the *Columbus* on 5 September 1933; from Hamburg on the *Hamburg* on 7 September 1934; and from Naples on the *Comte di Savoia* on 7 September 1935. She told her upstairs neighbor H. P. Lovecraft of the darkening situation in Germany under the Nazi dictatorship, and he began to modify his views based on her intelligence. After Lovecraft died, Miss Sheppard returned to New York City from one further European trip on 21 December 1938, having sailed from Trieste on the *Roma*.

Alice Rachel Sheppard was still living at 66 College Street in 1942, after Annie Gamwell had died on 29 January 1941. She had probably retired from teaching at Classical High School by the mid-1930s. She survived her friend Annie Gamwell by more than twenty years. The 1947–49 Providence directories listed her at 40 Benevolent Street. The 1953–60 Providence directories listed her at 389 Angell Street. She died on 2 July 1961, at the age

---

17. Most of this biographical information concerning Miss Sheppard derives from *General Alumni Catalogue of Boston University* (1918).

of ninety, and was buried with her parents and her brother William Carey Sheppard in Greenwood Cemetery in Coventry, R.I.

One more resident of 66 College Street with a tangential connection with H. P. Lovecraft remains: Mary Spink, who lived at 66 College from 1938 to 1947. She was a friend of Mrs. Gamwell, rather than of her nephew, who had died in 1937. Mary Spink had been born in Providence on 19 July 1877, the daughter of Judge Joseph Edwin Spink (1842–1910) and Emma Elizabeth Hudson (1848–1937). The 1900 census enumerated the following household (all born R.I.) at 150 South Angell Street in Providence: Joseph Spink (head), born July 1842, married 1873/74, municipal court judge; Emma R. Spink (wife), born January 1848, eight children borne, five living; Mary Spink (daughter), born July 1877, single; Alice G. Spink (daughter), born September 1879, single; Hope Spink (daughter), born July 1884, single; Martha E. Spink (daughter), born May 1887; and Agatha Spink (daughter), born May 1891, single. (Irish-born servant Julia A. Sullivan, born April 1875, was also in the household.) The family resided at the same address in 1910. All five surviving daughters remained single and members of their parents' household. Joseph Spink was now a probate judge. Daughter Alice G. Spink worked as assistant manager of a settlement house. Niece Dorothy E. Newton, age thirteen, born 1892/93 RI, had replaced servant Julia A. Sullivan.

Mary Spink had in the meantime obtained her A.B. degree from Wellesley College in 1899. She followed with an A.M. degree from Brown University in 1902. Perhaps she and Miss Sheppard were fellow graduate students at Brown. After the death of Judge Spink in 1910, Mary Spink lived with her widowed mother at 84 Cushing Street in Providence. In 1920, Emma Spink's niece Dorothy Newton, age twenty-three, single, born 1892/93 in Massachusetts of R.I.-born father and N.H.-

born mother, was residing with them and working as a government typist. Neither Emma Spink nor her daughter Mary Spink were then employed. By 1924, however, Mary Spink had become a notary public. She had probably already begun her longtime career as a title research clerk at Title Guarantee Co. of Rhode Island at 66 South Main. She continued to be listed at 84 Cushing Street until she removed to 230 Brown Street in 1936–37. Then, in 1938, she took up residence at 66 College Street, where she remained through 1947. She evidently became friends with Annie E. (Phillips) Gamwell, for in 1940 she compiled a rough catalogue of H. P. Lovecraft's library, which forms the basis for most of the listings in S. T. Joshi's *Lovecraft's Library*. After leaving 66 College Street, she lived at 34 Jenckes Street from 1949 onward. She continued to work for Title Guarantee Co. of Rhode Island through at least 1956. The 1964 Providence directory continued to list her at 34 Jenckes Street, but finally added the notation "retd." She died in December 1968, age ninety-one.

In 1940, Mrs. Gamwell's niece Helen M. Morrish, age fifty-five, a Canadian-born practical nurse, resided with Mrs. Gamwell in the second-story flat at 66 College Street. But by the mid-1940s, Brown University, which owned 66 College Street, began to rent the premises mainly to junior faculty and other staff members. Mary B. Gilson (1945–46) and Mary Spink (1938–47) may have been the last renters without direct Brown University connections. (Of course, Miss Spink was an alumna.) Assistant professor Juan Lopez-Morillas and his wife Frances M. were tenants in 1944–47. Assistant professor Edward J. Brown and his wife Catherine were tenants in 1952–57. The Browns must have liked the Garden House; they were still residing there in 1957, after Edward J. Brown had been promoted to full professor. Carroll Rikert, Jr., controller of accounts for Brown University, and his wife Jane W. were tenants in 1953–54. Assistant professor Gene B. Carpenter and his wife Elizabeth C. were tenants in 1956. Assistant professor William Deminoff and his wife Elizabeth were also tenants in 1956. Research associate Cornelius Haas was a tenant in 1957. He was the final tenant I found before the removal of the Garden House from 66 College Street to 65 Prospect Street in 1959.

One famous owner of the property at 65 Prospect Street was John C. A. Watkins (1912–2000), who served with distinction in World War II, joined the *Providence Journal* in 1950, and served as its publisher from 1954 to 1979, its CEO until 1983, and its chairman until 1985. He married (1) Helen Danforth (1922–2014), but they divorced and she married (2) Patrick B. Buchanan. John C. A. Watkins took the actress Jane Watkins (1915/16–1989) as his second wife in 1960. In more recent years, Edward R. Feller, M.D., Clinical Professor of Medicine at Brown University, a gastro-enterologist and internist, has been owner of 65 Prospect Street.[18] The "Garden House" at 65 Prospect Street is still maintained as beautifully as H. P. Lovecraft and Annie E. (Phillips) Gamwell might have wished. Brown University's starkly modern List Art Building now occupies the site where the Garden House once stood. I do not know whether mail addressed to 1 College Court or 1 Ely Court would reach Brown's art department.

Many questions relating to the Garden House remain. The

---

18. The magnificent mansion of Thomas Lloyd Halsey (1751–1838)—reportedly haunted by a piano-playing ghost in HPL's time—is only a few blocks north at 140 Prospect St. Halsey himself is buried in St. John's Churchyard, where HPL loved to take visitors to Providence. He and his wife are buried immediately west of the church building and have tall monuments. The Cathedral of St. John was closed by the Episcopal Diocese in 2012 because of rising maintenance costs and declining attendance. In 2014, the diocese announced its interest in partnering with the State of Rhode Island to reopen the former cathedral as a museum dedicated to the slave trade.

question of its dating should be considered in greater depth. Is it possible that the rear "ell" represents an older building to which the main part of the Garden House was later attached? The 1918 Providence atlas shows the immediate locale of the Garden House in much the same state as H. P. Lovecraft may have known it in 1933–37. The 1918 atlas shows an outbuilding adjoining the western property line of The Paxton (and the residence of I. Tucker). This outbuilding or shed would have been visible from the southwestern windows of Lovecraft's study, because of the setback of #66 from the north side of College Street. The 1918 atlas map shows clearly how deeply recessed the Garden House was from College Street. Nevertheless, questions about the detailed layout of the Garden House property doubtless remain. One wonders what delightful plantings may have earned the house its name. The history of all the wonderful cats who convened as the Kappa Alpha Tau fraternity on the shed rooftop also remains to be written. It could doubtlessly be reconstructed based on Lovecraft's letters to Miss Bonner and others.

It would be interesting to have more details concerning succession of ownership of the Garden House. At what time subsequent to 1875 was the property sold by the Mumford heirs? Could there have been owners before Samuel Brenton Mumford and his wife Louisa G. (Dexter) Mumford? Do the Colonial Dames of Rhode Island have photographs of the Garden House during the 1920s? Snapshots of Annie E. (Phillips) Gamwell and of H. P. Lovecraft in the doorway of the Garden House are the only known published exterior photographs from the 1930s, while Robert H. Barlow's photographs from 1937 are the only known published interior photographs from the same period. One can only go so far with Internet research.[19] The next stage

---

19. Sanborn fire maps of Providence RI are available on the Internet, but

of progress on the Garden House will require hands-on research using Providence resources.

Clark Ashton Smith expressed the wish that Lovecraft's study at 66 College St.—including all the books, paintings, furniture and mementos—might be preserved as a museum. The sad reality was that the only asset considered worthy of inclusion in the inventory of the author's estate was a $500 mortgage on a Providence quarry, which was not finally paid off until 1957, at which time Horace B. Knowles & Sons was probably paid the remaining unpaid balance due for the author's 1937 funeral.[20] Lovecraft's library—despite its 1940 cataloging by Mary Spink— was not sold until after the death of Annie E. (Phillips) Gamwell in 1941. I do not know how much the sale of the books to H. Douglass Dana raised for her estate. Fortunately, young Robert H. Barlow traveled to Providence shortly after the death of his mentor and assured the preservation of the author's manuscripts at the neighboring John Hay Library with the cooperation of Professor S. Foster Damon. Out of consideration for the privacy of the grieving Annie Gamwell, Barlow stayed at the downtown YMCA rather than at The Arsdale. The beauty of 65 Prospect Street (formerly 66 College Street) remains. We can share the joy of Annie E. (Phillips) Gamwell and H. P. Lovecraft in their final home. I hope it will remain a focus for Lovecraftian visitors to Providence for decades—if not for centuries—to come. Showing private property owners the same courtesy that Robert H. Barlow showed to Annie Gamwell in 1937 will help to assure the preservation of 65 Prospect St. and the other Lovecraft shrines of Providence.

---

only on a proprietary pay-for-use basis.
20. An excellent consideration of HPL's literary estate, including reproductions of many documents, is posted www.aetherial.net/lovecraft/index.html) by Chris J. Karr under the title "The Black Seas of Copyright."

I hope this essay has shed some light on the house where H. P. Lovecraft spent the last four years of his life. Alice Rachel Sheppard (1870–1961) and Mary Spink (1877–1968) were both well-educated ladies who deserve more than mere footnotes in the story of H. P. Lovecraft's life and posthumous literary reputation. I hope this essay has paid some justifiable tribute to their memory. It is more difficult to summon up the shades of figures more remotely involved in the history of the Garden House at 66 College Street—perhaps Samuel Brenton Mumford, Louisa G. (Dexter) Mumford, James Winchell Coleman Ely, Susan (Backus) Ely, and all the others who resided in the immediate locale will be difficult to rescue from the shadows. We can only hope that the other residents found as much happiness in living in the Garden House as did H. P. Lovecraft and his aunt.

Directory Abbreviations:
h. = house   bds. = boards   retd. = retired
r. = resides   rms. = rooms

Works Cited

Joshi, S. T., and David E. Schultz. *Lovecraft's Library: A Catalogue*. New York: Hippocampus Press, 4th ed. 2017.

Matthews, Margery I.; Benson, Virginia I.; and Wilson, Arthur E. *Churches of Foster: A History of Religious Life in Rural Rhode Island*. Foster, RI: North Foster Baptist Church, 1978.

Mitchell, Martha. *Encyclopedia Brunoniana*. Providence, RI: Brown University Library, 1993. Online at www.brown.edu/Administration/News_Bureau/Databases/Encyclopedia/search.php?serial=P0390

Wolf, Raymond A. *Foster*. Charleston, SC: Arcadia Publishing, 2012.

Note: Vital statistics quoted in this article can be confirmed using FamilySearch (LDS) and Ancestry.

The Fiction

John Osborne Austin's Seven Club Tales: Did They Inspire Lovecraft?

John Osborne Austin (1849–1918) is primarily remembered as an author of genealogical works, most notably *The Genealogical Dictionary of Rhode Island* (1887). However, he was also an author of fiction. His book-length works of fiction are listed in the appendix, "Works of Fiction by John Osborne Austin." Three of these books, as indicated in the appendix, were owned by H. P. Lovecraft—at least one of them an inheritance from his uncle Franklin C. Clark. It is these works of fiction that constitute the link between Austin and Lovecraft. I will begin with a short sketch of Austin's life and then discuss his fictional works and their possible influence on Lovecraft. I am grateful to the Rhode Island State Archives for some of the information concerning Austin and his relatives and to David E. Schultz for several citations of Lovecraft letters, but I remain solely responsible for any errors and all opinions in this paper.

The Life of John Osborne Austin

In his paternal line, Austin was of the seventh generation in descent from Robert Austin, of Kingstown, Rhode Island, in 1661. The four generations of paternal ancestors preceding John Osborne Austin were all members of the Quaker faith. His father, Samuel Austin (1816–1897), was born in Nantucket, Massachusetts, but came to Providence in 1828. He was a teacher at the Friends' School in Providence as early as 1838. He married Elizabeth Hanson (1820–1899) in Smithfield, Rhode Island, in 1843. From 1847 to 1868, he conducted the Union Hall School in Providence. From 1868 until his retirement in 1874, he served as agent for the Rhode Island Educational Union, which promoted the establishment of evening schools and public libraries in manufacturing villages.

John Osborne Austin had siblings Katharine Hanson Austin (1844–1926), Mary Louise Austin (1847–1936), William Samuel Austin (1854–1874), and Rachel Austin (1859–1917). None of his siblings ever married. By 1872, Samuel Austin lived at 85 Congdon Street in Providence.[1] His daughters continued to live there into the 1930s.

John Osborne Austin married Helen Augusta Whitaker (1853–1916), the daughter of William and Emma Louise (Barker) Whitaker, in 1878. They had two children, a son, Richard Sisson Austin (1885–1948), and a daughter, Rosamond Whitaker Austin (1879–1949).

Helen Augusta (Whitaker) Austin (1853–1916), from frontispiece of A Modern Love Chase/Peggy Rogers/ An Incompetent *(1916).*

Richard Sisson Austin (1885–1948).

---

1. As early as 1847, he had lived at 60 Congdon Street. Later addresses included 56 Congdon (1857–71) and 85 Congdon (1872–97).

The Austin family home at 85 Congdon Street, Providence.

A biographical sketch of John Osborne Austin appeared in *Representative Men and Old Families of Rhode Island* (Chicago: J. H. Beers & Co., 1908, 1.99–100). I extract the following passages, omitting the description of Austin's foreign travels in 1872–73 and 1893:

> John Osborne Austin, as stated in the foregoing, was born Dec. 28, 1849, in Providence, R.I. He received his education at the Primary, Intermediate and Grammar schools, leaving the latter after a few months, and then attending for some years the Union Hall School, on Westminster street, kept by his father. In 1866 he took a clerkship with the firm of Brownell & Rathbone, wool dealers, three years later becoming bookkeeper and salesman for D. L. Brownell. In 1871 he commenced business for himself as a wool dealer. Closing his business out in 1872 he took passage from New York to Glasgow in the steamer "Anglia . . ."
>
> In 1873 Mr. Austin resumed the wool business,[2] purchasing on commission in Maine that season, the next year on joint account in

---

2. He was a broker at 121 Dyer in 1872. He was a wool dealer at 25 South Water in 1874 and 23 South Water in 1877. He later kept offices as a publisher at 27 Custom House Street (1887) and 96 Westminster Street (1895–1914).

New York State, and in subsequent years on commission in Maine, New Hampshire, Vermont, New York, Georgia and Virginia. Spare intervals of his time (including many evenings) were used between 1873 and 1883, in preparing a family history of his own ancestors and later of his wife's ancestry, her father having left papers which showed an attempt in the same direction. During 1883 and nine subsequent years his time was devoted to the genealogy of Rhode Island families, resulting in the publication, in 1887, of "The Genealogical Dictionary of Rhode Island," in 1889 of "The Ancestry of Thirty-three Rhode Islanders," and in 1891 of "The Ancestral Dictionary." Much time was also given during the latter part of this period to developing the sale of these books. Contributions were frequently made to magazines, on genealogical subjects, and to newspapers advocating broader suffrage.

Helen (Whitaker) Austin died on 4 April 1916. Her husband followed her in death on 27 October 1918. They were both buried in Swan Point Cemetery in Providence.[3] In 1880, John O. Austin and his family lived with his mother-in-law, Mrs. William Whitaker, at 33 High Street in Providence; he was the householder there as late as 1887. However, by 1901 he and his wife and children had removed to 113 George Street.[4] After the death of his wife in 1916, he joined his sisters in the family home at 85 Congdon Street for the rest of his life.

The Fiction of John Osborne Austin

While Lovecraft also owned a copy of *Philip and Philippa* (1901), it was Austin's first two published book-length works of fiction, *The Journal of William Jefferay, Gentleman* (1899) and *More Seven Club Tales* (1900), which would have been of prima-

---

3. Their son, Richard Sisson Austin, and their daughter, Rosamond Whitaker Austin, are also buried at Swan Point.
4. This dwelling was demolished when Brown University constructed its Wriston Quadrangle.

ry interest to him. His copy of *The Journal of William Jefferay, Gentleman* had originally been presented to his uncle Franklin C. Clark (1847–1915) by the author.⁵ Clark, a noted antiquary in his own right, was the contemporary not only of Austin but of other Rhode Island historians such as Sidney S. Rider (1833–1917), James N. Arnold (1844–1927),⁶ and Thomas W. Bicknell (1834–1925). Whether Lovecraft himself ever had the occasion to meet Austin is not known. It would certainly have been natural that some of these local historians might have foregathered from time to time to discuss their research, but whether Dr. Clark's nephew was ever invited as a guest—even to a session held at Dr. Clark's final home at 38 Barnes Street—may be doubted.⁷

---

5. This copy was offered for sale by California Book Auction Galleries in their catalogue *Science Fiction & Fantasy with Manuscripts & Original Art,* item 584. The auction sale (number 218) was held on 4 May 1985. The item, estimated at $80–$120, actually sold for $37.50. The detailed description ran as follows: "584 [Lovecraft, Howard Phillips, his copy] Austin, John Osborne, ed. (but actually the author) THE JOURNAL OF WILLIAM JEFFERAY, GENTLEMAN . . . A DIARY THAT MIGHT HAVE BEEN. Rebound in cloth. First edition. (Providence: E. L. Freeman, 1909) This copy presented by the author to HPL's uncle F. C. Clark, with presentation letter inserted before title; with HPL's signature & address on front free endpaper, his bookplate on front pastedown. Dampstained throughout, seriously to title page & letter but curiously not affecting front endpapers, which are darkening, the free one split halfway up gutter edge; otherwise a good copy only." Collectors are often quite particular about condition, and perhaps this book's defects accounted for its relatively low hammer price. The bookseller's dating to 1909 is curious: I have not seen copies of this book as published by Austin (and printed for him by E. L. Freeman) dated other than 1899.

6. Arnold dedicated the first volume of his *Vital Record of Rhode Island* to Dr. Clark.

7. I posited such a meeting at Dr. Clark's home in 1912 or 1913 in my

There seem to be no references to Austin's fiction in Lovecraft's surviving letters. The only reference to Austin's work is to Lovecraft's consulting a copy of *The Genealogical Dictionary of Rhode Island* at the Rhode Island Historical Society cabinet on Waterman Street in his letter to Wilfred B. Talman dated 19 March 1929 (*WBT* 108–9).[8] Considering his strong interest in Rhode Island history, there is little doubt that Lovecraft delved into *The Journal of William Jefferay, Gentleman* and *More Seven Club Tales*. If he ever glanced over *Philip and Philippa* (1901), he would likely have been disappointed: two remotely related cousins fall in love, and chase each other over the globe until they find each other. Austin's other two subsequent volumes, *A Week's Wooing and Dolph and Dolly* (1902) and *A Modern Love Chase/Peggy Rogers/An Incompetent* (1916), are much the same sort of stuff, like the romances of Fred Jackson that Lovecraft excoriated in the letter column of *Argosy*.

The Journal of William Jefferay, Gentleman is woven around the life of early Rhode Island settler William Jefferay (1591–1675), who came to the New World in 1623. He settled first in Weymouth and married Mary Gould in 1640, but disagreeing with the Bay's harsh treatment of dissenters, he removed to Newport, Rhode Island, by 1641. He was encouraged by his wife to commence the keeping of a diary, which Austin has reconstructed from its beginning through its final entry made on 1

---

story "Collectors the Sixth and Seventh" in Kenneth W. Faig, Jr., *Lovecraft's Pillow and Other Strange Stories* (New York: Hippocampus Press, 2013), 107–28.

8. HPL indicated that he had never consulted this work before. He consulted it as part of researching his Casey line. Austin believed that HPL's Casey ancestors were of English origin, while other authorities such as John O'Hart (*Irish Pedigrees: or, The Origin and Stem of the Irish Nation* [New York: Murphy & McCarthy, 1923]) believed them to be of Irish origin.

January 1675, the day before Jefferay expired. If there is a fictional personage in *The Journal of William Jefferay, Gentleman*, I have not succeeded in identifying him or her. Jefferay records all the notable New England events of the day, including the excesses of the Quaker persecution, culminating in the hanging of Mary Dyer in 1660. However, it is sometimes his more domestic notes which touch the hearts of modern readers. A topical index (*Jefferay* 165–79) is a great aid in finding some of the more appealing passages. For example, Jefferay records the results of a blackberry-picking expedition:

> [1654] Sep. 1, Friday. Blackberrying with my wife, and brother Daniel Gould, and his wife. The berries are most large and sweet this year, the weather having favoured their growing. My wife gave us part of them in a pudding, for supper, her brother and his wife staying with us to help eat it. They agreed, as did all of us, that it was the best they had tasted, being of very light crust, with the berries massed together inside, and served with a sweet creamy sauce. (*Jefferay* 41)

Not all bounty came from the land:

> [1654] Mar. 27. . . . . In coming home from the cliffs where I had fished, I stopped upon the beach, and found that the late gale had thrown upon the shore some great sea clams, that though not fit for baking (like the smaller kind upon our bay), yet make a most excellent broth which my wife relisheth much. She hath not seemed of her usual health for a day or two, and this broth may hearten her. I had caught a few chogsets also in my fishing, which, though little esteemed by most, do make the best of chowder, from their sweetness, though 'tis true they be exceeding bony. (*Jefferay* 39–40)

Some of the most notable nature writing in *Jefferay* can be found in "The Rock Excursion" (47–50),[9] "The Woods Excursion" (50–53), and "The Bird Excursion" (53–56).

---

9. Part of the "rock excursion" was a visit to Purgatory Chasm, where ac-

But the central interest for Lovecraft in *Jefferay* must have been the group of tales with which Jefferay and six of his acquaintances, dubbed the Seven Club from their number, regaled themselves at weekly intervals in their respective homes, beginning on New Year's Day 1669. Jefferay himself explained the origin of the tale-telling:

> As the books we have are now mostly read, and some due unto us from England still delayed in the coming, it hath been proposed, this winter, that, for the next seven weeks, meetings shall be held of a Friday evening at seven of the clock, each member telling a tale at his own house. So now we are met, this New Year's Even, at my house, being somewhat the elder, and thus to tell the first tale. (*Jefferay* 80)

Mr. Jefferay[10] begins with "The Sea Serpent; or, The Strange Visitor" (*Jefferay* 80–86). On a fishing expedition to the Isles of

---

cording to legend an Indian maiden was murdered: "Coming now to the great fissure close by the western end of Sachuest Beach, my son would fain try to jump where the Indian maid did meet her fate; but this must not be, now or hereafter, as I shortly told him" (*Jefferay* 48). The site overlooks Sachuest [Second] Beach in Middletown, Rhode Island. The trailhead is on Tuckerman Avenue at 41° 29' 14.47" N, 71° 16' 9.89" W. A 0.3-mile trail leads to the chasm. A small pedestrian bridge allows viewing of the chasm. (Note: There is another Purgatory Chasm, with its own legend, in Sutton, Massachusetts.) Middletown's Purgatory Chasm is not among the places HPL mentions visiting during the visit of E. Hoffmann Price in early July 1933 (*JFM* 332–33; *IAP* 854), but HPL did subsequently visit Purgatory Chasm, when Robert E. Moe visited on 27–28 April 1935 (see HPL to E. Hoffmann Price, 4–7 May 1935, and HPL to Richard F. Searight, 31 May 1935). In both these letters he mentions visiting (on Saturday, 27 April 1935) "the strange rock cleft called 'Purgatory,' where the ocean ['sea' in the letter to Searight] pounds thunderously in."

10. William Jefferay, born 1591, died 2 January 1675. See Jefferay 142–43 and GDRI 111.

Shoals,[11] he and his friends are visited by a strange man of nautical appearance, with a large ring in his left ear only, who after demanding a pipe of tobacco, tells his tale in a haze of smoke. He warns Jefferay and his companions to depart before the end of the following day, lest they be eaten by a sea-serpent that lives in a cavern directly below them. The narrator had saved himself from drowning by floating on one of the serpent's scales, which rubbed off when the serpent squeezed into the hole leading to its den. He witnessed the serpent devour a group of mermaids: "Me thinks I can hear their shrieks now, and the noise of his crunching of them; and they of such exceeding beauty, and pretty, playful ways in their gambolling, that it seemed more the pity to have such a fate. It almost makes me weep, the thought of it." To this narration, Jefferay adds: "Yet I perceived not that he did weep, except a queer sniffling be that" (*Jefferay* 84). When Jefferay challenges the visitor with the suggestion that he might be trying to scare them away from his own fishing grounds, only the same sounds of oars which had announced the visitor's appearance announces his departure.

Mr. Arnold[12] follows with the second tale on 8 January, "The Goblin Land; or, The Devil's Healing" (*Jefferay* 86–91). The narrator encountered on one of his trading missions a Mohawk sachem who begged leave to accompany him home to Narragansett. While the narrator's cargo is being loaded, the sachem accompanies him to view the awesome falls at Niagara. The sachem tells him the story of an ancient Indian, who is kidnapped by another tribe from his home near Niagara. Carried far west by his captors, he falls ill, and they (having grown fond of

---

11. The Isles of Shoals are a group of small islands and tidal ledges about six miles off the coast of the border of Maine and New Hampshire.

12. Benedict Arnold, born 21 December 1615, died 19 June 1678. See Jefferay 142 and GDRI 242.

him) propose to take him to be healed by a hot spring in the "Goblin Land," or "Land of the Wicked Spirits." Traveling through snow-capped mountains, they come to a lush region, where he is quickly cured by bathing in the hot springs. He witnesses "great spouting springs" that recall for the modern reader the geysers of Yellowstone. Below the springs lives a ferocious goblin who loves to torture and then to devour his victims. The goblin bellows with rage when the visitors would fain escape from his domain, but their "spirits grew strong, and they hastened away from the cursed enchantment of a region which, only for the goblins, would be a wonder well worth a pilgrimage to try and find."

Mr. Coddington[13] follows with "The Secret Meeting; or, How a Good Baking May Come From a Cold Oven" (*Jefferay* 92–95) on January 15. In Boston, Lincolnshire, England, dissenters have to meet in secret during the days of King James I. The narrator's father helped to plan these secret meetings. Their strategy was as follows: "To hold one meeting, by a few, in a seeming secret place (but not unreadily found); while another, for the rest to worship, should be the real secret." The real secret meeting is held at the workplace of a baker belonging to the dissenters, who because of his connection with the group must keep one of his two large ovens cold on account of lack of patronage. The disused oven is the real secret meeting place. Feeling hungry, one of the sheriff's officers proposes to visit the dissenting baker, but eventually dismisses the sounds he hears from the disused oven as rats. The hungry official nearly loses his office as a result of his buying bread from the dissenting baker, so all the sheriff's men avoid future visits to the site of the secret meetings.

---

13. William Coddington, born 1601, died 1 November 1678. See Jefferay 142 and GDRI 276.

Mr. Brenton[14] follows with "The Witch of Hammersmith; or, How an Ill-Advised Journey Gained Not Honour or Profit" (*Jefferay* 95–102) on January 22. As an ambitious young man in Hammersmith, in Old England, the narrator makes bold to visit an evil witch to elicit knowledge as to what his future might be. When he comes to her dwelling at dusk, he refuses an invitation to drink from her evil brew and is dismissed with no prophecy, but with the command to circle a not too-distant oak tree three times, and if greeted with "To-whit! To-whit!" by the attending owl, to dig for a ring on the south side of the tree. He hears the owl's cries as predicted by the witch and recovers the ring, which bears the inscription "Go forth and prosper." So, with his father's permission, he ventures forth to the Levant, but prospers not, and returns only to find his dear father deceased for a month. He concludes by showing his ring to his fellow Seven Club members.

Mr. Brinley[15] follows with "The Ghostly Revel; or, The Fair Nun's Gift" (*Jefferay* 103–7) on January 22. A ruined castle and a ruined nunnery lie near Datchet, Buckinghamshire, where the narrator was born. Returning home from a neighboring village near midnight, he encounters a man in knight's attire near what appears to be a door to the nunnery. The knight says: "We had hoped to see you, and your partner is even now expecting you at her side, to dance a measure with her." A dozen beautiful nuns line one side of the hall, while eleven knights, whom he joins, line the other, and they proceed to dance, "most gravely and sedately at first, but with more liveliness and merriment soon." Knights and nuns enjoy "most excellent wine at one end of the

---

14. William Brenton, died 1 December 1674. See Jefferay 138–39 and GDRI 212.

15. Francis Brinley, born 15 November 1632, died autumn 1719. See Jefferay 142 and GDRI 256.

room, from a great silver flagon, to which we would, as occasion required, betake us, and pledge each other, in some curiously wrought silver cups." The narrator finds that his partner "was of such dainty ways and manners, as quite delighted me, the more I talked with her." The beautiful nun finally announces that they must soon part, and presses upon him a ring with the explanation: "My father dying, I vowed I would love no man, losing him, and so became a nun; yet have we one night in the year when we do dance this measure, which I have done but heavily, till to-night; but now, since meeting thee—" But the knight who invited him into the hall appears and announces that the narrator is called for at the door. When the narrator complies, the music falls silent, all goes dark, and the door closes behind him. When he returns by daylight, he finds only ruins; his friends speculate that he may have fallen in with robbers who wished to frighten everyone away from their lair. The ring bears the inscription: "None so fair." He tells his listeners: "My wife seemeth to set little store by this ring, and would fain have me melt it to a better shape and use than thus hanging to my chain; but I keep it there, as I do tell her, not for any love of it, now, but that, perchance, some one wiser, seeing it, may tell the meaning of it; none doing so yet, to my satisfaction."

Mr. Clark[e][16] continues with "The Wrecked Galleon; or, The Second Coming of the Strange Visitor" (*Jefferay* 107–15) on February 5. His tale features a second appearance by the strange nautical visitor with a ring in his left ear only who first appeared in Mr. Jefferay's tale on January 1. Mr. Clarke was lodging in

---

16. John Clark[e], died 20 April 1676. See Jefferay 142 and GDRI 45. For a full modern biography of John Clarke, see Cherry Fletcher Bamberg, FASG, and Judith Crandall Harbold, *John Clark's World* (Rhode Island Genealogical Society, 2018). John Clarke was probably not an ancestor of HPL's uncle Dr. Franklin C. Clark.

London, and negotiating for a royal charter on behalf of his fellow colonists. As when he visited Mr. Jefferay at his fishing outpost in the Isles of Shoals, the visitor demands tobacco and proceeds to raise a thick cloud of smoke from his pipe. He relates how he and his shipmates were captured by a richly laden Spanish galleon on a voyage from Bristol to the Barbadoes. The rest of his shipmates are set adrift in the captured ship's boats, but he is retained—perhaps for his knowledge of the locality—by his captors. Dismasted by a hurricane, the galleon drifts near a small rocky island. The crew members tow their ship into a harbor on the island, but are lifted with a roar by a great rising of the water and thrown into the sea to drown—all but the narrator, left on the ship. Left with plentiful food and useless wealth, the narrator finds a way to a hidden lake by way of terraced basins. He rides a boat made from the shell of a giant sea-turtle to a grotto, where he encounters a fairy with a single great diamond in her hair, who greets him with this speech: "Strange visitor, thou art welcome, and, after some refreshment and converse on other matters, I will escape thee from this island if that be still thy wish." Tempted to remain with the beautiful fairy, the narrator nevertheless departs, descending the basins in the turtle-shell boat and being picked up at last by a Dutch brig. A Dutch widow ("being still young and very comely") provides shelter for the nautical man and his strange boat, and he proposes to settle with her, if the narrator will accept his chart and go to claim the love of the beautiful fairy. But when the narrator expresses interest only in the chart, the nautical visitor vanishes as mysteriously as he first appeared. The narrator never seeks the turtle-shell boat left with the comely young Dutch widow, but keeps the chart, which he shows to his fellow Club members.

To conclude the series of tales, Mr. Vaughan[17] tells "The White Heron of Bedfordshire; or, How a White Feather May Not Show a Coward" (*Jefferay* 116–25) on February 12. This tale was not the experience of the teller, but of his father-in-law, who had served as the king's falconer. As a youth, he seeks determinedly for a mysterious white heron. The urgency of his search is intensified by the fact that he had pledged a feather from the heron to his beloved, so that she might fashion a pen from it. Finally, they admit their love to each other, and she excuses him from his unsuccessful quest, with the agreement that he may make one final attempt. The quest nearly costs him his life: the heron drags him over a cliff as he grasps one of its tail feathers. However, he accomplishes his mission and presents the feather to his beloved, who cuts herself with the feather and writes a message for her beloved in her blood, placing it in a locket. Only when the plume flies out the window and is recovered by the heron does her blood stanch. Having wed his beloved, the father returns to Bedfordshire after many years to finish his days. He sees the white heron one more time, but announces: "I follow him no more, and, giving him peace, only wish the same of him, and that he take not from me my locket, which, since it left my wife's heart, has ever been next to mine."

The diary's descriptions of historical events and of everyday life notwithstanding, readers evidently found the tales of the Seven Club one of the most fascinating parts of *The Journal of William Jefferay, Gentleman*;[18] so much so that Austin followed

---

17. William Vaughan, died 1677. See GDRI 211–12.
18. The book concludes with "Jefferay's Dream of True Values" (145–63), which he has written down at the insistence of his wife. Members of various professions seek to have the worth of their lives measured by a mysterious scale and be awarded with gold, silver, or brass medals according to their merit. Some of the results are unexpected: a bishop and a successful

the very next year with *More Seven Club Tales*. He explained the origin of these further tales as follows:

> It was doubtless Mr. Jefferay's intention to have read these tales at the Seven Club, though whether he ever did so is unknown. Evidently those who sent them to him were familiar with the tales already told at the club, and were acquainted with the members. The narrations heretofore published (as a part of Mr. Jefferay's Journal) were so favorably received, that it has been decided to print these later found stories, as a proper sequel. (*More* 3)

The first of the new tales, by Mr. Ray,[19] is entitled "An Indian Legend of Block Island" (*More* 5–16), and is a retelling, in an Indian voice, of the legend of the Palatine Light. An ancient Indian relates to Mr. Ray, upon his coming to Block Island in 1661, the story he had heard from his grandfather, who had heard it from his own grandfather. A great ship is driven into the harbor by a storm, only to find itself trapped when the entrance to the harbor is sealed by the storm. The trapped sailors commence a settlement and before long take Indian maidens as their partners. However, their leader rejects the attentions of the local sachem's daughter. Finally, another storm arrives and unseals the harbor. The settlers propose to return to their native land, but, fearing for the loss of her beloved, the sachem's daughter sets their ship afire. Afterward, a plague takes the lives of all the settlers except the leader, whom the sachem's daughter lovingly nurses to recovery. The leader at last relents and marries the sachem's daughter. The couple loses a daughter, and the mother follows her daughter to the grave. From time to time, the Indians go to the shore when the specter of the burning ship ap-

---

merchant each receive only a brass medal. Mr. Jefferay moralizes that steady work in one's own profession, without the objective of either wealth or fame, is the best path to be taken in life.

19. Simon Ray, born 1636, died 17 March 1737. See GDRI 160.

pears. Before his own death, the leader gives his ring to a trusted servitor, charging that it be handed down until it can be turned over to the first Englishman to appear in the locality. So the ring comes to Mr. Ray upon his arrival on Block Island. It bears the arms of the original English settler, which he is unable to identify. Mr. Ray closes with the ancient Indian's description of the sachem's daughter:

> Straight as an arrow, lissome as any fawn, hair black as night, but lustrous, and eyes like stars, yet melting (when turned toward one), teeth of pearl and voice sweet as wood thrush song, were only part that he told of her. In our plainer way, she was beautiful, tender and true; and those of us who believe love best of all, (as nearest like God who made us), will not pity too much the one whose heart was hers, e'en tho' his fate at first seemeth so hard to bear. (*More* 16)

The next tale is Mr. Smith's,[20] entitled "A Nameless Guest at Narragansett" (*More* 17–33). The narrator's father established his trading post at Narragansett as early as 1640. While the narrator is gathering seaweed at the shore to dress a field, a boat arrives and discharges a gentlemanly visitor, who begs leave to remain for three months and offers his services as a scribe to pay for his room and board. When asked to identify himself, he begs to be known as "The Nameless Guest," and his hosts agree to his stipulation. He offers to tutor any of the local youth in Hebrew, Greek, or Latin, but the settlement is too sparse to take advantage of his offer. A week before his anticipated departure, a king's ship is sighted, and "The Nameless Guest" goes into hiding in the

---

20. Richard Smith [Jr.], born 1636, died 1692. See GDRI 185. Following his father, he was a trader at Smith's Castle in Narragansett, Rhode Island. His trading house at Cocumscussoc (erected by him in 1678 after his father's original trading house was burned in King Philip's War in 1676) still survives in Wickford, Rhode Island.

woods. When the ship sails onward, he reappears and discloses that he had sided with the Protector during the late Civil War in England. The very eve before his scheduled departure, two of the king's officers appear at the door to arrest him; he escapes, shouting out that he intends to follow the Pequot Path to New London. The officers hasten away to follow him in their ship, but the very next day he reappears to meet his own ship and bid farewell to his hosts. In a note appended to the story, Austin speculates whether "The Nameless Guest" might have been one of the judges who condemned King Charles I to death in 1649.

Mr. Willett[21] follows with "A Strange Lading at the Kennebec" (*More* 34–45). Although he has no real economic need to do so, Mr. Willett decides to venture a last trading venture to Kennebec, with fine beaver pelts as his principal objective. But he finds even poorer quality pelts in scarce supply. An old Indian finally paddles to his boat and maintains that he will seek no pelts because of the Great Spirit's anger over the large number of beavers killed in previous years. Mr. Willett continues:

> When I pressed him for a method by which I might load my vessel, he would not allow he knew of any, until finally (finding me determined to stay the season out) he did admit there was one speedy and sure way. This could only be, however, by selling my soul to the Spirit of Evil; at which word he fell into such a trembling that I thought he might lose what few teeth were left him. (*More* 37)

After much persuading, the ancient Indian reluctantly provides directions to the pelts to be provided by the Evil Spirit. Mr. Ray follows the directions and he and his men discover "a pile of beaver skins that might not have their match for beauty anywhere" (*More* 39). Through seven days, including the Sabbath,

---

21. Thomas Willett, born 1605, died 4 August 1674. See GDRI 426–27. He was appointed the first English mayor of New York in 1665.

they continue to load the miraculously replenished pelts. Soon after setting out to return home they are overtaken by a terrific storm that sends pelts, ship, and all the men except Mr. Ray to the bottom of the sea. Mr. Ray manages to reach home in the ship's boat, which had come loose from the doomed vessel. He concludes his narration with the reflection:

> One thing I learned from this bitter experience; to be ever careful of taking something and giving nothing in exchange. Such may well prove the costliest kind of gift, as you have seen in my own case . . . within man much evil is engendered when once he setteth his mind upon following a short path to wealth. It were much wiser to keep in the old ways (well proved as good) even when toilsome and slow of travel. (*More* 44)

Mr. Blackstone[22] follows with his tale, entitled "Three Ghostly Appearings at Study Hill" (*More* 46–59), Study Hill being his own remote home just inside the Plymouth Colony bounds. One evening about dusk he witnesses "a sudden flaming up of fire, yet not like burning brush; spreading and playing differently and climbing not so high as that." He follows the flame through a mire to "a little pond that was all aflame, though water hath no quality to burn as I had ever been taught" (*More* 50). He hears a sudden wail behind him, and when he turns, he finds the fire extinguished and himself plunged into total darkness. With difficulty he manages to return safely to his home. A second ghostly appearance also involves fire. He has gone on an excursion to visit "Cobbling Rock" (a huge boulder perched precariously on a stone surface) with an Indian guide, and when returning he observes a "dancing light near the ground" toward Scott's Pond. He finds himself on a floating island in the pond when the light

---

22. William Blackstone, born 1595, died 26 May 1675. See GDRI 21–22. He arrived in America as early as 1623 and was noted as the first English settler of Boston and of Rhode Island.

suddenly goes out. Instead of diving into the water to attempt to swim to shore—which would surely have led to his death—he waits until the island drifts to shore and then finds his own way home (his Indian guide having declined to follow him to the pond). The final ghostly visitation is by Dr. Caius, his old tutor at Cambridge. They have a short converse, which ends with the spirit of Dr. Caius telling him:

> . . . I am well pleased to see thee placed in so sweet a retiracy for study of nature and books. I am much drawn to thee and this reposeful spot, but time presses, and duty now calls me far away; wherefore I must follow that call, for so I ever taught my lads that they must do. I came to see if thou hadst chosen as wisely as reported to me, and leave thee content in that. (*More* 58)

The spirit of Dr. Caius suddenly disappears. Although Mr. Blackstone was spared another visitation by fire in his lifetime, Mr. Austin noted that his home was burned during King Philip's War in 1676.

Dr. Cranston[23] follows with "A Marvelous Cure at Newport" (*More* 60–72). Late at night, after a long day of work, the doctor is disturbed in his home by a visitor who has broken his leg so severely that it must be amputated—the doctor's first amputation without supervision. He performs the work well, and the man curiously asks to take his severed leg with him, promising to return in a year and to pay the doctor double his customary fee, unless he has succeeded in reattaching his severed limb. He leaves a curious old snuff box as security for the fulfillment of his promise. He returns on the anniversary of his first visit, and, lo, the severed limb has miraculously rejoined itself to his body. He leaves as mysteriously as he first appeared, leaving the snuff box as payment for the services rendered by the doctor. He promises to publish the doc-

---

23. John Cranston, born 1626, died 12 March 1680. See GDRI 60.

tor's skill far and wide. Some speculate that the mysterious visitor has sent a twin brother to deceive the doctor; others, that the doctor has invented the whole tale in an effort to drum up business.

In Mr. Baulstone's[24] tale, "The First Caller to Mine Inn at Portsmouth" (*More* 73–85), we have a third appearance by the nautical man with the ring in his left ear only, who first appeared in Mr. Jefferey's and Mr. Clarke's tales in the first collection. Mr. Baulstone is just opening his first inn in 1638 when the incident occurs. The nautical man mysteriously appears seated next to Mr. Baulstone on his first day of business, accompanied by a heavy bag presumably filled with gold coins. As before, he asks for tobacco and soon sends up large clouds of smoke from his puffing. He tells his host: "I have traveled in this America of yours from the Isles of Shoals to the Carribees, and am lately come from the first, tho' how, thou shalt ne'er guess" (*More* 77). He claims to have arrived so swiftly on a magic boat fashioned from a sea serpent's scale, accompanied by a beautiful mermaid whom he deposits at Cormorant Rock lest she be eaten by the serpent. He boasts that his voice is "sweet and low to women, (who ever delight in my converse)" (*More* 78). (The nautical man has apparently lost none of his way with women since he consorted with the comely young Dutch widow in Mr. Clarke's tale.) The boat has been drawn so swiftly from the Isles of Shoals to Portsmouth by the serpent, whom the nautical man has commanded into service.

The visitor refuses all offers of refreshment, but before he retires to his bed he offers to pay for the entertainment of all first night visitors to the inn. Mr. Baulstone's neighbors celebrate the opening of his inn well and late because of the generous offer of the nautical man, but when he does not answer summons in the

---

24. William Baulstone, born 1600, died 14 March 1678. See GDRI 16.

morning, his room is found empty and he himself vanished. The nautical man has the effrontery to leave only a receipt reading: "Rec'd of mine host, Mr. Baulstone, a rare night's enjoyment (seeing all, yet myself unseen). I say received. (Signed) THE STRANGE VISITOR" (*More* 83). Mr. Baulstone offers for examination by the members of the Seven Club the receipt, which bears in one corner "a mark . . . like the Evil One's coat armour" (*More* 85), as also observed by Mr. Clarke on the chart he received. Despite his having been cheated by "The Mysterious Visitor," Mr. Baulstone allows that the added custom generated by the fame of the strange visit has benefitted his business.

Mistress Porter concludes with her tale, "My Husbands and Other Trials" (*More* 86–101). She was born Herodias Long, commonly known as "Horod." Losing her father at the age of ten, she comes to London with her mother. Not yet fourteen, she marries a handsome young apprentice, John Hicks, and they set out to the New World to seek their fortune, living first at Weymouth and then at Newport. But her husband absconds to Manhattan, taking with him most of her estate and their young son. She takes as her second husband George Gardiner, remaining with him for twenty years and bearing multiple children. Having joined the Quakers, she journeys with Mary Stanton to Weymouth to witness for her faith and is rewarded with ten lashes of the knotted cord on her bare back and a jail sentence. Later she returns to witness the martyrdom of Mary Dyer on Boston Common on 1 June 1660. Eventually, she decides to separate from Gardiner:

> Toward the last of it, however, there grew a feeling that an ill considered union had proved but an ill assorted one, the yoke too hard to bear; tho' fault not all of either, as I will freely say.
>
> Upon seeing (or fancying so) he wished no more of me, I resolved not to be left a second time, but e'en leave him; and desired

the most honored Assembly that I might have due allowance for my livelihood. (*More* 96)

Just turned forty, she decides to marry a third time, to Mr. Porter,[25] and they go to dwell at Narragansett. He has living a former wife, Margaret, of whom Horod writes:

> I do know this ancient dame as a most worthy woman, and would not have her rest in the belief some would fasten upon her, that this late husband (now mine) did plot with me in putting aside our former mates, to join ourselves. This is so false I would pass it by altogether, had not some assent been made by such as are always ready to believe the worst of their neighbours. (*More* 98–99)

She concludes by expressing a wish for her three living husbands:

> My husbands three (with wives having or had) shall believe this if no more of me: that I wish them such good health and sober happiness as God in his great mercy may vouchsafe them. . . . Ah! Who can tell (of us here) about the last weighing, and how it will go with self, friend or neighbor. Not always as we have deemed it. The Searcher of all things alone doth know, and we may but do our best and leave all judgment to Him. (*More* 99–101)

Analysis of Austin's Seven Club Tales and Their Possible Influence on Lovecraft

The Seven Club tales would certainly have been of interest to Lovecraft. All but three of the tales (Mr. Coddington's, Mr. Smith's, and Mistress Porter's) contain some elements of the supernatural. Seven of the tales involve some kind of token or legacy: rings in the cases of Mr. Brenton's, Mr. Brinley's, and Mr. Ray's tales; a mysterious boat and chart in Mr. Clark's; a locket in Mr. Vaughan's; a snuff box in Mr. Cranston's; and a receipt in Mr. Baulstone's. In the first collection, five of the tales were set

---

25. John Porter, died 1674+. He married (1) Margaret Odding and (2) Herodias Gardiner. See GDRI 155.

in Old England, while only two (Mr. Jefferay's and Mr. Arnold's) were set in North America. The situation is reversed in the second collection, where all the stories are set in New England (except for a small portion of Mistress Porter's tale, set in London, before she and her first husband leave for the New World). Mr. Ray's tale transpires on Block Island (Shoreham, Rhode Island); Mr. Smith's, in Narragansett, Rhode Island; Mr. Willett's, in Kennebec, Maine; Mr. Blackstone's, at his home at Study Hill, Blackstone, Massachusetts; Mr. Cranston's, in Newport, Rhode Island; Mr. Baulstone's, in Portsmouth, Rhode Island; and Mistress Porter's, in London, England, Weymouth, Massachusetts, and Newport, Rhode Island. The strong predominance of Rhode Island settings in the second volume is especially notable. All fourteen narrators were early Rhode Island settlers, and numerous references to them can be found in the works of Samuel G. Arnold, Thomas W. Bicknell, and other Rhode Island historians.

Since John Osborne Austin was himself born and bred in Providence, it is somewhat surprising that he did not choose to set any of his Seven Club tales in Providence. The predominance of southern Rhode Island homes among his own ancestors may account for this omission. We do not know when Lovecraft first read *The Journal of William Jefferay, Gentleman* or *More Seven Club Tales*. We know that the former was a presentation copy inscribed by Austin for Lovecraft's uncle Dr. Clark; so we may presume that the three volumes owned by Lovecraft—if all from Dr. Clark—came to him after his uncle's death in 1915. He did read extensively in Rhode Island history at the Providence Public Library in his early years and claimed to have perused the entire file of the *Providence Gazette and Country-Journal* (1762–95). So it is possible that he read some of Austin's works before he came to possess his own copies of three of them.

During his stay in New York City in 1924–26, Lovecraft carefully made his way through Gertrude Selwyn Kimball's *Providence in Colonial Times* (1912) at the main public library—the book was non-circulating, so he had to read it there. After his return to Providence in 1926, his interest in local history and genealogy was stoked by the enthusiasm of his young friend Wilfred B. Talman. They spent several sessions researching their family histories at the cabinet of the Rhode Island Historical Society. Unlike his uncle Dr. Clark, Lovecraft was never elected a member of the Rhode Island Historical Society. However, if less than an ardent devotee of family history, he remained vitally interested in Rhode Island history. He was delighted in July 1933 when with the help of visiting E. Hoffmann Price and Price's automobile Juggernaut, he was able to visit a number of southern Rhode Island sites he had never been able to see before (*JFM* 332–33; *IAP* 854).

While we do not have any surviving comment by Lovecraft on Austin's fiction, the appeal of the basic historical framework of *The Journal of William Jeffray, Gentleman* to Lovecraft as a devotee of Rhode Island history is readily apparent. The fact that eleven of the fourteen Seven Club tales involved some elements of the supernatural would also have appealed to him. While settings in England predominated in the first collection, four of the tales in the second collection have Rhode Island settings, while a fifth tale (Mr. Blackstone's) is set in Blackstone, Massachusetts—very close to Rhode Island—and a sixth tale (Mistress Porter's) is set partially in Newport, Rhode Island. Also, the motif of tangible relics of the mysterious events narrated—be they rings (Mr. Brenton, Mr. Brinley, Mr. Ray), receipt (Mr. Baulstone), boat and chart (Mr. Clark), or snuff box and crutches (Mr. Cranston)—would probably also have been a source of fascination for Lovecraft.

That Lovecraft did not exploit his wide historical knowledge of Providence in his early fiction is probably explained by the fact that he regarded Massachusetts Puritan theocracy as the darkest element in New England history. Massachusetts exiled Roger Williams, the founder of Providence, as early as 1636 and engaged in the cruel persecution of Quakers, including the hanging of Mary Dyer in 1660. Perhaps the cycle of persecution may be said to have culminated in the witchcraft persecution in Danvers in 1692. In any case, it is little wonder that Lovecraft saw his home state of Rhode Island as a place of refuge and toleration, while the Massachusetts theocracy engendered for him visions of darkness. Lovecraft had strong psychological motivation to set the secret horrors of early stories like "The Picture in the House" and "The Terrible Old Man" in Massachusetts. Even later, as he developed his fictional landscape, the principal foci of his horrors—Arkham, Innsmouth, Kingsport, Dunwich—were all situated in Massachusetts.

In Lovecraft's fiction, Rhode Island is often cast as a place of refuge or solace—as when the detective Thomas F. Malone retires to Chepachet in the attempt to recover from the shattering events he has experienced in "The Horror at Red Hook," or when Randolph Carter seeks refuge in memories of his ancestral home in Foster in "The Silver Key." It is possible that thoughts of creating some analogues of Austin's Seven Club tales percolated for some time in Lovecraft's mind. On 7 March 1920, he wrote his friend Rheinhart Kleiner: "I am at present full of various ideas, including a hideous novel to be entitled *The Club of the Seven Dreamers*" (*RK* 157). S. T. Joshi speculates that Lovecraft may have drawn inspiration for his projected novel (which is nonextant) from Austin's Seven Club tales (*IAP* 360–61).[26]

---

26. On 29 November 1933, HPL wrote to his friend Clark Ashton Smith of a dream he had experienced the prior week, involving twelve or thirteen strange, almost identical-appearing men who lived on a hillside street in Providence and visited his home (598 Angell Street) to demonstrate won-

Lovecraft probably noticed the absence of Providence settings in the Seven Club tales. The use of historical figures in Austin's tales and their solid grounding in local history probably charged his imagination. Why could he not craft his own historical fictions, with settings in his own beloved Providence, neglected by Austin? His reading of Gertrude Selwyn Kimball's *Providence in Colonial Times* in New York City in 1925 may have formed a principal inspiration for his great short novel *The Case of Charles Dexter Ward*, but I am of the opinion that the Seven Club tales of John Osborne Austin may have formed an ancillary inspiration—if not for the Providence setting, at least for the concept of weaving a solid budget of local history into a narration of supernatural events. The discovery of the hidden portrait of Joseph Curwen in the dilapidated house in Olney Court uses the same relic motif used by Austin in several of his Seven Club Tales. The idea of resurrecting historical figures from their remains is grotesque—but aligns with Austin's determined effort to recapture the past in the writing of historical fiction.

Because of the lack of any direct comment by Lovecraft, we will probably never know just how important the Seven Club tales of John Osborne Austin were for the writing of the stories that Lovecraft set against historical backgrounds in Providence. Doubtless, Dr. Clark's antiquarian interests also influenced Lovecraft in his use of historical Providence settings. The depth of his reading in other local historians such as William Staples, Samuel G. Arnold, Henry C. Dorr, Sidney S. Rider, James N. Arnold, and Thomas W. Bicknell, while not known exactly, was

---

ders to him (*DS* 484–86). August Derleth used HPL's account of his dream as the basis for his story "The Dark Brotherhood." While the number of the strange men is not seven, the idea of a group of men discussing mysteries is still suggestive of Austin's *The Diary of William Jefferay, Gentleman* and *More Seven Club Tales*.

probably considerable. I think, however, that it is incontrovertible that Austin's Seven Club tales showed that Rhode Island antiquities could provide an ample accommodation for supernatural happenings. Lovecraft probably felt that Austin had neglected Providence in these tales and determined to remedy the deficiency. How magnificently he did so in such tales as "The Shunned House" and "The Haunter of the Dark" and in the short novel *The Case of Charles Dexter Ward* is left for posterity to judge.

Bibliography

Austin, John Osborne. *The Genealogical Dictionary of Rhode Island*. Albany, NY: Joel Munsell's Sons, 1887. [Abbreviated in the text as GDRI. Available at archive.org.]

Kimball, Gertrude Selwyn. *Providence in Colonial Times* (Boston: Houghton Mifflin, 1912).

Appendix: Works of Fiction by John Osborne Austin
Note: Lovecraft-owned titles marked with an asterisk (*).
The Journal of William Jefferay, Gentleman. Providence, RI: Press of E. L. Freeman, 1899 (*LL* 63). [Abbreviated in the text as *Jefferay*. Available at hathitrust.org.]
A Modern Love Chase/Peggy Rogers/An Incompetent. Rahway, NJ: The Quinn & Boden Co. Press, n.d. [1916].[27] [Available at hathitrust.org.]

---

27. This work was privately printed for the author in a "Memorial Edition" of 10 copies. The 10 copies were given to Richard Sisson Austin (son), Rosamond Whitaker Austin (daughter), Rachel Austin (sister), British Museum, Providence Athenaeum, Providence Public Library, Redwood Library (Newport, R.I.), New York Public Library, and Library of Congress. The New York Public Library copy was received on 18 September 1916. The portrait of a young female serves as frontispiece for this book and probably depicts Austin's wife Helen Augusta Whitaker.

More Seven Club Tales. Newport, RI: Press of Newport Daily News, 1900 (*LL* 64). [Abbreviated in the text as *More*. Available at hathitrust.org.]

Philip and Philippa: A Genealogical Romance of Today. Newport, RI: Newport Daily News, 1901 (*LL* 65). [Available at loc.gov.]

A Week's Wooing and Dolph and Dolly. New York: Abbey Press, 1902. [Available at loc.org.]

Ethnic Names in Lovecraft's "The Dreams in the Witch House"

Viewing the Wild Claw Theater production of "The Dreams in the Witch House" on 14 December 2008 naturally sent me back to Lovecraft's original text, which I had not read for some years. It is certainly a magnificent story, although I found it somewhat uneven upon rereading. In some ways, the author's descriptions of all the bizarre scenery of hyperspace seems to clash with the dark, brooding setting in Arkham. The wealth of ethnic names—mostly Polish—in the story struck me especially, and I decided to spend an afternoon of research using Ancestry.com at the Glenview Public Library to see if I could gain any further insights. (Those of you who know me well may know that my wife Carol, née Gaber, is of Polish ancestry.)

Of course, the starting point for all commentary on the setting of "The Dreams in the Witch House" must be Salem's actual Witch House, known today more properly as the Jonathan Corwin House, after one of the judges (d. 1718) in the 1692 witch trials. Legend says that some of the proceedings took place in this very house at 310 Essex Street in Salem, although I do not know what history reveals in that regard. There is an excellent website on the house at www.corwinhouse.org/. Although some date the house as early as 1642, most believe it was originally built for Corwin himself c. 1675. His eldest grandson George Corwin inherited the house in 1740. George Corwin's daughter married merchant Richard Ward (yes, *Ward*) in 1764, and the house remained in the Ward family until sold to the pharmacist George Farrington in 1856. Eighteenth-century alterations were removed in the nineteenth century to adapt the house for commercial use on the ground floor (originally, a pharmacy operated by Farrington). Lovecraft would have known this house as a much-altered structure with businesses (e.g., an antiques shop) on the ground floor and apartments on the upper floors. In 1946, it was given to the City of Salem, after which it was restored to its seventeenth-century appearance. The house (open to tours) is still creating news. The Salem *News* of 19 December 2008 reported that the Salem Parks and Recreation Commission, by a vote of 3–0 (2 members absent), declined a request from the Rhode Island–based Spirit Finders Paranormal Investigators to conduct an investigation in the house. Witches are today a subject of sensitivity in Salem. Tourism is still centered on the 1692 witchcraft persecution. But the city and its citizens appear to be of divided mind as to how best to commemorate that unhappy episode of history.

But what can the U.S. census of 1930 tell us of the ethnic names used by Lovecraft in "Witch House"?

We'll start with the superstitious loom-fixer Joe Mazurewicz. Mazurewicz was actually quite a rare surname in the 1930 census. There was just one Mazurewicz household in the U.S. in that year, at 2501 Lotus Avenue in Chicago, Illinois. It was headed by Alexander Mazurewicz, a 46-year-old baker, born in Poland, who emigrated in 1903. His 42-year-old wife Antoinette, who worked as a saleslady in the bakery, had emigrated in 1908. Their children in that year were four daughters, all born in Illinois: Sophia, age 20; Stella, age 18; Irene, age 16; and Wanda, age 9. The two oldest daughters were employed in a candy factory in 1930. It seems unlikely that Lovecraft had any contact with this name. But who are we to say? His wife Sonia Haft Greene's brother Solomon, a tailor, was living in Chicago in 1930. Lovecraft and his wife continued to correspond after 1929. Maybe Sonia had some reason to mention a Mazurewicz bakery in her correspondence. Or maybe Lovecraft saw the name in a Chicago directory (although 1928–29 was the last year for Chicago directories). Or maybe he saw it in a Polish or a Canadian source, or maybe he simply invented a name that proved to be real. We do not know. As for Joe Mazurewicz's occupation, many Poles in New England were employed in the textile industry, especially in Rhode Island. Several of Lovecraft's young friends in the Providence Amateur Press Club in 1914–16 had family connections with the textile industry, e.g., Edmund Shehan and Caroline Miller.

On to Father Iwanicki, given name not mentioned. Iwanicki is actually a fairly common surname in the 1930 census. There were in that year 205 individuals with surname Iwanicki in places including Bridgeport, CT; Middletown, CT; Meriden, CT; Mansfield, CT; Chicago, IL; Taunton, MA; Chicopee, MA; Salem, MA; Blackman, MI; Dearborn, MI; Detroit, MI; Hamtramck, MI; South Hampton, NH; Wallington, NJ; Jersey City, NJ; Passaic, NJ; Auburn, NY; Buffalo, NY; Brooklyn, NY; Manhattan (NYC); Niagara Falls, NY; Lorain, OH; Youngstown, OH; Portland, OR; Emsworth, PA; Pittsburgh, PA; Upper Merion, PA; Milwaukee, WI; and Honolulu, HI. I was unable to check each name to see if any of them happened to be a priest. (Ancestry.com will not search the 1930 census by occupation.) Not every Iwanicki family was of Polish origin: the Iwanickis of Honolulu were of Japanese origin, as was 25-year-old Masao Iwanicki of Manhattan (NYC). In Salem, MA, in 1930 I found three Iwanicki households. There was the family of 57-year-old Wojceck Iwanicki at 26 Cross Street. Wojceck Iwanicki shared a common occupation with Lovecraft's fictional Mazurewicz: Wojceck was a loom-fixer, in a cotton mill. He had emigrated from Poland in 1903. His wife Carolina, age 53, had emigrated in 1906. In 1930, they had four children, all born in Massachusetts:

Michael, aged 23, who worked in a leather factory; Amelia, aged 19, who worked in the household; Jennie, aged 17, who worked as a stitcher in a shoe factory; and Stacia, aged 15, who had the same occupation as Jennie. At the same address was the household of Felix Iwanicki, age 30, employed as a driller in a shoe machinery shop. He had been born in Massachusetts of Polish-born parents. The third Salem, MA, Iwanicki household of 1930 was that of John Z. Iwanicki at 129 North Street. Born in Poland, John Z. Iwanicki, age 39, had emigrated in 1906 and was employed as a cotton mill foreman. His wife Mary, age 36, was also born in Poland and had emigrated in 1910. They had a daughter Alice P. Iwanicki, age 13, and a son Henry S. Iwanicki, age 4 years 11 months, both born in Massachusetts. Did Lovecraft encounter the name Iwanicki on a doorbell on one of his many visits to Salem? Or see it in a Salem directory? We do not know.

What about Gilman's neighbor Paul Choynski? Choynski was not a very common surname in the 1930 census. However, we do find in Salem at 10½ Herbert Street the household of John Choynski, age 43, born in Poland, emigrated 1914, employed as a finisher in a leather factory. His wife Wladyslans [*sic*], age 40, was also born in Poland and had emigrated in 1920. They had in 1930 a family of six children, the two eldest born in Poland, the four youngest in Massachusetts: Helen, age 21, emigrated 1920, coverer in a wood heel factory; Kazmier, age 18, emigrated 1920; Sally, age 7; Dorothy, age 5; Genevieve, age 4 years 6 months; John, Jr., age 7 months. Salem also had a Boleslaw Choynski, age 40, born in Poland, and a Maryan Choynski household at 27 Williams Street. Maryan, age 38, born in Poland, was a coremaker for an electrical supply firm. His wife Sophie, aged 35, born in Massachusetts, was a spinner in a cotton mill. They had in 1930 a daughter Hilda, age 6, and a son Hilary F., age 3, both born in Massachusetts.

The Choynski surname is also found in San Francisco and Chicago in 1930. Fanny Choynski, a 78-year-old widow, born in New York of German-born parents, lived at 404 Ashbury Street in San Francisco in that year, with her 55-year-old son Milton L. Choynski, single, born in California of a German-born father and a New York-born mother, employed as an attorney. Also in San Francisco in that year was the household (at 1000 Mason Street) of Herbert Choynski, age 67, born in California of a Polish-born father and an English-born mother, employed as a lawyer. Also in Herbert's household was his wife Ethel, age 48, born in Illinois of Russian-born parents. In Chicago we find at 854 North Clark Street the household of Maurice Choynski, age 64, born in California of a German-born father and an English-born mother, employed as owner of a movie theatre. Also in this household was his wife Sarah, age 50, born in Pennsylvania of an Irish-born father and a Scottish-born mother. I suspect that Maurice Choynski of Chicago and Herbert Choynski of San Francisco were brothers.

In Lansing, MI, there was an Irene Choynski, aged 19, born in New York. In Queens, NY, a John Choynski, age 35, born in Poland, and his wife Blanche, age 29. Finally, in Philadelphia, there was the household of Moses Choynski, age 59, born in Pennsylvania of German-born father and Polish-born mother, employed as a street railway operator. Also in this household was his wife Adelaide, age 58, also born in Pennsylvania, son Coleman Choynski, age 22, employed in construction, son Louis Choynski, age 17, employed as a helper, and daughter Rosa C. Krupnick, age 26, along with her husband Benjamin Krupnick, age 32, of Russian-born parents, employed as a commercial salesman, and grandson Albert C. Krupnick, age 2 years 2 months. Children, son-in-law and grandson were all born in Pennsylvania.

Maybe the Choynskis came from the Polish-German border region. From the names and occupations, my guess is that at least some of them were Jewish and spoke Yiddish in their households. How Lovecraft encountered the Choynski name, I have no idea. Perhaps he saw it on a Salem, MA, doorbell or encountered it in a Salem directory.

Dombrowski (given name not specified) was the Witch House landlord in Lovecraft's story. It is a pretty uncommon name in the 1930 census. However, in Providence, ward 8, there was a Stephen Dombrowski household at 21 Comerford Street in 1930. Stephen, age 39, was born in Poland and emigrated in 1910. In 1930, he worked as a weaver in a woollen mill. His wife Christina, age 35, born in Poland, emigrated in 1912 and worked as a winder in a woollen mill. They had three children in 1930, all born in Rhode Island: Helen, age 12; Anthony, age 10; and Stasia, age 8. Also in Providence Ward 10 in 1930 was the household of Joseph Andrukiewicz at 178 Amherst Street. Joseph, age 44, was born in Poland, and worked as a hardener in a file shop. His wife Eva, age 37, was born in Connecticut. Also in the household was Eva's mother Theophila Dombrowski, age 65, born in Poland. So, maybe Lovecraft encountered the Dombrowski name on a Providence doorbell or in a Providence directly.

The laundress Anastasia Wolejko has her baby stolen in Lovecraft's story. Her surname is quite rare in the 1930 census. I found only one Wolejko household, that of Anthony J. Wolejko, in Sunderland, Franklin Country, MA. Anthony, age 39, was born in Poland, as was his wife Stena I., age 38. In 1930, they had five children (all born in Massachusetts): Stella A., age 16; Anthony, age 13; Edward, age 11; Leon, age 7; and Blanche, age 2 years 10 months. Anthony J. Wolejko operated an onion farm. Wife and all but the two youngest children were employed as laborers on the farm. How Lovecraft encountered the Wolejko family name I have no idea.

Anastasia Wolejko had a friend Mary Czanek in Lovecraft's

story. Amazingly, Czanek is not found as a surname in the 1930 census. In the story, Anastasia also had a no-good boyfriend Pete Stowacki who had no use for Anastasia's child. The surname Stowacki is also unfound in the 1930 census. In the story, a Dr. Malkowski is called in to treat Walter Gilman. There are over six hundred occurrences of the Malkowski surname in the 1930 census, 33 in Massachusetts including Chicopee, Westfield, Granby, Boston, Oxford, and Worcester (none in Salem) and 12 in Rhode Island. The Providence Malkowski households included that of Stephan A. at 215 Common Street and that of Frank at 92 Pettis Street. Stephan Malkowski, age 48, born in Poland, operated a grocery store and had wife Anna, age 49, and children William, age 22; Sadie, age 19; Henry, age 17; and Edward, age 15. The two oldest children were born in Massachusetts, the two youngest in Rhode Island. Frank Malkowski, age 37, born in Poland, was a machinist in a machine shop, and had wife Helen, age 31, and children Edward, age 12; Adela, age 10, and Irene, age 2 years 3 months. Frank's wife and children were all born in Rhode Island. How did Lovecraft encounter the Malkowski surname? I do not know.

Intending no disrespect, I will pass over the non-Polish story names quite lightly. Desrochers was the boarder directly below Gilman in the Witch House. Desrochers is of course a common French and French-Canadian surname. Mason is a common English surname, but you will perhaps be relieved to know that "Keziah Mason" finds no exact match in the 1930 census. Walter Gilman gets 45 exact matches in the 1930 census, with 7 in Massachusetts alone. We have Walter F., age 16, of Danvers; Walter D., age 17, of Lynn; Walter, age 15, of Lynn; Walter, age 13, of Palmer; Walter H., age 25, of Boston; Walter, age 7, of Boston; and Walter H., age 76, of Lowell. Several of these are of proper age to figure in the events occurring in 1931 in Lovecraft's story.

In the story, Frank Elwood was Gilman's fellow student and Witch House lodger. Frank Elwood gets 25 exact matches in the 1930 census, but none in Massachusetts or Rhode Island. Upham is a common English name, including Lovecraft's childhood friend Ronald Upham. Professor Upham's given name is not provided in Lovecraft's story.

So much for the names found in "Dreams in the Witch House." It seems probable that Lovecraft encountered some of the surnames in his own life, albeit ephemerally, by seeing them on a doorbell or in a city directory. He was quite skilled in the invention of appropriate names for characters in his fiction. Lovecraft's friend Edith Miniter focussed much greater attention on Polish immigrants to New England in her novel *Our Natupski Neighbors* (Henry Holt, 1916), whose characters she modeled on her Nietupski neighbors in Wilbraham, Massachusetts. I think both Lovecraft and Miniter treat their Polish characters with sympathy. Although Lovecraft did not sympathize with their Roman Catholic faith, he doubtless had some grudging respect for the hard work, thrift, and family values of the Polish immigrants. Wilbraham's Nietupskis became very successful farmers.

II

Mazurewicz

I think Lovecraft probably had other inspiration for the superstitious loom-fixer Joe Mazurewicz than the one Mazurewicz family recorded in Chicago in the 1930 U.S. census. We may recall he had had some rough going in the amateur journalism hobby in 1921–23. His 1921–22 UAPA President Ida C. Haughton had accused him of mishandling official funds, prompting his rejoinder in the poem "Medusa: A Portrait." During the same period he was in conflict with NAPA President E. Dorothy Houtain over acceptance of a disputed laureate medal. Then, in

July 1922, to crown his amateur woes, the anti-literary faction in UAPA ousted the Lovecraft faction, installing the following slate (see *IAP* 396): Howard R. Conover, President; Edmund J. Mazurewicz, First Vice President; Stella V. Kellerman, Second Vice President; Edward Delbert Jones, Chairman, Department of Public Criticism; Leo Fritter, Official Editor; Secretary-Treasurer, Alma B. Sanger. But Lovecraft had his revenge. When William J. Dowdell resigned the presidency of the NAPA in November 1922, the Executive Judges, at the suggestion of James F. Morton, appointed Lovecraft to replace him. Then, in July 1923, just when his NAPA term was ending, Lovecraft and his supporters were returned to power in UAPA. Outgoing Secretary-Treasurer Alma B. Sanger refused to release funds to the new administration, causing a curtailed program.

So I suspect Lovecraft was thinking of his political opponent Mazurewicz in UAPA when he named the loom-fixer in "The Dreams in the Witch House." I only have a few issues of the *United Amateur* available to me, but in the May 1920 issue Edmund John Mazurewicz is listed as a member (number 2382b) in Korona, Florida. He was not so listed in July 1919. I suspect "Edward T." may be a mistranscription for "Edmund J.," but I might be wrong. In the 1920 U.S. census of Precinct 2, Dupont, Flagler County, Florida, we find the following Mazurewicz household: John J. head, white male aged 40, emigrated 1898, naturalized 1904, born Russian Poland, parents born Russian Poland, occupation farmer on a truck farm; Clara T., wife, white female aged 37, born Illinois, parents born Russian Poland, no occupation; Edmund J., son, white male aged 17, single, born Illinois, occupation school teacher, public school; John W., son, white male aged 11, single, born Illinois, no occupation; Clara, daughter, white female aged 4, single, born Florida, no occupation. The UAPA did a lot of recruiting among schoolteachers, so perhaps this is how Edmund J. Mazurewicz made his connection with amateur journalism. I don't believe that any correspondence from Edmund J. Mazurewicz survives in the Lovecraft Collection at Brown, but perhaps Lovecraft recalled the name from the slate of his political opponents and decided to get his revenge by naming the loom-fixer of "The Witch House" after him. Regrettably, I don't find any further trace of Edmund J. Mazurewicz. The Ancestry U.S. Public Records index includes an Edward Mazurewicz (born August 1950) residing in Fort Myers Beach, Florida.

Czanek

The surname Czanek makes more than one appearance in Lovecraft's fiction. In addition to Mary Czanek, who has a minor role as the friend of Anastasia Wolejko in "The Dreams in the Witch House," there is of course Joe Czanek, one of the three burglars in "The Terrible Old Man" (1920). If we go back one census from 1930, the 1920 U.S. census, we can find a Czanek family residing on 54th Avenue in Cicero, Cook County, Illinois, enumerated on 8–9 January 1920: Frank, white male age 35, emigrated 1916, naturalized 1917, born Bohemia of Bohemian-born parents, occupation tool and die maker (shop); Barbara [Necernany], wife, white female age 27, emigrated 1904, naturalized 1919, born Bohemia of Bohemian-born parents. They were then residing in the household of Barbara's father Anton Necernany, white male age 56, divorced, emigrated 1903, naturalized 1919, born Bohemia of Bohemian-born parents, occupation laborer (coal yard). Frank Czanek may also be found in the 1917–18 draft registrations: born 4 May 1884, residing 39th Street and 61st Avenue, Cicero, occupation tool and die maker, Addressograph Co., nearest relative Barbara Czanek. As of April 2009, the U.S. Social Security Death Master File contained no one with surname Czanek.

What may me say of Czanek? Like Mazurewicz, it seems to be a relatively uncommon name. From its occurrences, one may guess it is Bohemian-German in origin. How Lovecraft encountered the surname, I have no idea. Salem, MA, city directories might be a good source for checking all the ethnic names in "The Witch House." Maybe a Czanek lived or worked there at one point and Lovecraft saw the name on a doorbell. Anywhere on the Boston North Shore that Lovecraft loved so well to explore would be a good hunting ground.

Stowacki

Anastasia Wolejko's good-for-nothing boyfriend Pete Stowacki poses probably the toughest challenge of Lovecraft's ethnic names in "The Witch House." As with all ethnic names, one has to contend with mistranscriptions in census and other vital records. For example, in Polish, the letter "l" with a slash "ł" is pronounced like a "w" in English, while "w" is pronounced like a "v" in English. So the surname of the famous Polish poet and dramatist of the Romantic period Juliusz Słowacki (1809–1849) is actually pronounced "Swovatzky." One can find Słowacki's surname transcribed as Stowacki: for example, the Esperanto edition of his drama *Mazeppa* (1840), published as *Mazeppa: Tragedio en Kvin Aktos* (Paris, 1912), is cataloged under Juliusz Stowacki. The "t" here may or may not be a simple misinterpretation of the Polish "ł." Christopher John Murray's *Encyclopedia of the Romantic Era 1760–1850* (2003) has an excellent article on Juliusz Słowacki. A theatre named in honor of Słowacki is located in Krakow, Poland.

What is the important take-away concerning the ethnic names that Lovecraft used in "The Dreams in the Witch House"? Simply that he used suitable, authentic ethnic names, just as he used typical names for his Anglo-Saxon characters. He did not choose the most common names, but names that for whatever reason struck him as memorable. It is possible that Joe Mazurewicz the loom-fixer may be an echo of Edmund John Mazurewicz, a young school teacher who belonged to an opposing political faction in UAPA in the early 1920s. That's about all. The rest can fade to background.

Amateur Journalism

The Providence Amateur Press Club: 1914–16

With David Haden (now updated and expanded)[1]

In Memory of the Members of the Providence Amateur Press Club

Abbreviations used in this work:

de Camp L. Sprague de Camp, *Lovecraft: A Biography* (Garden City, NY: Doubleday, 1975)

JTD S. T. Joshi, David E. Schultz and John H. Stanley, "H. P. Lovecraft: Letters to John T. Dunn," *Books at Brown* 38–39 (1991–1992 [actually 1995]): 157–223.

YML L. Sprague de Camp, "Young Man Lovecraft," in *AAV* 172–74. Originally published in George Hay, ed., *The Necronomicon* (Jersey, UK: Neville Spearman, 1978).

Before you all, in apprehension stand
The timid members of a new-form'd band.
With awkward pen, but eager of success,
Our sev'ral failings must we here confess;
Let critics treat us with a kindly sense,
And frown not on our inexperience. [. . .]

Thus stand the club, to ev'ry eye reveal'd.
And not a fault or virtue left conceal'd.
If in your cultur'd ranks a place there be
For letter'd novices as crude as we,

---

1. As used in this article, "I" means co-author Faig. Co-author Haden furnished most of the illustrations for this article, along with other material.

The happy place we quickly would procure.
And each become a finish'd amateur.

> —H. P. LOVECRAFT, "To the Members of the United Amateur Press Ass'n From the Providence Amateur Press Club"

Introduction

By and large, local amateur press clubs have been relatively short-lived, Boston's Hub Club (fl. 1890–1924) and Brooklyn's Blue Pencil Club (fl. 1908–1960s) being notable exceptions. Among other relatively ephemeral local clubs, the Providence Amateur Press Club, which flourished for roughly two years between the fall of 1914 and the fall of 1916, was fortunate in having Howard Phillips Lovecraft as one of its members. Lovecraft's work has ascended to worldwide fame in the more than eighty years that have now elapsed since its first posthumous book publication by Arkham House in 1939. The first full-length biography of Lovecraft, written by L. Sprague de Camp, appeared in 1975, and a second biography by S. T. Joshi followed twenty-one years later in 1996. Both of Lovecraft's biographers gave generous attention to Lovecraft's involvement with the Providence Amateur Press Club in 1914–16. In addition, L. Sprague de Camp and his wife Catherine Crook de Camp traveled to Portsmouth, Ohio, to interview the aged Rev. John T. Dunn (1889–1983), one of the last surviving members of the Club, on 20–21 May 1975. The result of those interviews was de Camp's

EDWARD H. COLE

separate article "Young Man Lovecraft" (YML), first published in 1978. In due course, Father Dunn's surviving letters from Lovecraft came to the Lovecraft Collection at Brown University and they were published in 1995 in *Books at Brown* (JTD), with an extensive editorial apparatus by editors S. T. Joshi, David E. Schultz, and John H. Stanley. Earlier, Marc A. Michaud of Necronomicon Press (West Warwick, R.I.) reprinted the June 1915 and February 1916 issues of the *Providence Amateur* in facsimile editions (1976 and 1977, respectively).

Thus we begin by knowing a great deal about the Providence Amateur Press Club to which H. P. Lovecraft belonged. The club was founded by Providence amateur journalist Victor L. Basinet (1889–1956) among a group of seven or eight evening high school students at the urging of Edward H. Cole (1892–1966) of West Somerville, Mass.[2] Lovecraft wrote about the club at length in a letter to Cole of 23 November 1914:

> As Miss Hoffman has doubtless informed you, the members are recruited from the evening high school, and are scarcely representative of the intellectual life of Providence. Their environment has been distinctly plebeian, and their literary standards should not at this time be criticised too harshly [. . .]
>
> Their President, Victor L. Basinet, is a socialist of the extreme type, whose opinions have been formed through contact with the

---

2. The editors of JTD cite John T. Dunn and Caroline Miller as founders of the club (JTD 158). The exact citation from de Camp's account of his interview with Rev. John T. Dunn is as follows (YML 172): "Dunn, then 24, was earning his living as a plumber. He and his colleagues heard of the amateur-journalism movement. On the suggestion of the amateur journalist Edward H. Cole of Boston, they decided to form the Providence Amateur Press Club. The leading spirits were Victor Basinet and a Miss Miller, and Lovecraft was a founding member." Perhaps the best that one can say at this remove is that Basinet, Miller, and Dunn were the moving spirits in the club's formation, with encouragement from Cole.

most dangerous labour agitators in the country. He is, however, a man of much native intelligence, and I strongly hope that the influence of the press association may help to modify his conception of society. The Official Editor, John T. Dunn, is a wild Irishman with the usual offensive Popish and anti-English views; but he is of very fair education, and fired by real literary ambition. Of course, there is much frivolity in some of the members, which detracts from the dignity of the meetings. (*AG* 28–29)

The club members were apparently recruited primarily among young adults who were attending an evening high school course in English literature. Writing to Alfred Galpin on 29 August 1918, Lovecraft described the Club as "a 'literary' club of Micks who dwelt in the dingy 'North End' of the city" (*AG* 211). The Easter Rising against English rule intervened on 24–30 April 1916 and was harshly suppressed by England. This only exacerbated Irish feelings against England, and many Irish-Americans did not support the entry of the United States into the First World War in 1917. John Dunn refused to register for the draft and, when involuntarily registered, refused to serve, for which he was court-martialed by a military court and sentenced to twenty years' imprisonment in 1917. (He ultimately served about two years.) Basinet, of French extraction, succeeded in registering in New York as a conscientious objector. Dunn's case attracted national press coverage and Lovecraft vowed to his correspondent Alfred M. Galpin that he was "done with Dunn" (*AG* 212). By this time, however, the Club itself has ceased to be. Lovecraft's poem "Providence Amateur Press Club (Deceased) to the Athenaeum Club of Journalism" (A.Ms., John Hay Library) is dated 24 November 1916, and has generally been interpreted to mean that the Providence Amateur Press Club was deceased by that date (see *AT* 339–41, 505).

Perhaps the harsh feelings evoked by the Easter Rising of 1916 contributed to the club's demise by the latter part of that year. Nearly sixty years later, John T. Dunn vividly recalled Lovecraft's stiff bearing and staunch defense of England in his interviews with L. Sprague de Camp. De Camp described some of Dunn's recollections:

> Dunn's friends considered Lovecraft "laughable," never suspecting that he would one day be famous. "Among ourselves, we kind of made fun of him, not knowing his background." Now, said Dunn, he was sorry for his lack of sympathy with H.P.L., whose handicaps he had not been aware of. Dunn added that, if he had known that Lovecraft would become an important literary figure, he would have paid closer attention to him. (YML 173)

In correspondence with de Camp (16 November 1973), Father Dunn had recalled how Lovecraft's lifestyle contrasted with the blue-collar lifestyles of the members of the club: "He told me that he would think of a piece to write and he would stay up to finish it even if it took till six in the morning. He had an income and he did not have to get up as we did to go to work" (de Camp 88).

Lovecraft served as literary director of the club during the initial 1914–15 term and then as official editor during the 1915–16 term. Lovecraft wrote to Dunn on 14 October 1916 (JTD 192–93):

> Turning to amateur matters, I hope you will renew your membership in the United, and that you will be able in time to rehabilitate the Providence Amateur Press Club. Perhaps the lack of publishing activity this year has caused the members almost to forget that there is such a thing as amateur journalism. Many of my present duties are outside the association, in connection with the Symphony Literary Service, which is now handling a goodly amount of verse. Pres. Campbell [U.A.P.A. President 1916–1917] lately requested me to remind Messrs. Kelso and Wright of this State that their membership has expired; but judging from your club's attitude toward Kelso, and the rather hopeless nature of his verse, I think I will confine my persuasions to Mr. Wright, who never became really active.[3]

---

3. Wright had expressed interest in establishing an amateur press club in

The $1 annual dues payable to the United Amateur Press Association (UAPA) were undoubtedly an issue for many members of the Providence Amateur Press Club.[4] The average hourly wage in manufacturing in 1914 was 22 cents. A full work week of ten hours per day Monday–Friday and five hours on Saturday would produce a weekly paycheck of $12.10 and many workers (especially women) earned significantly less.

Across all kinds of manufacturing, the average annual wage, accounting for hours actually worked, was $580 in 1914, but textile industries, a significant component in Rhode Island, paid substantially less: $387 in cotton goods, $479 in wool and worsted, and $500 in men's clothing.[5] So investing $1 in annual UAPA dues was a major expenditure for the blue-collar mem-

---

Pawtucket, RI, but apparently never founded such a club. The editors of JTD (173) identify Wright as Herbert A. Wright of 301 Prospect Street, Pawtucket, RI. I found no Herbert Wright in Pawtucket 1913, 1916, and 1917 Directories maintained online by Ancestry.com. The 1920 and 1930 U.S. censuses recorded at least two Herbert Wrights in Rhode Island: an English-born Herbert Wright (b. 1893/94) who worked in a textile mill in North Providence and a Rhode Island-born Herbert Wright who resided in Riverside and worked as a public schoolteacher. The latter Herbert Wright (born 26 November 1889, died July 1969) appears in the Social Security Death Master File. However, there were other Herbert Wrights residing in Rhode Island and nearby Massachusetts during these years.

4. While some white-collar occupations were better-paid than manufacturing work, $1 annual association dues was nevertheless a significant commitment for white-collar members as well. Writing to John T. Dunn on 19 February 1917 (JTD 212–13), HPL reported that his recruit Louis E. Boutwell of Scottsville, NY, an English teacher in the Rochester High School, had declined to renew his U.A.P.A. membership on the grounds that he had not received "a dollar's worth of enjoyment."

5. The economic statistics cited in this paragraph are taken from Albert Rees, *Real Wages in Manufacturing: 1890–1914* (Princeton, NJ: Princeton University Press, 1961). The work can also now be consulted online.

bers of the Providence Amateur Press Club. Several of them never joined UAPA. Of the founding members of the club other than Lovecraft himself, we know that Basinet, Dunn, McManus, Miller, and Shehan belonged for various periods to UAPA. Writing to Dunn on 4 July 1916 (JTD 188), Lovecraft asked his correspondent to urge McManus and Shehan to get their UAPA election ballot proxies completed and mailed. Later, on 14 October 1916 (JTD 198), he urged Dunn to renew his own UAPA membership. On 20 July 1915 (JTD 171), he had expressed concern that Basinet, who had attended the July 1915 convention of the National Amateur Press Association (NAPA), might desert the ranks of the United for the National. Despite all his efforts, Lovecraft was again the sole Rhode Island resident on the UAPA roster by November 1917 (JTD 200).[6]

I cannot aspire to add a great deal to the vivid picture of the Providence Amateur Press Club in 1914–16 provided by de Camp and Joshi. It is really a matter of adding bits and pieces at this point. In the "Report of the President" in the *United Amateur* for November 1914, we find the following paragraph written by Dora M. Hepner (1888–1968)[7] (UAPA President 1914–15):

> On October 30th, the Providence Amateur Press Club was organized with eight members. Details concerning this club, its officers etc., will be found on another page of this paper. With such energetic amateurs as Mr. Lovecraft, Mr. Basinet and Mr. Dunn for members, this club will surely shine out as a bright spot in the Dom.

---

6. Writing to Dunn on 20 July 1915 (JTD 171), HPL had recalled that he had been the only Providence name in the UAPA membership list in the May 1914 *United Amateur*. (He had been recruited by Edward F. Daas on 6 April 1914.)

7. Later the first wife of Anthony F. Moitoret (1892–1979) and mother of the noted amateur journalist Victor A. Moitoret (1919–2005).

Regrettably, additional details concerning the Providence Amateur Press Club do not appear in this issue of the *United Amateur*. The only additional information is the name and address of the club secretary (Caroline Miller, 27 Henrietta St., Providence, R.I.) in the "Club Directory" (29) and the inclusion of one club member (Edmund L. Shehan, 30 Alverson Ave., Providence, R.I.) among the applicants for UAPA membership listed by Secretary H. B Darrow (28). Shehan was proposed for membership by Victor L. Basinet; his credential was "Some Objections to Motion Pictures."[8] Friday, 30 October 1914—the day before Halloween—was surely a fitting date for the foundation of a club in which the twentieth-century master of the supernatural tale was to play a prominent role. I do not know the place of the organizational meeting. According to Joshi (*AG* 28–29, citing Lovecraft's letter to Edward H. Cole dated 23 November 1914), the club generally met toward the end of each month. Friday does not appear to have been the regular meeting day, for we have the date of another meeting—Wednesday, 24 March 1915—in the article "Our Candidate" in the *Providence Amateur* for June 1915.

We have the names of nine members of the Club as printed in the *Providence Amateur* for June 1915: Victor L. Basinet, President; Eugene [Eugenie] M. Kern, Vice President; Caroline Miller, Secretary-Treasurer; Howard P. Lovecraft, Literary Director; John T. Dunn, Official Editor; Edmond L. Sheehan [*sic*, but corrected to Edmund L. Shehan in the second number]; Fred A. Byland; Mildred Metcalf; and Peter J. McManus. I am not sure which of these nine was not among the eight founders of 30 Oc-

---

8. Shehan wrote about the visit that he and Fred A. Byland paid to the Eastern Film Company in his essay "The Making of a Motion Picture" in the *Providence Amateur* for February 1916. I do not know if Shehan's credential was ever published.

tober 1914;[9] I have treated them all as founding members in the material that follows. Lovecraft's poem "To the Members of the United Amateur Press Ass'n from the Providence Amateur Press Club" (originally published in the *Providence Amateur*, June 1915; rpt. *AT* 336–38) provides verse sketches of many of these members and of an additional member, a Mr. Reilly, as well. We know that carpenter-poet Guy Harold Kelso was a somewhat troublesome member of the club in 1915–16. One final member of the Club, William Aloysius Henry, we know only from John T. Dunn's recollections:

> Another member of the Providence Amateur Press Club, living next door to Dunn, had a sister named Sadie Henry. Once Miss Henry, visiting at Dunn's house, as a joke among the circle of friends, telephoned Lovecraft and suggested that he take her out on a date. Lovecraft said: "I'll have to ask my mother," and nothing came of it. (YML 174)

I will leave the delectable story of the woman who asked Lovecraft for a date for my sketch of William Aloysius Henry. Suffice it to say that Sarah J. (Sadie) Henry, born 3 June 1879, was more than a decade older than Lovecraft. Young Misses Kern, Metcalf, and Miller may have found Lovecraft equally curious, but only the older woman Sadie Henry had enough interest to kid him about going out on a date. Generally speaking, it was older women who were most interested in Lovecraft: Winifred Virginia (Jackson) Jordan (1876–1959)[10] and Sonia (Haft)

---

9. I would be inclined to guess that HPL himself was the member missing from the founding eight, and only called in later by Edward H. Cole and Helene Hoffman to assist Victor L. Basinet and his fellow evening high school students. However, it should be noted that Rev. John T. Dunn himself recalled that HPL was a founding member of the club (see YML 172).

10. Divorced from her husband Mr. Jordan, Miss Jackson had resumed use of her maiden name around 1920.

Greene (1883–1972) being the two names most prominently connected with him within the amateur journalism hobby.

Father Dunn explained the origins of the club to L. Sprague de Camp as follows:

> Father Dunn told how he and seven or eight other students attended a night class at a high school in the northern part of Providence in 1914. They were working-class people in their twenties with literary ambitions, who wanted an advanced course in English. (YML 172)

The editors of JTD (158) put the high school in North Providence—a separate town—but I think we must defer to Father Dunn's crystal-clear recollections. Providence had opened its first public high school in 1843 at the corner of Angell and Benefit Streets (205 Benefit). A larger high school to replace the original was erected in 1877 at the corner of Summer and Pond Streets south and west of the immediate downtown Providence area. (The original Benefit Street high school subsequently served as a state normal school and as headquarters for the state Supreme Court.) The high school complex at Summer and Pond continued to grow through the years. The Manual Training School, subsequently the Technical High School, was built in 1893 and enlarged in 1908. (By 1936 it had become the School Department administration building.) The Classical High School was built on the southwest corner of Summer and Pond in 1897, around which time the original 1877 high school was renamed the English High School. (The final incarnation of the 1877 English High School before its demolition was as Central Annex A.)

In 1898, Hope Street High School—where Lovecraft attended—was added on the East Side of the city. Hope Street High School was replaced by a new school on the opposite side of the street (former site of Hope Reservoir) in 1936—the same year in which Mount Pleasant High School was opened in that section of the city—and eventually torn down in 1970–72. In 1923, Cen-

tral High School was erected on the block defined by Summer St., Pond St., Winter St., and Montcalm Court—immediately west of the existing high school complex. A gymnasium was erected at Pond and Spring Streets in 1924 and Central High was further expanded in 1926. Today, Central High and Classical High remain of the original downtown high school complex. Central High School still embodies some of the original 1920s architecture, but Classical High School is all modern architecture. Summer Street, Winter Street, and Pond Street no longer traverse the high school complex.[11]

Lovecraft had attended the 1898 Hope Street High School for the 1904–05, 1906–07, and 1907–08 terms with a reduced course load in the final term. He apparently had to skip the 1905–06 term on account of poor health. His high school transcript as summarized by de Camp (42, 45, 50–51) and Joshi (*IAP* 100–01) does not mention any subsequent pursuit of evening classes, although Lovecraft upon encountering the job mar-

---

11. The information concerning Providence high schools in this paragraph derives primarily from John H. Cady, *The Civic and Architectural Development of Providence* (Providence, RI: The Book Shop, 1957).

ket for clerical and other "white collar" occupations must have sorely felt the lack of a high school diploma. It is not impossible that he was among the evening high school students who formed the nucleus of the Providence Amateur Press Club—but I think it is more likely that he was called in to add some literary substance to the club after it had been founded by Victor L. Basinet and John T. Dunn among the evening high school students. The club members tended to be clustered around John T. Dunn's home at 83 Commodore Street on Providence's "North Side," but in actuality were widely scattered over the urban landscape in 1914. The following list shows the 1914 address of each member and the distance (in Mapquest miles) from the 83 Commodore Street focal point:

> Victor L. Basinet, 14 Gordon Ave., 4.25 miles
> Frederick A. Byland,[12] 29 Republican St., 3.38 miles
> John T. Dunn, 83 Commodore St., 0.00 mile
> Eugenie M. Kern, 372 Branch Ave., 0.14 mile
> Howard P. Lovecraft, 598 Angell St., 3.11 miles

---

12. Fred Byland does not appear in the 1914 Providence Directory under either Byland or Bylund, but his widowed mother Margaret (Margheret) Bylund was listed at 29 Republican Street in both the 1913 and 1915 Providence Directories, and I believe it is a safe assumption that Fred was living with her. A twentieth-century Democratic party stronghold like Providence could not allow a street name like Republican to endure and the street has been renamed; I have used its starting point at 286 Atwells Avenue to measure the distance from the Byland residence. It was certainly in close proximity to the present intersection of Atwells Avenue and Knight Street. Republican Street originally ended at Kent Street, which originated at Knight Street. An 1870 Providence Directory listed both Republican Street and Kent Street; an 1856 Providence Directory listed neither. The 1911 Providence House Directory indicated that Kent Street had been renamed Republican Street.

Peter J. McManus, 3 Jackson, 2.86 miles
Mildred G. Metcalf, 14 Catalpa St., 1.31 miles
Caroline Miller,[13] 45 Shiloh St., 1.06 miles
Edmund L. Shehan, 30 Alverson Ave., 4.57 miles
William A. Henry, 93 Commodore St., 0.02 mile
Guy H. Kelso, 56 Olney St., 1.53 miles

While strictly speaking only Dunn, Henry, Kern, and Miller lived within the "North End" (Wanskuck and Charles neighborhoods), Kelso and Metcalf were not far removed, within a mile and a half of the club's Commodore Street headquarters. Lovecraft, Byland, and McManus all lived about three miles from 83 Commodore Street—Lovecraft on the far East Side, Byland on Federal Hill, and McManus near Cathedral Square downtown. Basinet, on the south side of the city, and Shehan, on the west side, were farthest removed from the 83 Commodore Street focal point in the "North End." All things considered, if the members of the Providence Amateur Press Club were attending evening high school classes at one of the regular high school buildings, Hope Street High School would probably have been the most convenient. From the Dunn home at 83 Commodore Street, it was 1.85 miles to Hope Street High School (modern 324 Hope Street address) and 3.23 miles to Classical/English High School (modern 770 Westminster Street address). There is a modern high school at 1828 Mineral Spring Avenue in North Providence; this is 2.67 miles from 83 Commodore Street. On

---

13. Miss Miller's 1914 Providence Directory address is 45 Shiloh Street. However, her November 1914 *United Amateur* address (27 Henrietta Street) is in close proximity to 45 Shiloh Street, being 1.18 miles from 83 Commodore Street. Both the Shiloh Street and the Henrietta Street addresses were in the Wanskuck neighborhood of Providence, named for Wanskuck Pond.

the other hand, available transportation might have favored attending evening classes at the downtown high school complex at Summer and Pond. It is certainly possible that the public schools held evening high school classes in locations other than the four existing high schools in 1914. Unless the Providence Public School system has retained records of enrollments in evening high school classes, I fear that we may never know for certain where the club members attended their evening classes.[14]

Despite their separation in miles, an excellent public streetcar system would probably have made club meetings in individual homes a possibility. We do not know for a fact where the club meetings were held; certainly there does not appear to be any surviving record to indicate that Lovecraft hosted any club meeting at 598 Angell Street. The response provoked in Susie Lovecraft by a lively mixed-sex group of working-class people in their twenties would not have been difficult to predict; if she had been offended by the crudities of Arthur Fredlund in 1905, she—who nearly turned W. Paul Cook away from the door of 598 Angell Street because of his dress—would surely have reacted adversely to the lively members of the Providence Amateur Press Club. It is possible that a friendly teacher allowed club meetings consist-

---

14. It may be noted that club member (and 1914–15 Vice President) Eugenie [Eugene] M. Kern was already listed with occupation teacher in the 1914 Providence Directory. However, I do not find her listed among the faculty shown for the Providence High Schools in that Directory (45). In the 1920s, Kern taught at Knightsville School in Cranston, in the 1930s at Samuel Slater Junior High School in Pawtucket, and in the 1940s at West High School (now Charles E. Shea High School) in Pawtucket. Born 25 December 1893, Kern was probably just commencing her teaching career when the Providence Amateur Press Club was founded. I do not think it is likely that she was actually the teacher of the evening high school class in advanced English which many of the club members attended. However, I'm willing to be surprised!

ing primarily of evening high school students to take place at the high school facility. However, administrators, janitors, and insurance policy provisions are perennially hostile to such "extraneous" use of public facilities.

Is it accurate to refer to the club members as "working class"? Overall, I do not believe it is unfair. The following list shows the 1914 occupation and the longtime occupation for each club member:

> Victor L. Basinet: (1914) designer; (longtime) nurse, artist
> Frederick A. Byland: (1914) [not found];[15] (longtime) silversmith, tea and coffee merchant, state employee
> John T. Dunn: (1914) plumber; (longtime) Roman Catholic priest
> Eugenie M. Kern: (1914) teacher; (longtime) teacher
> Howard P. Lovecraft: (1914) student; (longtime) writer & reviser
> Peter J. McManus: (1914) [none listed];[16] (longtime) public school janitor
> Mildred G. Metcalf: (1914) [not found];[17] (longtime) hat shop proprietor
> Caroline Miller: (1914) stenographer; (longtime) homemaker
> Edmund L. Shehan: (1914) [none listed];[18] (longtime) machinist

---

15. Probably living at home with his widowed mother at 29 Republican Street. His 1914 occupation is unknown but he was already at Gorham when he registered for the draft in 1917–18.
16. Probably a laborer or janitor if employed.
17. Probably living at home with her parents at 14 Catalpa Street.
18. He was a loom maker in 1910 and a reed maker in 1917–18; if employed in 1914, he was probably still employed in some branch of the textile industry, in which his father worked as a wool-sorter.

William A. Henry: (1914) express company clerk; (longtime) sporting goods store proprietor

Guy H. Kelso: (1914) carpenter; (longtime) carpenter

Surprisingly, all the known club members were Rhode Island natives except for Guy Kelso (born in Maine), Peter J. McManus (born in Ireland), and Caroline Miller (born in Pennsylvania). Of their parents I can say the following from census records:

Victor L. Basinet: father (born Canada), mother (born RI)
Frederick A. Byland: father (born Sweden), mother (born Ireland)
John T. Dunn: father (born Ireland), mother (born Ireland)
Eugenie M. Kern: father (born Germany), mother (born NJ)
Peter J. McManus: father (born Ireland), mother (born Ireland)
Mildred G. Metcalf: father (born Rhode Island), mother (born MA)
Caroline Miller: father (born France), mother (born France)
Edmund L. Shehan: father (born New York), mother (born RI)
William A. Henry: father (born Ireland), mother (born Ireland)
Guy H. Kelso: father (born New Brunswick, Canada), mother (born ME)

Father Dunn's remembrance of the club members as twenty-year-olds during the club's active period is accurate. I list below known club members, from the earliest-born to the latest-born:

Guy H. Kelso, born 28 June 1878, Island Falls, ME
William A. Henry, born 3 April 1884, Providence, RI
Peter J. McManus, born 4 August 1888, Rooskey, County Roscommon, Ireland
John T. Dunn, born 2 January 1889, Providence, RI
Victor L. Basinet, born 14 March 1889, Providence, RI
Howard P. Lovecraft, born 20 August 1890, Providence, RI

Edmund L. Shehan, born 12 March 1891, Johnston, RI
Caroline Miller, born 16 July 1891, Pennsylvania
Eugenie M. Kern, born 25 December 1893, Providence, RI
Mildred G. Metcalf, born 5 January 1894, Providence, RI
Frederick A. Byland, born 5 June 1894, Providence, RI

By and large, the club members were long-lived. I list below known club members, from the earliest-deceased to the latest-deceased:

Howard P. Lovecraft, died 15 March 1937, Providence, RI
Guy Harold Kelso died 1950, Providence RI
Victor L. Basinet, died 9 October 1956, Los Angeles, CA
Mildred G. (Metcalf) died 19 September 1964, Warren, RI.
William A. Henry died January 1966, Providence RI.[19]
Frederick A. Byland, February 1967, Providence, RI
Peter J. McManus, October 1971, Providence, RI
Edmund L. Shehan, May 1972, Warwick, RI
Eugenie M. Kern, April 1977, Providence, RI
Caroline (Miller) Barlow, July 1979, Sudbury, MA
John T. Dunn, 24 May 1983, Portsmouth, OH

It is amazing to think that a fiftieth reunion of the Providence Amateur Press Club on 30 October 1964 would have found six club members still living: Fred Byland, Peter McManus, Edmund Shehan, Eugenie Kern, Caroline (Miller) Barlow, and John T. Dunn. A sixtieth reunion on 30 October 1974 would have found three club members still living: Eugenie Kern, Caroline (Miller) Barlow, and John T. Dunn. However, from July 1979 until his death in May 1983, there was only one survivor remaining: John T. Dunn. We are richly blessed that Father Dunn was interviewed by L. Sprague de Camp about the Provi-

---

19. This information from an Ancestry Family Tree was not verified by RI State Archives.

dence Amateur Press Club in 1975. His crystal-clear memories are the best picture we have of the club, its members, and the young lady who dared to ask H. P. Lovecraft for a date. Hopefully, the tapes of the de Camp interviews of Father Dunn[20]—or at least transcripts thereof—survive.

Lovecraft was probably right to remember Victor L. Basinet and John T. Dunn as the best intellects of the club, and both of them went on to careers of accomplishment—Basinet as an artist and Dunn as a Roman Catholic priest. But the others certainly did not lead lives worthy of contempt. William A. Henry became the proprietor of his own sporting goods business, and his sister Sarah J. Henry (she who dared ask Lovecraft for a date) was a jewelry saleswoman for the prestigious Cherry & Webb department store. Caroline (Miller) Barlow married a university professor and raised a family. Eugenie M. Kern never married and ended a lifelong teaching career at West High School in Pawtucket, RI. Mildred (Metcalf) Heald took over her deceased husband's hat business in Providence and continued it for over twenty years. Edmund L. Shehan was a skilled machinist, Guy H. Kelso a carpenter, and Peter J. McManus a public school janitor. Fred A. Byland had a varied career, working for many years at Gorham, then as a coffee and tea merchant, then as a state of Rhode Island employee. Byland and his wife Winifred were minor figures in the Democratic party machine in Providence.

I do not make any representation that the bare vital statistics that comprise the majority of this article succeed in bringing to life the erstwhile members of the Providence Amateur Press Club. We can only imagine the lively meetings of those twenty-year-olds in 1914–16 with the help of Father Dunn's recollec-

---

20. De Camp (YML 172) specifically noted that much of his two-hour interview with Rev. John T. Dunn on the afternoon of 20 May 1975 was tape-recorded.

tions and the other facts developed by Lovecraft's biographers. However, I hope this article does achieve the objective of informing us about the members of the club from the perspective of the outer events of their lives. Of the club members other than Lovecraft, I had—until the pictures found for this second edition—seen only the photograph of Victor L. Basinet at the 1915 NAPA convention. The club fiftieth reunion on 30 October 1964 must remain forever a fantasy. As a poor substitute I offer in the remainder of this article what little I have been able to discover about the erstwhile members of the Providence Amateur Press Club. I have relied primarily on the electronic records of Ancestry.com, consulted at the Glenview Public Library, and on the New England Historic Genealogical Society's online database of the Providence, R.I., vital records. I could have done better work had I had access to a complete set of Rhode Island directories. I am grateful to bookseller Jim Weyant for selling me a copy of the 1914 Providence Directory—this purchase inspired me to continue research on the members of the Providence Amateur Press Club in 1914–16.

I hope there will be more advances in research regarding the club in future years. Perhaps the Providence School Department does retain records of evening high school enrollees, which include various club members. If so, we may be able to find out where they attended their advanced English course. It may even be possible that H. P. Lovecraft attended such a course, if the record would be separate from his regular high school transcript at Hope Street High School. Perhaps other researchers interviewed other members of the Providence Amateur Press Club before they died. It is only a shame that Edward H. Cole's vast correspondence files, apart from his correspondence with H. P. Lovecraft, were destroyed. They would probably have contained correspondence with Victor L. Basinet and John T. Dunn that would shed further light upon the Club. Lovecraft's own surviving letters need to be reviewed further for more references to the Providence Amateur Press Club and its members. Perhaps we can even find the given name of club member —— Reilly in a surviving Lovecraft letter. A more skilled family history researcher than I with complete access to local resources in Providence can undoubtedly clear up some of my doubts and correct some of my errors. In the meantime, we can only imagine what fun those young members of the Providence Amateur Press Club must have had back in 1914–16. What a strange creature most of them must have found Howard Phillips Lovecraft! If they made fun of him, I nevertheless doubt that they were very cruel. Lovecraft's biographer L. Sprague de Camp believed that Lovecraft's involvement with these young, blue-collar contemporaries probably helped to broaden his horizons at an earlier stage than might otherwise have occurred.

In the following sketches, the lines at the beginning of each sketch derive from Lovecraft's poem "To the Members of the United Amateur Press Ass'n From the Providence Amateur Press Club," first published in the June 1915 number of the *Providence Amateur*.

Founding Members

Victor L. Basinet

> As President above the others set,
> Firm in his rule, see gifted Basinet,
> By his bright genius all the club was made;
> In every act his wisdom is displayed.
> Of broadest sympathy, he seeks to lend
> A pitying ear to all, and all befriend;
> With fearless mien he scorns oppressive laws,
> And stands a champion of the people's cause.

Date and Place of Birth: 14 March 1889, Providence, RI
Date and Place of Death: 9 October 1956, Los Angeles, CA
1914 Providence Directory Address: 14 Gordon Avenue
Club Offices: President, 1914–15
Writings in the *Providence Amateur:* [none]

Victor L. Basinet served as the first president of the Providence Amateur Press Club and was one of the prime movers in its foundation.[21] He was the son of the veteran printer Louis A. and his wife Effie R. Basinet. In 1914, Louis Basinet was operating the Atlantic Printing Company at his father's print shop at 35 Cranston Street in Providence. The display advertisement on page 1198 of the 1914 Providence Directory indicated that the company performed "book and job printing" and indicated a specialty in "translating and printing in French." His father had been raised in Quebec, so must have known French well. The 1914 and 1915 directories list Victor as a designer boarding in his parents' home at 14 Gordon Avenue in Providence; in the 1913 directory, Victor had been listed as an artist at the same address. He had been enumerated as an artist boarding in the Providence home of his 49-year-old Canadian-born father Louis A. and 45-

Victor L. Basinet, in 1912.

---

21. Next to HPL himself, Basinet was probably the club member who was most active in the amateur journalism hobby. He attended the convention of the NAPA in Brooklyn in July 1915, which caused HPL to express concern about his loyalties to John T. Dunn (JTD 171). The October 1915 number of HPL's own amateur journal, the *Conservative,* mentioned that Basinet intended to issue his own amateur journal, the *Rebel* (see JTD 166n8). I do not know whether Basinet ever actually published any numbers of the *Rebel.*

year-old Rhode Island–born mother Effi R. when the 1910 census was taken. When Victor registered for the draft on 5 June 1917, he was residing at 431 East 26th Street in New York City and was working as a nurse at Bellevue Hospital. He had brown eyes and black hair and classified himself as a conscientious objector. Lovecraft remarked in his letter to Edward H. Cole of 23 November 1914 that Basinet was an extreme socialist; his name can be found in FBI "Old German Files 1909–1921" available on a fee basis on the Internet. By January 1920, when the U.S. census was enumerated, Basinet had removed to Los Angeles, where he was living in the home of physician William D. Judge and working as a hospital orderly. He claimed birth in Kentucky of a Canadian-born father and an Irish-born mother.

Changing his name to "Victor Hugo Basinet" (perhaps in admiration for the famous French writer), Basinet did eventually attain recognition as an artist. A short biography on the Ask/ART site on the Internet, citing Edna Hughes's "Artists in California, 1786–1940," *Who's Who in American Art 1938–41* and *Artists of the American West* (Doris Dawdy), provides the following information:

> Born in Providence, RI on March 14, 1889. Basinet was a pupil of Hugo Bruel, Jean Goucher, Antonio Cremonini, Angelo Carducci, and David Siqueiros. He lived in both Monterey and Los Angeles during the late 1930s. He died in the latter Oct. 9, 1956. Member: LA AA; Charcoal Club (LA); Bloc Mural Painters (LA), American Artists Congress (LA), 1938. In: USC; NMAA; Gaelic School (Dublin Ireland).

Who's Who in American Art (1935) gives further details:

> BASINET, Victor Hugo, 2600 So. Hoover St.; h. 1008 West Adams St., Los Angeles; summer, Monterey, Calif. Mural p. Des. Dec— Born Providence, R.I., March 14.

Basinet is also listed in Peter Hastings Falk, ed., *Who Was Who in American Art* (1999). He illustrated Ernest R. Trattner's *The Autobiography of God* (New York: Scribner, 1930). Four of his paintings are owned by the Smithsonian Museum of American Art: "Don Francisco Avila House, Los Angeles" (1936) [1979.10.2], "Fisherman's Wharf" (1936) [1964.1.170], "Point Lobos" (1935) [1967.74.2], and "Wharf Markets" (1936) [1964.1.171]. The painting "Point Lobos" had formerly been in the collection of the U.S. Department of Public Welfare, Receiving Home for Children, Washington, D.C.

Frederick Aloysius Byland

> Next of the band, the quiet Byland see,
> Whose gifts are mix'd with gentle dignity.
> With forceful logic does the scholar think;
> With pleasing style his thoughts are trac'd in ink.

Date and Place of Birth: 5 June 1894, Providence, RI
Date and Place of Death: February 1967, Providence, RI
1914 Providence Directory Address: [not listed; but probably living with his widowed mother at 29 Republican St. (her address in 1913 and 1915 directories)]
Club Offices: [none known]
Writings in the *Providence Amateur*: [none]

Fred was the son of Swedish-born Albert and Irish-born Margaret Byland. His father Albert was listed as a watchman boarding at 46 South Main Street in the 1892 Providence Directory. Albert (last name spelled "Bylund") married Margaret Sullivan in Providence on 17 May 1892. They had a son Albert W. Bylund, born in Providence on 3 March 1893, who died there on 5 October 1893, aged seven months. Younger brother Frederick was born in Providence on 5 June 1894. Albert apparently returned to Sweden for a visit in 1897. A 1900 Providence Business Directory lists Albert as proprietor of a wine and liquor business at 334 Atwell's Avenue; another directory of the same year lists Albert as a clerk at 64 Fountain Street, residing at 33 Spruce Street. In the 1900 U.S. census, Albert and his family were enumerated at 4 Brayton Avenue in Ward 4. Albert, born August 1861 in Sweden, was a naturalized citizen, having emigrated to the United States in 1882, and was working as a bartender. His wife Margaret, born in Ireland in May 1867, had emigrated to the United States in 1886. Albert, aged 46, died in Providence on 6 October 1906. I did not find either Fred or his widowed mother Margaret (Sullivan) Byland in the 1914 Providence Directory. However, Margheret Bylund, widow, was listed at 29 Republican Street in the 1913 Providence Directory and listed there again in the 1915 Providence Directory. I conclude that Fred and his mother were probably at 29 Republican Street when the club was founded in 1914. Fred's mother Margaret followed her husband in death at age 58 in Providence, Rhode Island on 11 March 1926.

Frederick Aloysius Byland, in 1912.

When Fred registered for the World War I draft in 1917–18, he was residing at 1 Ericsson Place (off Atwells Avenue) and working as a metal turner for the Gorham Manufacturing Company in the Elmwood section of Providence; he listed his widowed mother as a dependent. When the 1920 census was enumerated, Fred was recorded with his widowed mother Margaret at 1 Ericsson Place and his occupation listed as a jeweler at Gorham; in this census

Fred claimed that both his mother and his father were born in Ireland. (The home at 1 Ericsson Place was shared for many years with members of the Vallely family, who may have been relatives.) Providence directories through 1930 continued to list Fred at this address. On 14 September 1922 Fred married Winifred C. Hand in Providence. The 1930 census recorded Fred residing at 1 Giles Place with his wife Winifred; he was apparently still at Gorham, since his occupation was listed as silver worker in a silver factory; the 1931 Providence Directory also reflects Fred's changed address. Fred continued to be listed as a silversmith in the Providence directories through 1935; beginning in the 1938 Providence Directory, however, Fred was listed as proprietor of a tea and coffee business operating from his home at 1 Giles Place. Fred and his wife Winifred continued to be listed in the tea and coffee business at 1 Giles Place through the 1947 Providence Directory. It's interesting to note that from 1900 onward the Byland [Bylund] family resided in the Atwells Avenue area, gradually moving westward along the avenue from Spruce Street, to Republican Street, to Ericsson Place, and finally to Giles Place.

Gorham Silversmiths, Providence, 1906. Gorham was one of the biggest local employers in Providence, and the possible employer of H. P. Lovecraft's father as a salesman.

The 1932 Providence Directory reflects Fred's service as secretary of the Irish American Club at 767 Westminster Street and the Ancient Order of Hibernians. By 1941 and 1942, he was serving as secretary of Hope Council no. 398 of the Knights of Columbus at 14 Greene Street. When registering for the draft again in 1942, Fred listed his employer as the State Department of Public Works in the State Office Building in Providence. The 1942 directory also listed his wife as president of the Rhode Island Women's Democratic Club meeting at 340 Weybosset Street the fourth Thursday of every month. In the 1952 and 1957 directories, Fred was listed as coordinator in the state Division of Automotive Equipment. In the 1964 Providence Directory, Fred was listed as superintendent of the State Automotive Maintenance Unit—perhaps he had received a promotion. During all this time he and his wife remained at 1 Giles Place in Providence. The Social Security Death Master File records Fred's death in Providence in February 1967. His widow Winifred (born 11 May 1895) died in Pawtucket, RI, in July 1981.

John Thomas Dunn

> Next Dunn behold, whose active, well-stocked mind
> Is worth a hundred of the pompous kind.
> Learned but modest, sure of what he knows,
> His wit and sense in endless ways he shows.
> Skilled in dispute, with none he fears to vie,
> But picks up L——'s faults in history.
> From his quick tongue the proofs abundant roll,
> And Hugo's quoted 'gainst the mighty C——!

Date and Place of Birth: 2 January 1889, Providence, RI
Date and Place of Death: 24 May 1983, Portsmouth, OH
1914 Providence Directory Address: 83 Commodore Street
Club Offices: Official Editor, 1914–15

Writings in the *Providence Amateur*:
[unsigned editorial material], June 1915
"Editorial," June 1915 [signed J.T.D.]
"On Acknowledgments," June 1915 [signed J.T.D.]
"A Post-Christmas Lament," February 1916

John Thomas Dunn, in 1912

John was the son of Patrick and Mary Dunn. His father Patrick Dunn, the son of Thomas and Mary Dunn, was born in Ireland in December 1847 and died in Providence on 4 June 1908. Patrick Dunn was a house builder, which probably explains why his sons James and John became plumbers. John's mother Mary Dunn was born in Ireland in March 1847 and followed her husband in death in Providence on 3 February 1911. In the 1900 census, John was enumerated in his parents' home at 83 Commodore Street in Providence along with siblings Mary (b. June 1874, bench hand), James (born August 1878, plumber), Anna (born March 1883, at school), and Margaret (born August 1886, at school). All the children had been born in Rhode Island. When the 1910 U.S. census was taken, the widowed Mary Dunn was the head of household at 83 Commodore Street, where her children Anna L. (saleswoman, shoe store), Margery

C. (dressmaker), and John T. (plumber) were also enumerated. Providence directories from 1915 to 1923 continued to list John T. Dunn as a plumber at 83 Commodore Street. His sister Margaret was also listed there in the 1917, 1919, and 1921 directories and his brother James (also a plumber) in the 1917 directory. In the 1921 and 1923 Providence directories, there was apparently another John T. Dunn in Providence, a salesman at 88 Massachusetts Avenue.

Dunn refused to register for the draft in 1917, and was sentenced to twenty years in the federal penitentiary in Atlanta. Dunn was, however, released after two years of imprisonment and apparently returned to the plumbing trade in Providence. However, he eventually entered Mount St. Mary's College and Seminary in Emmitsburg, Maryland, and was ordained to the Roman Catholic priesthood on 29 May 1930. Assigned to the Diocese of Columbus, Ohio, he worked as chaplain at Mercy Hospital from 1932 until his retirement in 1969. Late in life, he was interviewed by L. Sprague de Camp regarding his association with Lovecraft for de Camp's 1975 biography of the author.

Lovecraft ghostwrote the poem "Lines on Graduation from the R.I. Hospital's School of Nurses" (*AT* 104–6) for Dunn's sister Anna L. Dunn to read at her graduation; the poem was published under the name of John T. Dunn in the *Tryout* for February 1917. Lovecraft sent the poem to Dunn along with his letter dated 31 January 1917 (JTD 210–11). Lovecraft's letter to Dunn dated 19 February 1917 (JTD 212–13) further noted that the author had sent the poem to Charles W. Smith for publication in the *Tryout* under Dunn's name. I do not know whether Anna L. Dunn actually read the poem before her graduating class at the Rhode Island Hospital School of Nursing, nor do I know whether Lovecraft ever had the opportunity to meet the proud graduate.

I have not found John T. Dunn in the 1920 or 1930 U.S. censuses. He did not repeat his refusal to register for the draft in 1942. His registration reflect his employment as chaplain at Mercy Hospital in Portsmouth, Ohio. He gave the name of Anna L. Dunn of 33 Ardmore Avenue in Providence, Rhode Island, as his nearest relative.

Eugene [Eugenie] M. Kern

> Amongst the throng a shining light discern:
> 'Tis Kipling's own disciple, Mistress Kern.
> The instructed fair, with ev'ry talent grac'd,
> Decides the mode in literary taste.

Date and Place of Birth: 25 December 1893, Providence, RI
Date and Place of Death: April 1977, Providence, RI
1914 Providence Directory Address: 372 Branch Avenue Club Offices: Vice President, 1914–15
Writings in the *Providence Amateur*: [none]

The club member was of German ancestry; in German, Eugene is the female form of the male name Eugen. I will use Eugenie here to make her sex clear, although both Eugene and Eugenie appear in the vital records. Her father Augustus M. Kern was born in Germany in October 1870, the son of Michael and Eugene Kern. Her mother Susan J. (McGirl) Kern was born in New Jersey in January 1871, the

Eugene M. Kern, in 1912.

daughter of an Irish-born father and a Nova Scotia–born mother. Eugenie's parents wed in Providence on 4 June 1890. They had a large family, all born in Providence, including Joseph (born 17 October 1891), Eugenie (born Christmas Day 1893), Helen L. (born 15 February 1896, died 15 December 1911); Augustus F. (born 18 November 1897), Rosa (born 17 August 1899), Susan (born 10 September 1901), Charles (born 8 September 1903), George A. (born 21 April 1905), William (born 15 June 1908, died 10 May 1910), and Mary (born 7 December 1910). When the 1900 census was taken, Augustus M. Kern was recorded with his large family at 605 Charles Street in Providence; his occupation was given as teamster. By the time of the 1910 census, August had moved his large family to 21 Touro Street. However, Augustus M. Kern died young, aged only 41 years, on 16 May 1912 in Providence.

In the 1914 directory, widow Susan J. Kern remained in the home at 21 Touro Street while Augustus F. Kern, a clerk, and Eugenie M. Kern, a teacher, were boarding at 372 Branch Avenue. When the 1920 census was enumerated in January 1920, Susan Kern and her children Augustus F. (accountant in bleachery), Eugenie M. (teacher), Rosa (hooker in bleachery), Charles (stretcher in bleachery), and George were are all recorded at 372 Branch Avenue. Augustus F. Kern married Anna V. Sullivan in Providence on 16 February 1920 and their daughter Eileen A. Kern was born in Providence on 21 August 1920.

The widowed Susan J. Kern continued to reside at 372 Branch Avenue through the 1931 Providence Directory. Her daughter Eugenie M. Kern was recorded in the Cranston directories in 1924 and 1926; she was teaching at Knightsville School under Principal Mildred L. Watrous and residing in Providence. The 1928 Pawtucket Directory recorded Eugenie M. Kern as a teacher at Samuel Slater Junior High School at 23 Abbott Street under Principal Albert L. Copeland and Dean S. Wilhelmina Bennett. She was still at Samuel Slater Junior High School in 1935, residing at 225 Lowden Street in Pawtucket, but had transferred to West Senior High School (now Charles E. Shea High School) by 1942.[22] Her residence address from 1938 onward appears to have been 14 Hillside Avenue in Providence. Her brother Augustus Ferdinand Kern died in East Providence, Rhode Island, in September 1971. At least two other siblings married in Providence: Rosa L. Kern and Dennis A. Lawton on 14 April 1926 and George A. Kern and Evelyn L. Shea on 22 June 1929.

Howard Phillips Lovecraft

Howard Phillips Lovecraft, in 1915.

Gaze last on H.P.L., whose bookish speech
But bores the auditors he tries to teach:
Whose stiff heroics ev'ry ear annoy;

---

22. I thank Robin Panchuk, Library Media Specialist at Charles E. Shea High School, who searched the school yearbooks from the 1940s through the 1950s for a photograph of Eugenie M. Kern for me. Unfortunately, the yearbooks from this period did not include faculty photographs.

Whose polysyllables our peace destroy.
The stilted pedant now can do no worse,
For he it is that writ this wretched verse!

Date and Place of Birth: 20 August 1890, Providence, RI
Date and Place of Death: 15 March 1937, Providence, RI
1914 Providence Directory Address: 598 Angell Street
Club Offices: Literary Director, 1914–15; Official Editor, 1915–16
Writings in the *Providence Amateur*:
"To the Members of the United Amateur Press Ass'n from the Providence Amateur Press Club," June 1915
"Editor's Note" [prefacing "The Irish and the Fairies"], February 1916 [signed H.P.L.]
"Editorial," February 1916
"To Charlie of the Comics," February 1916 [as by "Lewis Theobald Jr."]
"The Bride of the Sea," February 1916 [as by "Lewis Theobald Jr."]

Lovecraft also wrote a note on a club member in the "Department of Public Criticism" column of the *United Amateur*, May 1915:

> "Some Objections to Moving Pictures", by Edmund L. Shehan [as printed in Daas's amateur journal *The Lake Breeze*, March 1915], presents a strong array of evidence against one of the most popular and instructive amusements of today. We do not believe, however, that the objections here offered are vital. The moving picture has infinite possibilities for literary and artistic good when rightly presented, and having achieved a permanent place, seems destined eventually to convey the liberal arts to multitudes hitherto denied their enjoyment. Mr. Shehan's prose style is clear and forceful, capable of highly advantageous development. (*CE* 1.39)

Peter Joseph McManus

[Not included in Lovecraft's poem on the members of the Club.]
Date and Place of Birth: 4 August 1888, Mullagh, Rooskey, County Roscommon, Ireland
Date and Place of Death: October 1971, Providence, RI
1914 Providence Directory Address: 3 Jackson Street[23]
Club Offices:[none known]
Writings in the *Providence Amateur*:
"The Irish and the Fairies," February 1916

It seems appropriate that the author of "The Irish and the Fairies" was the only one of the original eight members of the club to be born in Ireland. Listed as a laborer, he sailed on the *S.S. Majestic* from Queenstown on 20 May 1909, arriving in New York City 27 May 1909, with final destination in Providence. His contact person was "Mrs. McManus" at his birthplace address. Peter appears to have engaged in janitorial work for most of his working lifetime in Providence and was employed in this capacity for many years by the Providence Public Schools. He married Margaret M. Aldworth in Providence on 11 June 1918. There were at least two Peter McManuses in Providence during these years, both of whom registered for the draft in 1942: (1) our Peter Joseph McManus, residing at 90 Moore Street and

---

23. Since there were at least two men named Peter McManus in Providence during these years, this identification is only tentative. The 1914 Directory listing for Peter McManus at 3 Jackson Street does not provide any additional information. In the 1913 and 1915 Providence House Directories, 3 Jackson Street was identified as "The Laurence"—a boarding house. By 1917, it was occupied by Mrs. Mary Fuller, who operated a rooming house at the adjoining address 5 Jackson Street. Today Jackson Street remains as Jackson Walkway ending at Cathedral Square.

working at the Providence School Department Administration Building at 20 Summer Street; and (2) Peter Francis McManus (born 2 December 1890, Fall River, MA), residing at 86 Comstock Avenue, and working for Merritt-Chapman-Scott & George A. Fuller at the Naval Air Base in Quonset, Rhode Island.

So care must be taken and I am not absolutely sure that the sole "Peter McManus" of the 1914 Providence Directory (see above) was our Peter. I have not found our Peter in either the 1910 U.S. census or the 1920 U.S. census, nor have I found him in the 1917–18 World War I draft registrations. There were three Peter McManuses listed in the 1913 Providence Directory: a laborer residing at 191 Lockwood Street; a porter residing at 9 Alphonso Street; and another laborer boarding at 49 Robinson Street. By way of contrast, the 1914 Providence Directory listed only one Peter McManus, boarding at 3 Jackson Street. The Ancestry.com database of Rhode Island city directories includes the 1915 and 1917 Providence House Directories, but at the time of writing they were not searchable. I am reasonably confident that the Peter J. McManus who resided at 54 Canton Street in the 1919, 1921, 1923, 1925, and 1926 Providence Directories was our Peter—in 1919 and 1921, Peter's occupation was recorded as "clerk," in 1923, 1925, and 1926 as "packer." In the 1927 Directory, Peter J. McManus, residing at 73 Regent Street, was listed as janitor at Althea School at 245 Althea Street. In 1929 and 1930, Peter J. was janitor at the Hammond Street School and still resided at 73 Regent Avenue. By 1930, there was another Peter J. McManus (wife Elizabeth) residing at 235 Dean Street. (To make things even more interesting, there was a Peter McManus, clerk, residing at 110 Prairie Avenue as well.) When the 1930 U.S. census was taken, Peter J. McManus and his wife Margaret were recorded at 73 Regent Avenue on 10 April 1930. Peter was paying $20 monthly rent and working as a public school janitor. He was a naturalized U.S. citizen and gave 1908 as his emigration year. Both he and his wife Margaret gave their ages as 42 and stated that they were born in the Irish Free State of parents also born there. Margaret did not work outside the home and was also a naturalized U.S. citizen and gave 1908 as her year of emigration. They had no children in their household and both stated they had been married at age 30. Regrettably, the 1930 U.S. census did not ask for number of children born and number of children living.

In 1933, our Peter J. was listed at 32 Canton Street and in 1935 at 17 Huron Street, with occupation listed as janitor in both years. In the 1938 Directory, Peter J. McManus and his wife Margaret M. were listed at 68 Regent Avenue; Peter's occupation was listed as "helper" at 20 Summer Street room 105 (this was the administration building for the Providence School Department). By 1940, Peter and his wife had removed to their longtime address at 90 Moore Street, where he was residing when he registered for the draft in 1942. In the 1942, 1943, and 1944 directories, Peter's occupation was given as assistant janitor for the School Department. In the 1947, 1952, 1953, and 1956 directories, Peter and Margaret remained at 90 Moore Street. Peter's occupation was listed as custodian for the School Department. In the 1957 directory, Peter's occupation was listed simply as janitor, and starting with the 1958 directory Peter no longer had any occupation listed—perhaps he had finally retired at age seventy. Peter's wife Margaret M. McManus continued to be listed with him in directories through 1960; however, she is missing from the 1964 directory and presumably died between 1960 and 1964. In the 1964 directory—the last available to me on Ancestry—Peter was listed as retired, with home at 90 Moore Street.

For a club that had its origins in an evening high school class, it seems appropriate that one of the last survivors, Peter Joseph McManus, spent most of his working career as a janitor for the Providence School Department. He seems to have worked at the central high school complex in downtown Providence during the final years of his career with the School Department.

Mildred Gardiner Metcalf [married name Heald]

[Not included in Lovecraft's poem on the members of the Club.]
Date and Place of Birth: 5 January 1894, Providence, RI
Date and Place of Death: 19 September 1964, Warren, RI
1914 Providence Directory Address: 14 Catalpa Road[24]
Club Offices: [none known]
Writings in the *Providence Amateur:* [none]

Mildred's parents Edward P. Metcalf and Mary E. Gardiner married in Providence on 18 June 1885. Edward, the son of Franklin and Narcissa S. (Potter) Metcalf, was born in Providence on 6 September 1859. Franklin, the son of Jesse and Eunice H. (Horton) Metcalf, married Narcissa S. Potter in Providence on 11 July 1855 and died in Providence on 28 January 1908, aged 75 years. Jesse Metcalf and Eunice D. Horton (daughter of John) had married in Providence on 19 April 1812; Eunice died as Jesse's widow in Providence on 17 May 1858, aged 65. So Mildred G. Metcalf came from a long line of Providence Metcalfs. When the 1900 census was taken in June 1900, Edward P. Metcalf and his family were enumerated

---

24. Mildred Metcalf has no listing in the 1914 Providence Directory, but was probably living with her parents Edward p. and Mary E. (Gardiner) Metcalf at this address.

at 179 Pocasset Avenue in Providence. Edward was working as a bank examiner. In addition to his wife Mary (born April 1864, New Jersey), there were three daughters: Alice B. (born October 1888, New Jersey), Margaret (born April 1890, New Jersey), and Mildred G. (born January 1894, Rhode Island).

Mildred was a 1911 graduate of Hope Street High School. Her portrait as reproduced herein comes from the school's 1911 yearbook *Blue and White* (28). She married Herbert S. Heald in Providence on 28 January 1919. Herbert Shepley Heald had been born in Valisburg, New Jersey, on 11 May 1894, the son of another Herbert Heald. When the family was enumerated in Orange, New Jersey, on 11 June 1900 for the U.S. census, the senior Herbert Heald (born September 1865 in England) was residing at 17 Berwick Street and working as a hat finisher. With him were his wife Maria Heald (born December 1870 in England) and their children Herbert Jr. (born May 1894, New Jersey) and Alice M. (born February 1898, New Jersey). By 1910, Herbert Sr. and his family had removed to 105 Jenkins Street in Providence. Herbert Jr. soon took over the hat finishing business at 103 Westminster Street in Providence from his father. However, his 1919 marriage ended tragically; for Herbert Shepley Heald, aged only 25, died in Providence on 28 August 1919, after only seven months of marriage.

As Herbert's widow, Mildred M. Heald, continued the hatting business at 103 Westminster Street. When the 1920 census was taken on 8 January 1920, she was enumerated with her parents at 14 Catalpa Road. Her occupation was listed as "proprietor—hat store."

> Mildred M. Heald, Raymond H. Burton and Thomas Z. Lee have received a charter under the name of the Heald Hat Works, Providence, R. I., and will continue the business of making and repairing hats at the present location in that city. The company is capitalized at $10,000.

Heald in the journal *America Hatter*, c.1919.

Her father Edward P. Metcalf died in Providence on 20 July 1924, aged 64 years, but Mildred continued to reside at 14 Catalpa Road. In Providence directories from 1929 to 1938 her business at 103 Westminster Street was listed as "Heald Hat Works." When the 1930 U.S. census was taken, Mildred was listed with her widowed mother at 14 Catalpa Road; her occupation was given as "proprietor millinery shop." In the 1933 and 1935 Providence directories, Mildred M. Heald was also listed as an active member of the Providence Quota Club.

Between the compilation of the 1938 and 1940 Providence directories, Mildred sold the Heald Hat Works at 103 Westminster Street (room 1) to Benjamin F. Bachand. Mr. Bachand was still listed as proprietor of this business in the 1944 Providence Directory, but the business disappeared from the Providence directories in 1947 and later. Perhaps like many small service businesses it fell victim to societal changes in the postwar years. Mildred M. Heald, widow of Herbert S. Heald, continued to be listed at 14 Catalpa Road through the 1947 Providence Directory; beginning with the 1952 Providence Directory, she was listed at 161 Medway Street. In the 1964 Providence Directory, she had removed a few doors to 159 Medway Street.

Caroline Miller [married name Barlow]

> Prepare ye now to shed unwonted tears,
> As Mistress Miller with her pen appears:
> The Queen of Fiction; with pathetic art

She melts the coldest and the hardest heart.
The reader tries to leave such scenes of pain,
Yet, charm'd against his will, he reads again.

Date and Place of Birth: 16 July 1891, PA
Date and Place of Death: July 1979, Sudbury, MA
1914 Providence Directory Address: 45 Shiloh Street
Club Offices: Secretary-Treasurer, 1914–15
Writings in the *Providence Amateur*: [none]

Caroline Miller, in 1912

A Caroline Miller was born to Charles and Margaret S. Miller in Providence on 18 October 1881, but I do not believe she is our Caroline Miller. Perhaps this other Caroline Miller was the one who married Charles Harris on Providence on 26 September 1900. Our Caroline Miller was a stenographer at 327 Westminster Street in the 1914 Providence Directory, but it is her residence address "bds. 45 Shiloh" that provides the crucial clue. In the same directory, we also find at 45 Shiloh Street Mrs. Mary Miller (head) and additional boarders Marie and Louise (working as sewer). The 1910 census taken in April 1910 provides additional information about this family. Enumerated on Shiloh Street in that census were Marie Miller (head), widow, aged 57, born in France; her daughter Marie, aged 29, also born in France; her daughter Caroline, aged 18, born in Pennsylvania; her daughter Louise, aged 16, born in Pennsylvania; and her son Henry J., aged 8, born in Rhode Island. All three daughters were working in a woollen mill when the 1910 census was enumerated. Caroline Miller was the secretary-treasurer of the club for the 1914–15 term.

The *United Amateur* for November 1914 gave her address as 27 Henrietta Street, which is not far from Shiloh Street in the Wanskuck neighborhood of Providence. (The 1915 Providence House Directory listed Joseph Curran (weaver) and James Appleton (laborer) at 27 Henrietta Street; neither man was listed at this address in the 1914 Providence Directory. So perhaps Caroline Miller was at 27 Henrietta Street briefly in 1914–15.) The 1915 Providence House Directory listed Mrs. Marie Miller at 45 Shiloh Street, and indeed the entire street was full of weavers and spinners. A Mrs. Marie Miller was also listed at 1497 Broad Street as housekeeper for traveling salesman William L. C. Potter; if the housekeeper at 1497 Broad was live-in she was probably Caroline's sister Marie rather than her mother Marie, although the residence at 45 Shiloh could still have been listed under the elder Marie's name even in her absence. The Marie Miller, widow of John, aged 64 years, who died in Providence on 16 April 1918 was in all likelihood the elder Marie.

In the meantime, daughter Caroline Miller had married John Barlow in Providence on 20 December 1917. That our Caroline was indeed the 1917 bride is shown by the 1920 U.S. census of

South Kingstown, Rhode Island, taken in January 1920. Therein, John Barlow, aged 50 (born New York), teacher in the agricultural college, was enumerated with his wife Caroline Barlow, aged 28 (born Pennsylvania of French-born parents) and their son John P. Barlow, aged 1 year 2 months (born Rhode Island). I think the wife's French-born parents (i.e., the elder Marie and her husband) make our identification of the 1917 bride very likely. In the 1917 South Kingstown and Narragansett Directory, John A. M. Barlow (wife Caroline) was listed as a professor of zoology at RISC with home on South Road in Kingstown. In the 1930 census, John Barlow, aged 56, college professor, was enumerated on South Road in South Kingstown with his family: wife Caroline, aged 39 (born Pennsylvania, parents born in France), son John P., aged 11, born Rhode Island; son David E., aged 9, born Rhode Island; and daughter Caroline M., aged 3, born Rhode Island. The dates of birth and death and place of death for our Caroline Barlow are taken from the Social Security Death Master File record. Caroline F. Barlow, born 13 August 1927, died 10 November 1993 in Harmony, Rhode Island, also appears in this file and may very likely be the daughter of John and Caroline (Miller) Barlow.

Edmund Leo Shehan

> Turn now to Shehan; his pointed prose reveals
> A man whose mind the censor's duty feels.
> The flickering film the moving picture stage,
> Are lash'd in scorn by his discerning rage.
> The bold reformer naught of vigour lacks,
> And idle Pleasure shakes at his attacks.

Date and Place of Birth: 12 March 1891, Johnston, RI
Date and Place of Death: May 1972, Warwick, RI
1914 Providence Directory Address: 30 Alverson Avenue
Club Offices: [none known]

Writings in the *Providence Amateur*:
"Death," February 1916
"The Making of a Motion Picture," February 1916

In the 1900 U.S. census of Providence (ward 8) taken in June 1900 we find enumerated on Whittier Avenue the household of John Shehan (born November 1859, New York), wool-sorter, including: wife Caroline Shehan (born March 1864, Rhode Island); son Edmund Shehan (born March 1891, Rhode Island); and son Thomas Shehan (born March 1893, Rhode Island). In the 1910 U.S. census, taken in April 1910, the same family was still at 224 Whittier Avenue. John Shehan was still working as a wool-sorter at a woollen mill while son Edmund L., aged 19, was working as a loommaker at the loom works and son Thomas E., aged 14, was working as a clerk in a drug store. The 1914 Providence Directory recorded John H. Shehan, wool sorter, residing at 30 Alverson Avenue, and sons Edmund L. and Thomas E. (steamfitter) boarding at the same address, far out the Plainfield Pike near Neutaconkanut Hill Park. When he registered for the draft in 1917–18, Edmund L. Shehan, still single, was still residing at 30 Alverson Avenue and working as a reed maker for Crompton E. Knowles in Providence. When brother Thomas E. Shehan (born 4 March 1893, Johnston, Rhode Island) registered for the 1917–18 draft, he was also residing at 30 Alverson Avenue, he was also still single and listed his occupation as steamfitter, although he was currently unemployed. John H. Shehan (wool sorter) was still head of household at 30 Alverson Avenue in the 1917 Providence Directory, with son Edmund L. Shehan (lensmaker) as a boarder.

Sometime before 9 May 1920, Edmund L. Shehan married, because Catherine Shehan, daughter of Edmund L. and Ida Shehan, was born in Providence on that date. Daughter Helen was born in Providence on 14 May 1922, and an unnamed son was born (and died the same day) in Providence on 12 August 1926. In the 1921 Providence Directory, Edmund L. Shehan, machinist, was residing at 135 River Avenue. In the 1941 Providence Directory, we find residing at 50 River Avenue: Catherine Shehan, widow of John; Catherine E. Shehan, clerk; Edmund L. Shehan, clerk; and Helen Shehan, hairdresser. When he registered for the draft in 1942, Edmund Shehan was still residing at 50 River Avenue and working for the Department of Public Works (sewer maintenance) at 37 Ernest Street. In the 1953 Providence Directory, Catherine E. Shehan was recorded as secretary for the Imperial Knife Company, residing at Cranston, Rhode Island. Perhaps her father had removed from Providence by this time as well; he would have been approaching retirement age by 1953.

Additional Members

William Aloysius Henry

[*Not included in Lovecraft's poem on the members of the Club.*]
Date and Place of Birth: 3 April 1884, Providence, RI
Date and Place of Death: January 1966, Providence, RI
1914 Providence Directory Address: 93 Commodore Street
Club Offices: [none known]
Writings in the *Providence Amateur*: [none]

Our sole reference from this member of the Club is L. Sprague de Camp's interviews with Rev. John T. Dunn, M.F., on 20–21 May 1975, as reported in his essay "Young Man Lovecraft." Dunn, of course, had been one of the leaders of the Providence Amateur Press Club in 1914–16 and shared his vivid memories of Lovecraft with de Camp.

Dunn acknowledged in his interviews with de Camp that the twenty-somethings who made up the club tended to make fun of the staid Lovecraft. De Camp reported:

> Another member of the Providence Amateur Press Club, living next door to Dunn, had a sister named Sadie Henry. Once Miss Henry, visiting at Dunn's house, as a joke among the circle of friends, telephoned Lovecraft and suggested that he take her out on a date. Lovecraft said: `I'll have to ask my mother,' and nothing came of it. (YML 174)

William's birth record in the Providence vital records (3 April 1884) specific his middle initial as "J," not "A"—perhaps he adopted a confirmation name for use as a middle initial in adult life. William was working as a clerk for Adams Express and boarding at his father's home at 93 Commodore Street when the 1914 Providence Directory was compiled. When he registered for the draft in 1917–18, he was living at 60 Pinehurst Avenue in Providence and working as a clerk for the U.S. Finishing Company in Pawtucket, Rhode Island. He had married Mary C. Sullivan in Providence on 8 November 1916.

William A. Henry was later, according to the *Providence Magazine* 34 (1922) one of the Town Criers publicists: "The Town Criers by William F. Baker, William A. Henry, Edward Sartorius, Samuel Burchiel, and H. Harold Price" (161). The group appears in the online record as early as 1912. The book *Music, Sound, and Technology in America* (2012) tells us more of this group, in respect of the experience of a musician in March 1924: "The first intimation of the widespread interest in this trip was the receipt by Mr. Rothafel of hundreds and hundreds of postal cards from an organization known as the Town Criers welcoming him to Providence . . ." The book *Making Time: Lillian Moller Gilbreth* (2004) notes the group as "the Town Criers, a Providence 'booster' club." The contemporary journal *Gas Age-Record* 53 (1924) is a tad more specific noting the group as:

> The Town Criers of Rhode Island, the advertising club of Providence R.I., is one of the livest clubs of its kind in the United States. It has a large membership and holds weekly noon-day luncheons at the largest hotel in the city. (22)

By the time of the 1930 census, William and his wife Mary were residing at 38 Gentian Avenue in Providence and their household included a daughter Barbara A. Henry, aged 12 (born 18 November 1917, Providence), and a son William A. Henry [Jr.], aged 3 years 10 months (born 28 June 1926, Providence). William was then working as manager of a sporting goods store.

In the 1942 and 1947 Providence Directories, William was recorded as president-treasurer of W. A. Henry, Inc. (incorporated under Rhode Island law in 1936), a sporting goods business operating at 8 Weybosset Street in Providence. His home remained at 38 Gentian Avenue in Providence. When the 1952 Providence Directory was compiled, Mary C. Henry, still residing at 38 Gentian Avenue, was serving as president-treasurer of the sporting goods business at 8 Weybosset Street. In the 1957 and 1964 Providence Directories, Mary remained at the same home and in the same business. Son William A. Henry Jr., also in the sporting goods business, was recorded with his wife Hope L. Henry, residing at 98 Kentland Avenue. In the 1964 Providence Directory—the most recent accessible to me online—William A. Henry, Jr. had replaced his mother as president-treasurer of the athletic goods business at 8 Weybosset Street and Mrs. Barbara A. Powers (probably William's daughter Barbara) had joined the firm as secretary. The Mary Henry (born 10 April

1896) who died in March 1982, with last residence East Providence, Rhode Island, may possibly have been William's widow.

William A. Henry, Jr. served in the U.S. armed forces in the Pacific theatre during World War II and was a 1951 graduate of Brown University. After closing or selling the family sporting goods business, he worked for twenty years for the Rhode Island Department of Employment and Training. He and his wife were the parents of five sons. He died on 1 October 2005 in North Providence. He was a longtime parishioner of St. Augustine Church in North Providence.

It is really speculation that William Aloysius Henry, the youngest son and Charles H. and Catherine Henry, was a member of the Providence Amateur Press Club in 1914–16, but he seems by far the most likely candidate among the five Henry brothers. In the 1914 Providence Directory, the sons listed in the family of Charles H. Henry at 93 Commodore were Arthur E. (laborer), and William A. (clerk, Adams Express Company). Son John F. Henry (laborer) had his own home at 71 Commodore Street. Son Charles S. Henry (car repairer) had his own home at 34 Waling Street. Son Robert J. Henry had his own home at 363 Manton Avenue. Daughter Mary E. Henry had married John J. O'Haire in Providence on 25 September 1912 and she and her husband also made their home at 93 Commodore Street. Daughter Margaret E. Henry had married neighbor William Shierson in Providence on 16 April 1896; she and her husband made their home at 49 Commodore Street. Unmarried daughter Sarah J. Henry (of whom more anon) remained at home at 93 Commodore Street. So we are left with the youngest son William Aloysius Henry as the probable member of the Providence Amateur Press Club in 1914–16.

What then of Rev. John T. Dunn's "Sadie" Henry, sister of William Aloysius, who made bold to ask Lovecraft for a date over the telephone? As remarked above, our best date of birth for Sarah J. Henry (3 June 1879) comes from the published Providence vital records. Some sources give her middle initial as "L" rather than "J"—perhaps reflect a variation in name preference between second baptismal name and confirmation name. Sarah was enumerated in the parental home at 93 Commodore Street (numbered 22 in 1880) in the 1880, 1900, 1910, and 1920 U.S. censuses. She was also enumerated in this home with her sister Mary E. (Henry) O'Haire (with her husband John J. O'Haire and three sons) and her brother Arthur E. Henry in the 1930 census. In all these censuses, her marital status was single—never married. In 1900 and 1910, her occupation was given as stone setter in the jewelry business. In 1920, she was an inspector in a machine shop. In the 1923 Providence Directory, she was listed (as Sadie L. Henry) as a jeweler residing at 93 Commodore Street. By 1930, however, she had become a saleslady in a department store, in which occupation she remained for the rest of her working lifetime. The 1940 and 1941 Providence directories listed her at 93 Commodore Street and listed her occupation as saleswoman at Cherry & Webb. The 1947 Providence Directory was the last to list Sarah J. Henry's occupation as saleswoman; she was still listed as residing at 93 Commodore Street in the 1952 Providence Directory but with no occupation given. The 1958 Providence Directory listed Sarah J. Henry for the last time, giving her residence as 93 Commodore Street and her date of death as 26 June 1957.

Whether H. P. Lovecraft ever ventured within the portals of the Henry family home at 93 Commodore Street is unknown. One wonders what the family patriarch Charles H. Henry would have made of the young Anglophile, especially in the wake of the bloody suppression of the 1916 Easter Rising by England. Of his numerous children, the youngest son William Aloysius Henry and the middle daughter Sarah J. ("Sadie") Henry (born between her sisters Margaret E. and Mary E.) seem to have been the most ambitious and upwardly mobile. William became the proprietor of his own sporting goods business and Sarah worked the jewelry counter at the prestigious Cherry & Webb department store. It is wonderful that John T. Dunn's recollections make it possible for us to identify these early acquaintances of H. P. Lovecraft in the amateur journalism hobby.

It should be noted that the Providence directories for many years listed "Sadie G. Henry" as a dressmaker or milliner at 851 Atwells Avenue. This Sadie G. Henry (Sarah Henry) was born in July 1876 according to the 1900 census. According to the 1952 Providence Directory, this Sarah G. Henry died on 20 May 1951. It should also be noted that the William Alan Henry (1867–1941) of 111 Priscilla Avenue in Providence who married into Lovecraft's branch of the Phillips family came from a completely different family from that of Charles and Catherine Henry of 93 Commodore Street; his parents were of Scottish rather than Irish birth.[25]

Guy Harold Kelso

[Not included in Lovecraft's poem on the members of the Club, but note the following poem "[On Kelso the Poet]"]
Date and Place of Birth: 28 June 1878, Island Falls, ME
Date and Place of Death: 1950, Providence, RI
1914 Providence Directory Address: 56 Olney Street
Club Offices: [none known]
Writings in the *Providence Amateur:* [none]

---

25. For the William Alan Henry who married into HPL's branch of the Phillips family, refer to Kenneth Faig, *Some of the Descendants of Asaph Phillips and Esther Whipple of Foster, Rhode Island* (Glenview, IL: Moshassuck Press, 1993), 144–46.

H. P. Lovecraft wrote to John T. Dunn on 14 October 1916: "Pres. Campbell lately requested me to remind Messrs. Kelso and Wright of this State that their membership has expired; but judging from your club's attitude toward Kelso, and the rather hopeless nature of his verse, I think I will confine my persuasions to Mr. Wright, who never became really active" (JTD 199). Paul J. Campbell was president of the UAPA in 1915–16 and had written Lovecraft to ask that he encourage Messrs. Kelso and Wright to renew their memberships. Guy Kelso may be found in the 1909 Cranston Directory, boarding at 45 Wilbur; his occupation was given as carpenter. In the 1910 U.S. census of Providence, he was enumerated as a lodger on Walnut Street, occupation carpenter. Guy Kelso married Elizabeth A. Kelley in Providence on 5 October 1911. In the 1914 and 1915 Providence Directories, he was listed at 56 Olney Street. In 1915, a clerk James Kelly, perhaps a relation of Guy's wife, was residing at the same address.

When he registered for the draft on 10 September 1918, Guy was residing at 49 Grand View Street in Providence. He worked as a carpenter for Charles Maguire in Newport, Rhode Island. His contact person was Lily A. Kelso, also residing at 49 Grand View Street. In the 1920 U.S. census of Providence, taken in January 1920, Guy was enumerated with his wife Elizabeth A. Kelso (aged 42, born Rhode Island) and his son Harold J. Kelso (aged 7, born Rhode Island). Guy was still working as a carpenter. He was born in Maine of a New Brunswick–born father and a Maine-born mother. He appears to have briefly tried his hand at songwriting for the music halls and recording industry, as evidenced by *The Catalog of Copyright Entries* 1922 recording the song "Kissing Is the Soul of Love," with music by A. Leopold Richard, and words by Guy H. Kelso. Keslo died in 1950, according to a family tree inquiry found by co-author Haden at genforum.genealogy.com.

The 1929 Providence House Directory recorded Guy Kelso at 99 Doyle Avenue and gave his occupation as "internal revenue." (This is the only record I have found where he is not identified as a carpenter by trade—perhaps he had secured government employment as a carpenter.) In 1930, he was recorded in the Cranston Directory at 62 Tucker Avenue. When he registered for the draft again in 1942, Guy was residing at 4 Mallett Street in Providence. He gave his birthplace was Island Falls, Maine, and designated Lily A. Kelso as his contact person. His employer at the time was Merritt-Chapman-Scott on Quonset Point in North Kingstown, Rhode Island. In the 1947 Providence Directory, Guy H. Kelso, carpenter, with wife Elizabeth, was listed at 4 Mallett Street. The 1952 Providence Directory listed Elizabeth Kelso, widow of Guy H., at the same address.

> Poor Kelso the poet, defending his verse,
> Forbids us to laugh, since we're like to write worse.
> Sure, 'tis horribly rough, and unmanly as well,
> To sneer at a bard whom you cannot excel!
> But I'm thinking myself, that although I am told
> That my rhyming is bad, and my manner be old,
> It would hardly be difficult dull tho' I be,
> To prove I'm not quite such a bungler as he.
> So in spite of his warning, I must, for a while,
> Give vent to my feelings by cracking a smile!
> "[On Kelso the Poet]" *AT* 231 from AMS, JHL]

—— *Reilly*

> Observe skilled Reilly, erudite and wise.
> Who all his art to stately prose applies.
> Of matchless culture, and refinement rare.
> His polish'd page reflects the author's care.

Date and Place of Birth: [missing]
Date and Place of Death: [missing]
1914 Providence Directory Address: [missing]
Club Offices:[none known]
Writings in the *Providence Amateur:* [none]

The 1914 Providence Directory recorded 114 males with the surname Reilly, distributed as follows: Andrew, 1; Bernard, 4; Charles, 9; Clarence, 1; Cornelius, 1; Daniel, 2; Edward, 5; Felix, 1; Francis, 6; Frank, 3; George, 5; James, 14; John, 18; Joseph, 4; Lawrence, 2; Mathew or Matthew, 2; Michael, 3; Nicholas, 1; Owen, 2; Patrick, 5; Peter, 7; Philip, 1; Richard, 1; Robert, 1; Sylvester, 1; Terrence, 1; Thomas, 9; William, 4. In the Providence births for the period 1875–1900, there are 62 males with surname Reilly. Identification of club member —— Reilly appears unlikely unless we can find a Lovecraft letter or another source that provides his given name (or better yet, full name and address). Since the home of John T. Dunn at 83 Commodore Street served as something of a center for club activities, I did search for male Reillys living on nearby streets in the 1914 Providence Directory and came up with John P. Reilly, clerk, residing at 192 Silver Spring Street, located about 0.40 Mapquest miles from the Dunn home at 83 Commodore Street. Margaret Reilly, clerk, was listed as a boarder at 192 Silver Spring Street in the 1914 Providence Directory. The only John Reillys born in Providence without conflicting middle initials whom I found in the 1875–1900 period surveyed were: John of John W. and Mary E., born 19 November 1889, and John of John P. and Catherine M., born 14 November 1891. (In all, there were twelve John Reillys born in Providence during the period surveyed but all but these two and John P. J. Reilly had conflicting middle initials. John P. J. Reilly, of Patrick and Mary, born 13 September 1891, alas, died 11 May 1896, aged 4 years.) I have not been able to find a sister Margaret with the same parents as either of the two John Reillys identified as candidates. With only propinquity of residence to the Dunn household as an identifying factor, it does not seem worthwhile to pursue further research concerning John p. Reilly of 192 Silver Spring Street. The next step would surely be to look for him in the U.S. censuses and additional Providence Directories. It is quite possible that he was not born in Providence.

The Lovecraft–Gidlow Centenary

The arrival of July 2017 provides occasion to celebrate the centenaries of the commencement of two notable presidencies of amateur journalism organizations: the election of H. P. Lovecraft to the presidency of the so-called Hoffman-Daas faction of the United Amateur Press Association in Chicago, Illinois, and the election of Elsie Alice Gidlow (1898–1986) (later known as Elsa Gidlow) to the presidency of the so-called Erford–Noel faction of the same association in Montreal, Canada, at about the same time. Verna McGeoch was elected as official editor of Lovecraft's faction and dutifully produced six bimonthly numbers of the *United Amateur* during her term, while Gidlow's official editor, Chester O. Hoisington, managed only one number of the rival official organ.

Lovecraft had been recruited for the Hoffman–Daas faction of UAPA in April 1914 by Edward F. Daas (1879–1962), as a result of his participation in a long-running "war" over the romantic fiction of Fred Jackson in the letter column of *Argosy*. He was appointed chair of the Department of Public Criticism by President Dora Hepner as early as October 1914 and continued in that office through 1919, with the exception of his presidential term in 1917–18, when the work was taken over by his friend and fellow poet Rheinhart Kleiner. Edward H. Cole (1892–1966) of Somerville, Mass., early on connected Lovecraft with the Providence Amateur Press Club founded by evening high school alumni and alumnae in Providence at the end of October 1914. Irishman John T. Dunn (1889–1983) was probably the central figure in the club; Lovecraft eventually broke with him because of his refusal to register for the draft and his resulting imprisonment.

Lovecraft became known for intellectual controversies with Charles D. Isaacson, Elsa Gidlow, F. Graeme Davis and others in the columns of his own amateur journal, the *Conservative*, of which he published thirteen numbers between 1915 and 1923. Lovecraft was advanced to First Vice President of his association as early as its Rocky Mount, N.C., convention in July 1915. Curiously, however, he was never to attend any of the conventions of his faction of UAPA. Perhaps his mother's fragile health and her unfavorable opinion of the hobby inhibited his attendance.

Perhaps the most notable event of Lovecraft's 1917–18 UAPA presidency was his decision to join NAPA in early November 1917. NAPA stalwart F. Graeme Davis had been railing against UAPA in the editorials in his *Lingerer* in 1917. However, when he became NAPA official editor in July 1917, Davis agreed to forego attacks on UAPA if Lovecraft would do the same regarding NAPA. UAPA hardliners like Edward F. Daas were furious with Lovecraft for joining NAPA, but the president maintained that his action would help to promote inter-association cooperation and to dampen feuding and raiding for members. Lovecraft was succeeded by three friendly UAPA presidents: his friend Rheinhart Kleiner (1918–19), Mary Faye Durr (1919–20), and his protégé Alfred M. Galpin (1920–21). He served as official editor in Galpin's administration and carried over to the same position under the succeeding president Ida C. Haughton (1921–22). Lovecraft and Haughton, however, had a rocky relationship. She wanted him to broaden the appeal of the *United Amateur* and to open its columns to contributors other than his own circle of literary friends. In addition, she infuriated him by accusing him of mishandling the official organ fund. In a stinging rebuke, the members of UAPA voted Lovecraft and his faction out of office in the succeeding administration of Howard Conover (1922–23). When his old opponent William B. Dowdell resigned the presidency of NAPA at the end of November 1922, Lovecraft's friend James F. Morton, as a member of NAPA's board of executive judges, recruited Lovecraft to assume the NAPA presidency. Edward H. Cole wanted Lovecraft to stand for a full term as NAPA president in 1923–24, but Lovecraft declined the honor. His future wife Sonia H. Greene was elected UAPA president in July 1923, and Lovecraft served as her official editor. They were returned to the same offices for the 1924–25, after Lovecraft had married Mrs. Greene on 3 March 1924. But the United of which they assumed the helm in 1923–25 was a pale shadow of lively association of 1915. Alma Sanger, the former treasurer in the Howard Conover administration (1922–23), refused to turn over the funds in the treasury. As a result, Mr. and Mrs. Lovecraft were able to produce only a few, thin issues of the *United Amateur*. For the 1925–26 term, Lovecraft's friend Edgar J. Davis was elected president, and his recruit Victor F. Bacon official editor, but activity virtually ceased. No officers were ever elected for the 1926–27 year, and the so-called Hoffman–Daas United perished. The only United left in the field was the one presided over by Roy Erford and Clyde Noel from Seattle, Washington. After having lived in New York City since his marriage, Lovecraft moved back to Providence in April 1926. He did not involve himself again actively in amateur affairs until he attended Boston's NAPA convention in 1930. He did yeoman's service on NAPA's board of critics in 1931–35, serving as chair in 1933–35, and was elected an executive judge in 1935–36 in honor of his service. (He had previously served in that role in 1923–24—a traditional role for the retiring president.) He died, aged only forty-six, of cancer on 15 March 1937. Of course, his professional writings, beginning in *Weird Tales* in 1923, eventually secured his fame. His *Tales*, selected by Peter Straub, were published as a volume in the prestigious Library of America in 2005.

Lovecraft's rival president, Elsa Gidlow, became famous in her own right. She became active in the rival United association about the same time as Lovecraft. At age nineteen, she served as in-house editor for a company paper, *Factory Facts*. By 1917, she had gathered around herself a literary circle including students at McGill University in Montreal. They began to publish a spirit-duplicated paper, initially titled *Coal from Hades,* but eventually retitled *Les Mouches Fantastiques* (*The Fantastic Flies*). Gidlow and her associate Roswell George Mills (1896–1966) also published work in W. Paul Cook's *Vagrant*. Aesthetically, Gidlow was an advocate of free verse. Philosophically, she and her circle attacked traditional religious values and advocated a materialistic, hedonistic outlook on life, including advocacy of same-sex love.

Gidlow had published her poem "Two Lovers" and Mills his poem "Once" in Cook's *Vagrant* for June 1918. Writing to his friend Rheinhart Kleiner on 5 May 1918, Lovecraft commented:

> Cook's latest *Vagrant* is assuredly a marvel. The literary standard is this time even higher than before, I think. The esthetic Elsa Gidlow's outburst could undoubtedly be a great deal worse, as free verse is reckoned. Of the "two lovers that woo her unceasingly," I advise her to choose oblivion. That is the best way for all *vers-libristes*. Her colleague, Rossy George, tangles himself all up in some words & phrases, in which a trace of metre is observable. His spasms, however, are less definite in thought (if, indeed, there be any definiteness in imagistical chaos!) & less meritorious altogether. (*RK* 111)

Lovecraft's protégé Alfred Galpin wrote a parody of Gidlow's poem entitled "Two Loves"; eventually, Lovecraft published Galpin's poem, as by "Consul Hasting," in the *Conservative* for July 1918. In the same number, Lovecraft commented:

> It seems to The Conservative that Miss Gidlow and Mr. Mills, instead of being divinely endowed seers in sole possession of all

Life's truths, are a pair of rather youthful persons suffering from a sadly distorted philosophical perspective. Instead of seeing Life In its entirety, they see but one tiny phase, which they mistake for the whole. What worlds of beauty—pure Uranian beauty—are utterly denied them on account of their bondage to the lower regions of the senses! It is almost pitiful to hear superficial allusions to "Truth" from the lips of those whose eyes are sealed to the intellectual Absolute: who know not the upper altitudes of pure thought, in which empirical forms and material aspects are as nothing. (*CE* 1.204)

Gidlow published her signature essay "Life for Life's Sake" in Horace L. Lawson's *Wolverine* for October 1919. She wrote of her life-centered philosophy:

The usual accusation of materialism need not be advanced to meet Life for Life's sake for it is too absurd. If logic and scientific truth are materialism, we need more materialism, for it is healthy and strong and selfish, and antagonistic to the sentimental idealism that the weak-willed, weak-charactered, weak-minded lean to, and that is the cause, or one of the causes, as well as the effect of their weakness.[1]

In the same month, Mills had published his lesbian play "Tea Flowers," dedicated to "Sappho" (Gidlow's nickname among her associates), in Cook's *Vagrant*. Earlier the same year, F. Graeme Davis had published an extended defense of *Les Mouches Fantastiques* in his *Lingerer*. "Life for Life's Sake" drew several rebuttals, including Lovecraft's "Life for Humanity's Sake," eventually published in John Heins's *American Amateur* for September 1920.

Davis had risen to the NAPA presidency for the 1918–19 term, but he skipped NAPA's July 1919 Newark convention to spend a month with Gidlow and her circle in Montreal. Davis fell in love with Mills, whom he hoped to make his permanent partner. However, Gidlow's Montreal ménage was not to endure

---

1. Elsa A. Gidlow, "Life for Life's Sake," *Wolverine* No. 5 (October 1919); rpt. in *Fossil* No. 329 (July 2006): 33.

much longer. In March 1920, Gidlow and Mills issued a final, typeset number of *Les Mouches Fantastiques*. They were planning to relocate to New York City and perhaps intended the typeset number of *Les Mouches* as a calling card for American amateurs. Gidlow finally broke away to New York in April 1920, and Mills followed her there a few months later. He subsequently broke Davis's heart by taking Khagendrenath Ghose as his lover.

Young John Milton Heins, son of Charles W. Heins, cultivated the friendship of Gidlow and Mills. Young Heins met Gidlow, Edna Hyde ("Vondy") and Hyde's fiancé Philip B. McDonald for a May Day outing in Central Park on 1 May 1920. Heins and his father both visited Gidlow in her apartment on 34th Street on 25 September 1920. Later, Gidlow and Mills both attended the famous gathering at the Heins home in Ridgefield, N.J., on 17 October 1920. This gathering was made famous by Edna Hyde's alleged rude treatment of her hosts, which young John Milton Heins publicized in his magazine, the *American Amateur,* where he was also publishing the works of Gidlow and Mills. Heins had published a scathing article by Gidlow, entitled "The Literary Decadence of E. G.," in his number dated July 1920. She declared:

> That is what is wrong with amateur journalism—it is futile. None of its members appear to have anything to say, yet they write unceasingly. I have read all amateur journals that have appeared during the past six years and I can truly say that I have not found in those journals, in all that time, as many as six original ideas, or six artistic expressions of any sort of ideas.[2]

She wrote scathingly of amateurdom's poets:

---

2. Elsa A. Gidlow, "The Literary Decadence of E. G.," *American Amateur* 1, No. 5 (July 1920); rpt. in *Fossil* No. 329 (July 2006): 35.

> All amateurdom is pervaded by an atmosphere of middle age, mustiness, fossilism. Every pseudo-poet writing in AJ imitates or plagiarizes Poe, Shelley, Keats, Wordsworth or Pope, and some bend their muse to lengthy pastorals. The favorite subjects of the prose writers are mysticism, politics or theosophy, evidently culled and rehashed from Sunday afternoon forums and newspapers.
>
> If these were the first fluttering attempts of younglings, one could be tolerant, trustful of development, but this is not so. Most of these offenders are middle-aged, settled and hopeless and they will ride their wooden "hobby" at a dull, satisfied joy-trot till it or they shall crumble.
>
> There is Mr. Goodenough with his rhymed very-moral maxims; Mr. Lovecraft with his morbid imitations of artists he seems not even able to understand; Mr. Ward Phillips who admires Poe wisely and far too well, since he mimics him so laboriously, and a host of others, male and female, who apart from having no new word to speak, cannot write three consecutive rhymed verses in even metre, although they raise their voices continuously and wildly against "modern" poetry and that in their opinion heretical expression of a perverted intellect, *vers libre*.[3]

Pearl K. Merritt, James F. Morton, and Lovecraft all replied to Gidlow's essay in the pages of the *American Amateur*. Lovecraft's response in "Life for Humanity's Sake" was fairly measured:

> Miss Gidlow has discovered the fact that there is no vast supernatural intelligence governing the cosmos—a thing Democritus could have told her several centuries B.C.—and is amazingly disturbed thereat. Without stopping to consider the possibility of acquiescence in a purposeless, mechanical universe, she at once strives to invent a substitute for the mythology she has cast aside; and preaches as a new and surprising discovery the ancient selfish hedonism whose folly was manifest before the death of its founder Aristippus. (*CE* 5.45)

---

3. Ibid., 36.

Perhaps he revealed his real feelings toward Gidlow more clearly in his comments in "Lucubrations Lovecraftian" in *The United Cooperative* for April 1921:

> In the July *American Amateur*, the precocious Miss Elsie (alias Elsa) A. Gidlow of *Les Mouches* fame refers with admirable courtesy to "Mr. Lovecraft with his morbid imitations of artists he seems not even able to understand." Perhaps Mistress Elsie-Elsa would prefer that the amateurs follow her own example, and perpetrate morbid imitations of morbid artists whom nobody outside the asylum is able to understand. (*CE* 1.284)

Lovecraft made his hatred of Mills even clearer in his letter to Rheinhart Kleiner dated 21 May 1920:

> As to day-dreams & Rossie George—I am afraid that the wildest of his flights is rather tame compared with what I have seen in other universes whilst asleep. He can't even get off this one poor planet, or rise much above the animal instincts here. Carcass-worshippers like Rossie & Elsie make me so infernally sick & tired that I lack patience with them. This reminds me—I never shewed you that putrid fellow's letter, which he wrote me last summer. I promised to do so, & will enclose it herewith. My personal comment is twofold: (a) Nobody home. (b) Throw it in the garbage pail behind the house & cover well with chloride of lime. Kindly return this bit of mental & moral aberration for preservation as a horrible example in my private museum of mental pathology. (*RK* 164)

Mills's letter to Lovecraft does not appear to survive among Lovecraft's papers as preserved in the Lovecraft Collection at Brown University.

Gidlow and Lovecraft were both residents of New York City in 1924–26, but there is no evidence that they ever met. For part of this time, Gidlow worked as a cataloguer for the antiquarian bookseller W. A. Gough. While she resided in New York, Will Ransom of Chicago published Gidlow's first collection of poetry, *On a Grey Thread* (1923), often described as the first collection of explicitly lesbian poetry published in the United States. In 1926, the same year Lovecraft returned to Providence, Gidlow migrated to the San Francisco Bay Area, where she spent the rest of her life. She published a further poetry collection *Sapphic Songs* (1976) and her autobiography, *Elsa: I Come with My Songs* (1986). On 9 February 1937, she wrote to Edwin Hadley Smith of her involvement in the amateur journalism hobby:

> I have pleasant memories of amateur days and some friendships grew out of them. Some of us had fun editing and publishing. I imagine the members did not realize what a child I was when they were corresponding—about 15 or 16 when invited to join the association. Since 1921 I have been a professional writer, editor, or journalist of one sort or another.[4]

Gidlow numbered Kenneth Rexroth and Alan Watts among her friends in San Francisco. She devoted much time to her artists' community at Druid Heights. In old age, she traveled to Japan and China and was admired as a spokesperson for women's rights. She had two long-term lovers, Violet W. L. Henry-Anderson, who died in 1935, and Isabel Grenfell Quallo.

As for the other players, Roswell George Mills spent much time in Europe in the 1920s, but eventually returned to the New York area. He was working as a reporter for the Brooklyn *Eagle* and resided with his widowed mother when he registered for the draft in 1942. Eventually, he retired to Miami, Florida, where he died in 1966. F. Graeme Davis, who had been ordained as an Episcopal priest in 1910, was deposed from the priesthood in 1925. He subsequently became a Liberal Catholic priest, then an Old Catholic bishop in Chicago. He attended NAPA's 1934 Chicago convention in full bishop's regalia, and published one

---

4. Cited in Kenneth W. Faig, Jr., "Were Il Duce's Sons Amateur Journalists?" *Fossil* No. 345 (July 2010): 20–21.

last amateur journal, *Letters from the Lingerer,* in 1937, the year before his death.

I don't know how many amateur journalists of today will find much to remark in the lives or the work of Lovecraft and Gidlow. For me, they remain two of the most interesting figures who ever participated in our hobby.

Sources

Note: All essays have been revised for publication in this collection.

"Can You Direct Me to Ely Court? Some Notes on 66 College Street." *Lovecraft Annual* No. 9 (2015): 54–69.

Devonshire Ancestry of Howard Phillips Lovecraft. By Chris J. Docherty, A. Langley Searles, and Kenneth W. Faig, Jr. Moshassuck Monograph Series No. 9. Glenview, IL: Moshassuck Press, 2003.

Edward Francis Gamwell and His Family. Glenview IL: Published by the Author, 1991. Also circulated in the Esoteric Order of Dagon Amateur Press Association, Lammas 1991.

"Ethnic Names in Lovecraft's "The Dreams in the Witch House." *EOD Letter* No. 10 [Esoteric Order of Dagon Amateur Press Association] (May Eve 2009; mailing 146): 5–9; No. 11 (Lammas 2009; mailing 147): 1–5.

George Elliott Lovecraft: Lost Scion of the House of Lovecraft. Moshassuck Monograph Series No. 14. Glenview, IL: Moshassuck Press, May 31, 2010. [Contains an appendix of facsimile plates.]

"John Osborne Austin's Seven Club Tales: Did They Inspire Lovecraft?" *Lovecraft Annual* No. 14 (2020): 83–108.

"The Lovecraft–Gidlow Centenary." *Lovecraft Annual* No. 12 (2018): 66–74 (as "Two Centenaries: H. P. Lovecraft and Elsa Gidlow").

Lovecraft Was Our Neighbor: The People of the Arsdale. Glenview IL: Moshassuck Press (Monograph No. 17), 2019.

The People of 598–600 Angell Street. Glenview IL: Moshassuck Preds (Monograph No. 25), 2020.

The Providence Amateur Press Club, 1914–1916. Moshassuck Monograph Series No. 11. Glenview, IL: Moshassuck Press, 2008. Rev. ed. (with David Haden). Moshassuck Press and Burslem Books, 2014.

The Site of Joseph Curwen's Home in The Case of Charles Dexter Ward. Moshassuck Monograph Series No. 15. Glenview, IL: Moshassuck Press, 2013.

"The Story of 454 Angell Street: The Birthplace of Howard Phillips Lovecraft." *454 Angell Street: The Birthplace of Howard Phillips Lovecraft*, Glenview IL: Moshassuck Press (Monograph No. 22), 2020.

www.ingramcontent.com/pod-product-compliance
Lightning Source LLC
Chambersburg PA
CBHW060107170426
43198CB00010B/805